Developing a Lifelong Contract in the Sports Marketplace

Greg J. Cylkowski, M.A.

Athletic Achievements
3036 Ontario Road
Little Canada, Minnesota 55117

Copyright © 1992; 1994 Greg J. Cylkowski.
Printed and bound in the United States of America. All rights reserved. No part of this book may be reproduced or transmitted in any form or by any means, electronic or mechanical, including photocopying, recording, or by an information and retrieval system—except by a reviewer who may quote brief passages in a review to be printed in a magazine or newspaper—without permission in writing from the author.

Although the author has made every effort to ensure the accuracy and completeness of information contained in this book, he assumes no responsibility for errors, inaccuracies, omissions, or any inconsistency herein. Any slights of people or organizations are unintentional.

**Attention Sports Organizations,
Teachers, Seminar Leaders,
Colleges and Universities:**
Quantity discounts are available on bulk purchases of this book for sales promotions, educational purposes, premiums, or fund raising.

For information, please contact, Athletic Achievements, 3036 Ontario Road, Little Canada, MN 55117. (612) 484-8299.
ISBN # 0-9636449-0-4

This Book is Dedicated To

My wife, Michele, who has unconditionally supported me through the peaks and valleys of my sports practice and who has shared with me an appreciation for America's favorite pastime - sports.

My children, Nicole, Cameron, Lance and Anna Belle, who serve as the inspiration for all my professional endeavors. My hope is that they too will be able to enjoy sport for what it truly was meant to be - a healthy love affair with one of life's most exciting avocations.

My mentors, Tom House and Jerry Gill, who have guided and motivated me by example to be a professional in the truest sense of the word.

Acknowledgments To

Sports Careers, Inc., for serving as a source of pertinent information and research data on the sports marketplace.

The Women's Sports Foundation, for its many informative editorials and statistical analysis.

Mark Tudi, President of **Sports Search**, for his many insights and perspectives about the sports industry.

Gary Roberts, Editor of **Sports Lawyer** for providing permission to reprint his manuscript.

Jacqueline Blais and Beth Krodel of *USA Today*, for their editorial insights on women in sport.

Special Thanks To

Jim Templin, a sports administration intern, who laboriously researched and updated the book's content material for a second printing.

Contents

Chapter 1

Planning Your Career In Sports — 1

Why a Career in Sports?	2
Life Changing Tips for a Sports Career	6
Choosing A Career That's Really You	6
Life Planning	7
Game Plan for a Complete and Fulfilling Life	10
Conduct a Self-Analysis	11
Goal-Setting	12
The Fantasy Career Model	15
Define Your Career Direction	16
Job Factors Inventory	17
Gather Career Information	18
Occupational Research Worksheet	19
Action Plans for Long-Term Success	20
Validating a Career Choice	20
For Further Reading	22

Chapter 2

The Networking Process — 25

How to Identify Your Network	25
Develop a Contact List	25
Building Your Network	27
Prospecting	28
Networking	28
Informational Interviewing	29
Putting Your Network to Work	29
The Hidden Job Market	30
Key Elements in the Approach Letter	31
Informational Interview Questions	31
Seven Rules for Networking Success	32
Expanding Your Network	33
Network on the Job	34
Developing Personal and Professional Associations	35
Maximize the Job Search Process by Being in Demand	35
Resources	36
Creating a Personal Advisory Team	36

Chapter 3

Job Acquisition Strategies — 41

Developing a Game Plan That Maximizes Your Efforts	41
The Job Acquisition Process	43
Taking Matters Into Your Own Hands	45
Before You Begin	45
Keys to Success	47
Application Techniques	47
Designing a #1 Draft Choice Cover Letter	48
Creating an MVP Resume	51
Some Basic Guidelines	55
Accomplishments: The key to what's in it for the Employer	55
Broadcast Letter in Reply to an Ad	59
Making it Happen with a Game-Winning Interview	60
Interview Strategy Checklist	60
During the Interview	62
If You Get the Job	63
If You Don't Get the Job	63
Becoming Your Own Marketing Agent	63
A few words of encouragement...	70
Career Steps: Summing It All Up	71

Chapter 4

Increasing Your Marketability — 74

Acquiring Experience: A Key Job Seeking Attribute	75
The Value of an Internship	78
Why Employers Want Interns	79
Other Avenues to Pursue for Practical Know-How	79
Switching Careers to a Sports Related Occupation	81
Do You Need a Mentor?	84
Choosing the Right Mentor	85

Chapter 5

Women in Sports — 89

The Need for Role Models in Coaching	90
Education and Training	92
Going For It	93
There's More to Television Than A Pretty Face	94
The New Wave Sports Executives	95
The Prototype Sports Agent - And YES, She Is A Woman!	97
More Success Stories: Women in Sports Administration, TV	99
Areas of Growth for Women: Sports Broadcasting	100
Where to Look for your First Job	101

Don't Get Discouraged	101
Career Steps: Summing it All Up	102
Women's Sports Resources	104
Publications	107
A/V Learning Materials	107
Reference Guides	108

Chapter 6

Is the Professional Athlete's Lifestyle for You? *111*

Professional Athletes	112
What It Takes To Be A Pro	114
Playing Professionally For the Wrong Reasons	115
Resources	118
Publications	119

Chapter 7

Playing the Professional Game *121*

Professional Baseball	121
Resources	122
Publications	123
Professional Basketball	123
Resources	124
Publications	124
Professional Football	124
Resources	125
Professional Hockey	126
Resources	127
Publication	127
Golf	127
Caddying	129
Major Golf Associations	130
Academic Institutions Offering Golf Programs	131
Bowling	133
Resources	134
Bowling Publications	134
Tennis	135
Resources	136
Specialized Training/Educational Curriculums	136

Chapter 8

Competing in Professional Sports As An Avocation — 139

Auto Racing	139
Resources	140
Body Building	140
Resources	140
Boxing	141
Resources	141
Publications	142
Equine Sports—The Horse Industry	142
Horse Racing	144
The Jockey	145
Resources	146
Ice Skating	147
Skating Shows	148
Resources	148
Racquetball	149
Resources	149
Rodeo	149
Resources	150
Publications	150
Downhill Skiing	150
Resources	151
Soccer	151
Resources	151
Surfing	152
Resources	152
Triathalons	152
Resources	153
Volleyball	153
Resources	153
Publications	153
Water-skiing	154
Resources	154

Chapter 9

The Sports Marketplace — 157

The Professional Ranks	158
College Sports Administration	160
Sports Marketplace Salary Survey	164
Specializing Training Profile	165
Resources for Collegiate Athletic Directors	166
Conferences and Meetings	166
Publications	166

Contents　　v

Resources and Publications for Business Managers	167
Organizations	167
Arena & Stadium Management	167
Resources	168
Publications	168
Training Opportunities	169

Chapter 10

Sports Communications & Mass Media　　171

Public Relations	171
The Mass Media	175
Print Media	176
Television	181
Brown Institute	183
Television Support Personnel	184
Public Relations Resources	188
Resources- Print Media	189
Sports & Media Publications	190
Resources – Television and Radio Broadcasting	190
Photography Resources	191

Chapter 11

Coaching　　193

The Art of Mentorship	194
The Most Unique Position in Sports	195
Do You Have the right Stuff?	196
Key Attributes of Coaching	197
Where the Jobs Are	199
Coaching in the College Ranks	200
Professional Coaching	201
Other Coaching Opportunities	202
Resources	203
Publications	204
Resources	206
Recommended Reading	206

Chapter 12

Sports Agents & Legal Representation　　209

On Becoming a Sports Lawyer	211
Educational Profile	215
Associations	216
Publications	217

Periodicals 218
Financial Services 219
Traps to Avoid 220
Game Plan 221
Opportunities 221

Chapter 13

The Business of Sport — 223

The Sporting Good Industry	223
Resources	226
Trade Journal & Publications	226
Sports Entrepreneurship: Franchising	232
What is Franchising	232
Is Franchising For You?	233
The Advantages	233
The Top Ten Entrepreneurial Schools	236
Marketing Consultants	237
Advertising Agents	238
Sports Marketing Agencies vs. Sports Marketing Firms	239
Specialized Training Programs	243
Career and Job Placement Services	243
Insurance Reps	244

Chapter 14

Sports Medicine — 247

Sports Injuries	247
Sports Physicians	249
Orthopedists	250
Education	251
Resources	251
Certification in the American College of Sports Medicine	252
Preventive Certifications	252
Rehabilitative Certifications	253
Doctor of Osteopathy	255
Resources	255
Doctor of Chiropractic	256
Resources	257
Physical Therapy	257
Resources	258
Athletic Trainers	258
Resources	262
Sports Nutrition	263
Resources	263
Podiatry	264
Resources	264

Schools With Podiatric Medicine Curriculums	264
Other Sports Medicine Related Careers	265
Resources	265
Sports Vision	265
Resources	266
Sports Medicine Paraprofessionals	266
Sports Dentistry	266
Resources	267
Sports Massage	267
Publications	270

Chapter 15

Sports Education & Performance Consultants — 273

Physical Education	274
Weight Training Instructor	276
Sports Psychology	277
Sport Psychology Resources	278
Sports Psychology Education	278
Resources	279
Conferences	279
Exercise Physiology	280
Biomechanics	281
Sports Sociology	281
Publications	281

Chapter 16

Health & Fitness — 285

Resources	287
Dance Therapist	287
Resources	288
Corporate Fitness Director	289
Resources	289
Health Club Administrative Personnel	290
Job Placement Services	291
Resources	291

Chapter 17

Recreation & Leisure — 293

Opportunities	293
Leisure Related Occupations	295
Top 50 Recreation and Leisure Careers	296
Professional Preparation	298

Specialized Educational Training	299
Employment	301
Federal Government Employment	301
State Government Positions	303
Recreation Therapy	303
Industrial Recreation	304
Commercial Recreation	304
Tourism	305
Employment Conditions	306
The Future	307
Recent Changes and Current Trends	307
Future Participation Trends	308
Trends and Issues	308
Publications	309
Federal Agencies	310
State Divisions with Parks and Recreation Responsibilities	310
Additional Resources	311

Chapter 18

Specialty Sports Careers 313

Sports Officiating	313
Publications	321
Doing It	321
Strength and Conditioning Coaches	322
Groundskeepers	323
Equipment Managers	324
Cinematographers	325
Resources	325
Trainers as a Para-Professional	325

Chapter 19

Specialized Training & Education in Sports Administration 329

The Curriculum in Sport Management	330
Durham College	333
Robert Morris College	334
St. Thomas University	335
Western Illinois University	336
Other Sports Administration Programs	337
Additional Program Listings	343

Chapter 20

Specialized Job Search Services   353

Career Development Firms	353
National Job Search Conference	354
Conference Format	355
Who Should Attend	355
Professional Baseball Training and Placement Program	357
SportSearch... Retained Career Development Consulting	358
Job Search Agencies	358
Additional Placement Resources	360
Additional Job Listing Agencies	360
Athletic Administration	360
Telephone Job Placement Agencies	361
International Conference on Sports Business	362
Newsletters	363

Chapter 21

Sports Magazines, Newspapers & Periodicals   365

Nationally Sold Publications (listed alphabetically)	367

Chapter 22

Resources Directory   373

General Resources	374
Head Offices - Amateur Organizations	374
Arenas	375
Major League Baseball	375
Minor League Baseball	377
Class AAA	377
Class AA	378
Class A	378
Rookie Classification	379
Basketball	379
College Basketball	381
Major College Conferences	382
Football	384
American Football Conference	384
National Football Conference	385
Canadian Football League	386
Hockey	387
Soccer	389
Sports and Athletic Organizations	390
Billiards Organizations	391

Preface

The growing emphasis placed on athletics, coupled with the increasing amount of leisure time the public now enjoys, have made the world of sports one of the fastest growing segments of American business. Formation of new sports leagues, expansion of franchises to untapped markets, and legislative enactments opening the door for female athletics all aided the evolution of new sports markets in the 1980s. With the enactment of Title IX, and the increased television exposure for such non-traditional sports as soccer, additional career opportunities have dramatically risen as well.

Watching and participating in sports is an important part of life for many sports enthusiasts. Sports is often the main topic of conversation between friends and acquaintances. For those who participate, sport serves as a rewarding form of relaxation and recreation. Since many dream of active involvement in athletics on a daily basis, sports enthusiasts are constantly looking for a way to turn their preoccupation into a well-paying occupation.

The professional athlete has done what most sports fanatics dream of doing. He/she participates in athletics on a year-round basis and earns a living by doing it. Unfortunately, the proportion of our population qualified for this vocation, which has an average career life-span of only 4.5 years, is minute. But, a little known fact is that many other sports career options exist. The world of sports has become a 75 billion dollar a year entertainment industry, and the demand today for working men and women in this field has expanded greatly. From the field of sports administration to exercise physiology, to special event managers and contract advisors, the need for qualified individuals in select areas seems to be forever growing.

Contrary to public perception, positions in sports are not all glamour and, as in any other highly competitive field, the "big rewards" are not easily attainable. The reality of finding an opportunity in sports is largely a matter of "who you know." Still, one of the basic concepts in this book is that "you have to be good before you can be lucky." Quality people who are persistent will eventually be noticed. Any athlete or successful sports administrator will tell you that sports demands much from its people, but the rewards can be substantial for those who are willing to pay the price.

It has been said that there are three kinds of people in the world: those who watch it happen; those who wonder what happened; and those who make it happen. Whichever category you fall in will determine the success you will experience with this guide.

Greg J. Cylkowski,

Author & Sports Analyst

Developing a Lifelong Contract in the Sports Marketplace

Brandy Johnson, former international competitor in gymnastics, epitomizes the dedication and commitment necessary to fulfill a dream in sports. Photo: courtesy of the **U.S. Olympic Festival.**

Planning Your Career In Sports

*It's five minutes before the start of the **Super Bowl**. Even though you find the pre-game show interesting, you can't wait for the kick-off...*

...You're one of the 75,000 cheering fans. You can't decide if you want the manager to shorten his talk on the mound and let the pitcher throw, or if you want the conversation to go on and give the ace right hander more time to settle down...

...The center leaps high, grabs the defensive rebound, lets loose a bullet of a pass. It's caught by the quick forward, who puts it up from 15 feet out. Two more points. Now we're down by three...

...What is the darn coach saying in the dressing room? Intermission is lasting too long. Why don't they come back on the ice for the third period and break this scoreless tie...

...You go to school or to work. That's OK, but when you go to a game or watch one on television - that's excitement. You're lucky if your friend or spouse likes it too. Maybe that's partially why you get along so well. When you get the paper you open to the sports section first. You can't wait for the television weatherman to finish his forecast so you can get the latest scores.

Why a Career in Sports?

Let's face it. You're a sports fan. Some, who don't understand, even call you a *sports addict*.

Often you think about how great it would be to actually work for a team or athletic organization. You're discouraged by comments like "Only ex-athletes get front office jobs," or "You have to be the boss' son to get a job with the team." While the ex-athlete does get an opportunity and the owner's child can have the job if he wants it, the fact remains that with all the new teams and franchises, there just aren't enough ex-athletes or owners' children qualified to fill the growing number of athletic organization positions.

But did you know that *most* sports career opportunities exist *outside* professional athletic organizations (Figure 1A). You will soon realize that it requires a great deal of imagination and ability to find your niche in sports. For instance, let's assume that you've been an academic whiz in organic chemistry and a dedicated gymnast after school — you could conceivably be the **U.S. Olympic Team's** physical therapist, rehabilitating injuries and mending gold medal careers at the same time (Figure 1B). Or if

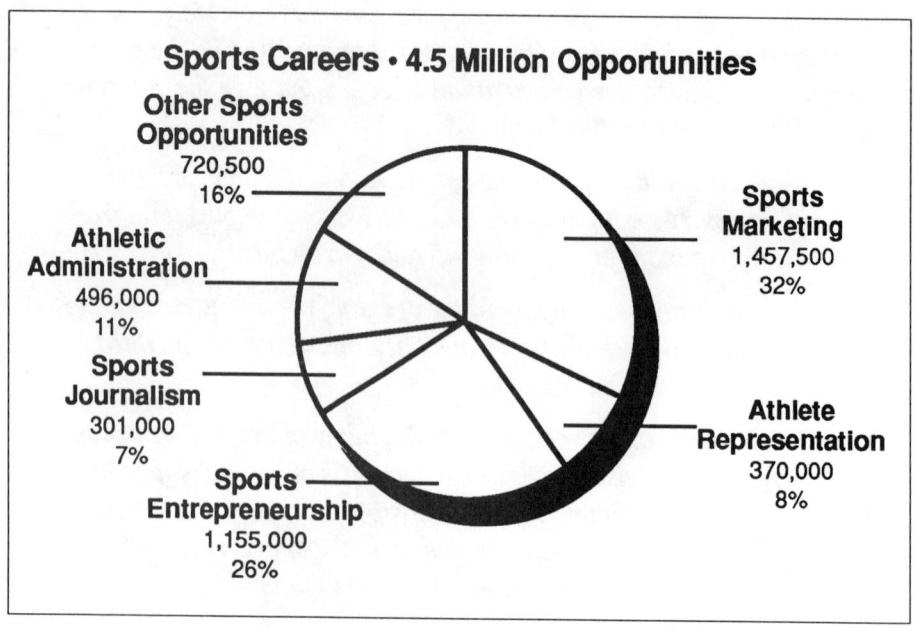

Figure 1A.   **Sports Marketing Opportunities**

communications skills are your forte with a nose for news and a batting average of .465 on your college team, you may wind up holding post-game interviews at the **1995 World Series** (See Figure 1C). You don't even have to be a youthful student gearing up for the specialized training, or even be pursuing a career for the first time to be able to realize your dreams. Consider this. If you are a highly organized horse fanatic with 15 years financial consulting experience, you possibly could step in and manage the racetrack at Gulf-Stream! What better way for a Masters Marathoner with the patience of a research scientist to contribute to the well-being of future runners than by developing the ultimate shoe as a biomechanical engineer (See Figure 1D).

These dreams and fascinations are not as far-fetched as you may think. But if you allow others to discourage you and stifle your creativity, you could be passing up on the opportunity of a lifetime.

All over the world people are preoccupied with sports. Millions of dollars are spent preparing **Olympic** teams to go for the gold. In many countries like the United States, professional sports has become a billion dollar enterprise supported by millions of spectators annually.

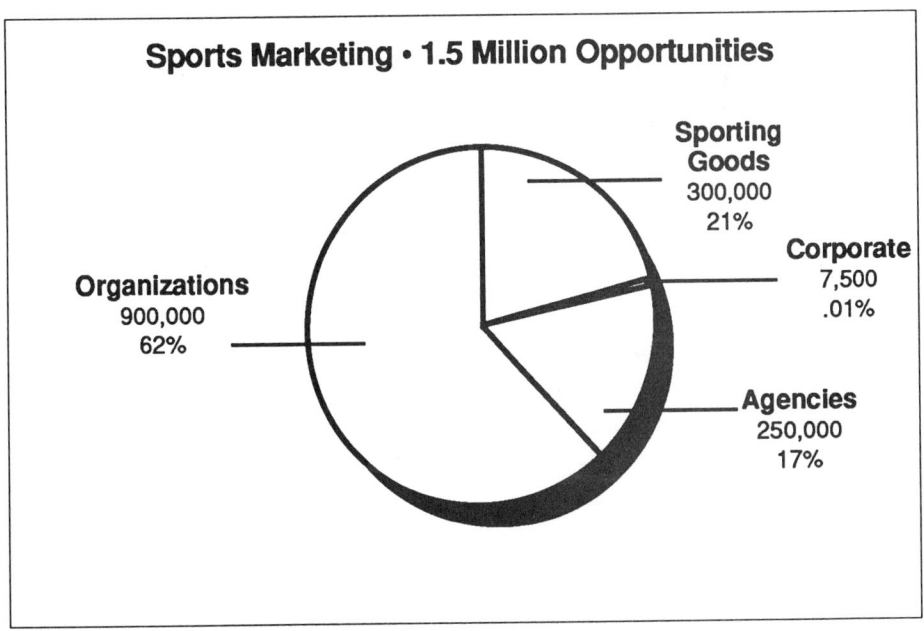

Figure 1B.   Sports Marketing Opportunities

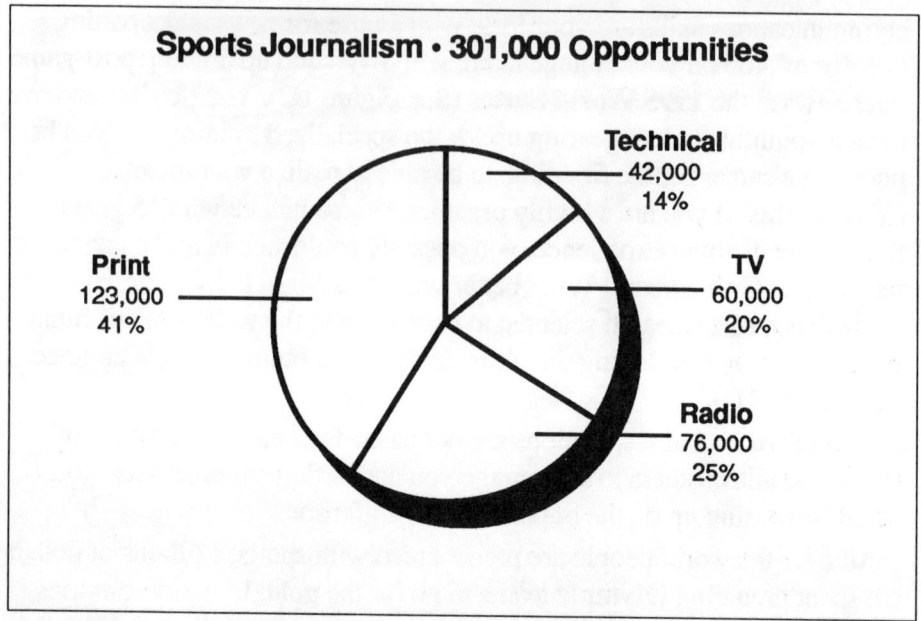

Figure 1C.   Sports Journalism Opportunities

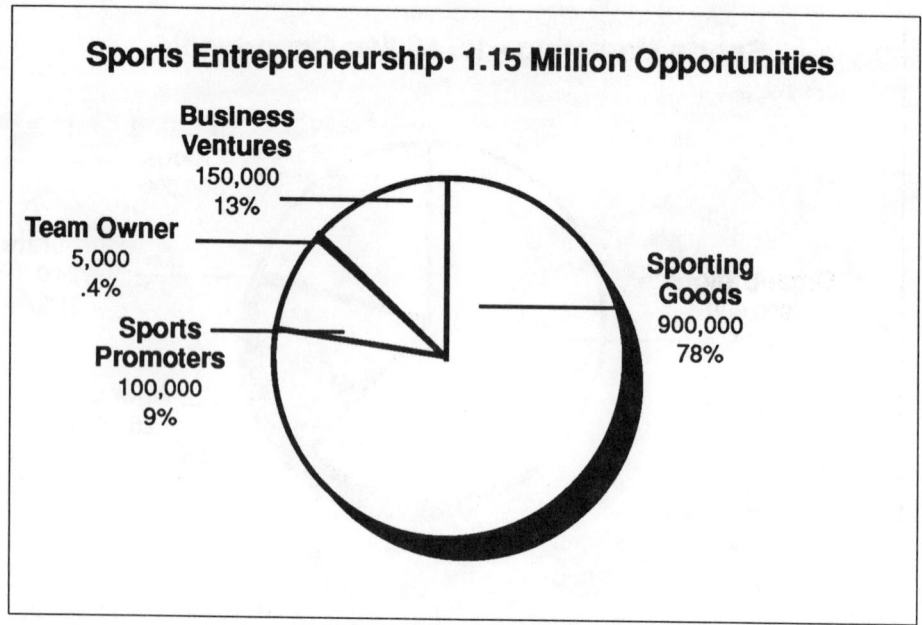

Figure 1D.   Sports Entrepreneurship Opportunities

This country's fascination with sports has reached epidemic proportions. Today thousands of leagues exist in dozens of sports ranging from those for elementary school students to the pros and beyond. In fact, organized team sports are available for just about everyone in today's society: young, middle-aged, elderly, men, women, and persons with special needs. Although most of us participate in some form of recreational activity, we are also a great nation of fans. Each weekend, over 150 million of us fanatically cheer for our home team. The willingness to watch athletic events for a fee has created the fastest growing entertainment field in our country today.

You may be well aware of these realities: The field is fiercely competitive, with a many qualified candidates seeking a limited number of available positions. Salaries are low when compared to similar level positions in private industry since there is always someone who is willing to work twice as hard for half the compensation just to get a foot in the door. *However, there are plenty of opportunities for those who are focused, patient, and equipped with a long-term plan.*

Sports can very well be the most rewarding of all industries. However, you need to know what opportunities are available, which particular opportunities you want and how to acquire those opportunities. Basically, what you need is information and direction. This book will assist you by explaining the variety of positions available today. It will provide helpful guidelines for acquiring the necessary training, identify application techniques, and list the specific contact information for existing franchises, leagues, and athletic organizations. Perseverance is the key to success in any vocation. The sports market of the future will be dominated by creative, dedicated individuals who are equipped to deal with tomorrow's trends and issues.

This book eliminates the mystique surrounding how to develop your own sports career path. Veteran sports business executives and administrators may confess that their successful careers were built more on circumstance than plan. Many wouldn't be able to tell you exactly how their careers blossomed. However, what they *can* tell you is that they absolutely have a passion for what they are doing for a living and will never leave the sports marketplace. That's a central theme you'll find repeated again and again in this book: If you naturally enjoy and have a high degree of interest in sports, then every facet of your life will be strengthened by your pursuit of that passion.

The industry has finally recognized the need for career development guidance in the sports business. Let this book serve as a methodical guide as you realize the endless niches available to you in sports.

First, you will need to identify what career is best suited for you. Then you can strategically plan a long-term approach with realistic expectations.

Life Changing Tips for a Sports Career

- Work your passion and make it happen!
  Ask yourself: "If I had every need fulfilled in my life right now, how would I spend each day and still be productive and excited?"
- Don't ever leave the sports industry for a job in a completely different career field on a whim, merely for security or monetary purposes. If so, you may never have the opportunity to return to the sports marketplace. Worse still, you may regret the decision for the rest of your life.
- The happiest people in the world are those who have attained peace of mind, and have realized *what they are destined to do* and *what they are actually doing* are one in the same.

Choosing A Career That's Really You

How often do you see people who have been working at the same position for many years and simply dread going to their jobs in the morning? Worse yet, think of the individuals you know who have spent countless dollars, time and effort in their educational training only to realize shortly after accepting that mythical dream position that they have chosen the wrong field?

One of the main concerns in industry today is that too much of the work force are unhappy with their present jobs, or are ill-qualified for their present positions. The result is discontented employees who are only marginally productive, have low initiative, and possess low self-esteem. Studies have shown that nearly 50% of the American work force in the 80s were dissatisfied with their jobs. In addition, continued automation coupled with a more demanding economy, has caused more people to either lose their jobs, or find themselves transferred to positions unrelated to their field of study due to corporate restructuring. Making a career change is difficult for anybody—but especially for someone who either has too many lifestyle responsibilities to risk a career change, lacks advanced skills, or is perceived too old to be retrained in his/her chosen career.

One method to help you identify career options is to determine what activities you pursue for pure enjoyment and satisfaction. This may sound somewhat idealistic, but remember, we're talking about how you plan to dedicate anywhere from one third to one half of each working day of your life! If you carefully choose a career that incorporates what you love to do, *you will be more productive at your work and more satisfied with yourself and your life.* You may not be able to realize goals such as being professional athletes, due to physical limitations. However, if you have clearly identified a particular professional sport as a goal, you will find in this book other ways to establish a career related to that particular sport. How do you develop a career plan that incorporates an ideal lifestyle and is realistically attainable? It boils down to your priorities regarding salary, travel, self-esteem and personal investment. It becomes a matter of what are you willing to accept and sacrifice in both your own, and, if applicable, your family's situation.

Life Planning

Before you even consider any particular career or vocation, you need to formulate life planning goals. Life planning involves a comprehensive approach for satisfying all areas of a balanced, integrated lifestyle. If any one of your lifestyle goals remains unfulfilled, frustration and dissatisfaction will ultimately result. The higher the emphasis or priority placed upon an unmet goal, the greater the degree of frustration that will persist. If a career decision is made without taking all aspects of your life-plan into consideration, even though the career choice appears appropriate, it may very well trigger a disruption in other areas of your life.

Take for example, a father who accepts a career-changing position as a sports administrator in southern Florida. Though he couldn't be happier, his wife and family may be disenchanted since they despise hot climates and find humid summers very unhealthy. In addition, they may resent moving away from cherished relatives or friends and their home. In this case, what appeared to be an excellent career move for the individual turns out to be a disaster because all aspects of the life-plan were not considered.

Only you can identify what elements belong in your life-plan and the importance each has for you. Relationships, material acquisitions, and commitments all need to be factored into your life-plan. Remember, life-plans are dynamic. As you grow and change, so do your life-planning goals. The considerations of a college graduate are different from someone making a mid-life career change.

To further assist you in forming a system of lifestyle and career goals, review Maslow's hierarchy of needs (see Figure 2). According to motivational psychologist Abraham Maslow, human needs can be classified into five levels. We need to satisfy needs at the lowest level before we can move to the next level. Unsatisfied needs will influence behavior and dictate how we approach a life-style game plan.

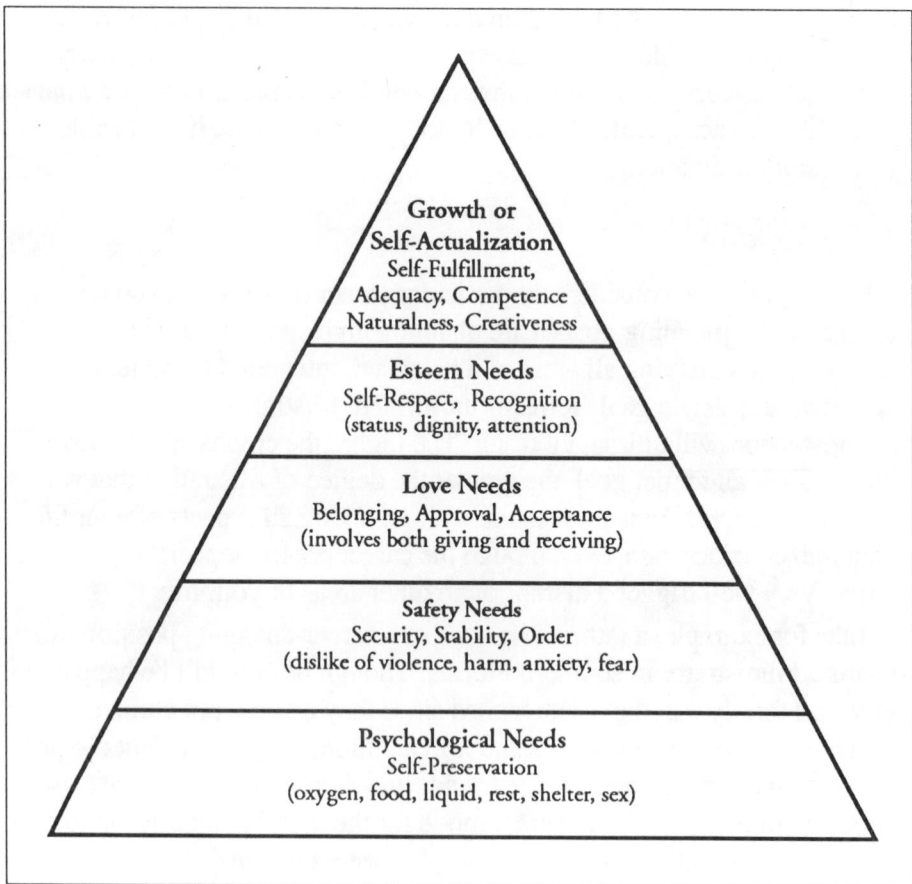

Figure 2. **Maslow's Hierarchy of Needs**
Needs at the lowest level of Maslow's hierarchy must be met before one can work toward meeting needs at the next level.

Maslow has designed a general model for achieving personal satisfaction, however, you need to identify and prioritize your own particular needs. It's important to remember that the many different models are just that — guides. What is important is not that you are able to specifically identify all the stages shown in this model, but rather that you form your own system for identifying and prioritizing your needs so that you can form a life-plan.

Super, an industrial psychologist, has developed another model which illustrates the various age stages in a life-work cycle (See Figure 3).

Individual development undoubtedly varies due to such factors as the timeliness of discovering one's destined career or the number of severity of obstacles that may be encountered. Both these models should be viewed as general guides. Industrial psychologists have concluded that people are generally underpaid in relation to their training and work efforts during their first 10 years of formal work experience In contrast, these same individuals are overpaid during their last 10 years of employment.

The life planning process is not intended to push anyone in a particular

Age	Stage	Development
0 - 14	Growth	Physical, Social, Mental
15 - 25	Exploratory	Soul Searching, choices based on education and practical experience
26 - 45	Establishment	Career -meshed, Creation of a work identity
46 - 65	Maintenance	Status quo, Financial and career security
65 +	Decline	Exit from work force, Increased delegation of responsibilities

Figure 3. **Super's Model of the Stages in a Life-Work Cycle**

Game Plan for a Complete and Fulfilling Life:

Write down in a notebook your thoughts about each of the following issues. Be sure to outline what your needs will be in the three different time frames specified.

In regards to the following areas, what will my needs be

	In 1 year? from now?	3 years from now?	5 years
Family Concerns			
Physical Needs			
Intellectual Challenges			
Creativity			
Financial Security			
Personal Power			

These goals are a measure of your value system as they exist today. Expect that they will change. Keep this list handy so you can check your progress toward your goals, as well as monitor and record how your goals and values change. That way, you alter your game plan to satisfy new goals as they evolve. Change is a natural force. Awareness of your own development will keep you focused on what is important (and most comfortable) for you. You are now in a position to begin shaping the future.

Figure 4.   Goal Setting
This form should help you more fully evaluate your needs.

career direction. People and their careers are dynamic and will change over time. Therefore, the life-planning process is a tool to help prepare you for meeting the challenges you face today, as well as those you anticipate for the future. Figure 4 provides a short sampling of some of the major needs and concerns that you may be evaluating when making your own life-plans.

More than 15 million people find themselves unemployed each year while millions of others try to increase their satisfaction within the workplace as well as advance their careers by looking for alternate career opportunities. Statistics reveal that the average individual will make more than 10 job changes which will include between three to five career changes during his/her lifetime!

It is not entirely clear how many of these job changes are career-planned advancements, or changes made to provide an individual with a more satisfying career. What is clear, however, is that life-plans help you map out a course so you don't make unnecessary or unproductive job changes.

More so than not, people find themselves in career transitions by accident. Some job changes are forced (termination, lack of work or layoff), or others just are unexpected opportunities. Even though it appears that chance and luck can play important but uncontrollable role in finding employment, when you properly prepare and plan for future job changes, you increase the probability that luck or new opportunities come your way. Many athletic coaches would say, "good luck and breaks are the result of sound preparation," or simply, "you have to be good before you're lucky!"

Developing your career path or seeking a career change will require a systematic and well-defined game plan that will be laborious, yet rewarding work.

Conduct a Self-Analysis

Assess your skills, abilities, motivations, interests, values, temperament, experience and accomplishments. You need this information before proceeding to other stages in the career development process. This helps you develop the necessary self-awareness with which you can effectively communicate your qualifications to employers as well as build your career. Know your strengths and weaknesses: This allows you to develop a personal strategy for not only putting your best foot forward, but preparing for any potentially embarrassing or difficult questions which may come up during the interview process. Reviewing your weaknesses will help you identify areas where you need to develop control, educational abilities or seek outside assistance. Minimizing your potential weaknesses will help you become completely marketable.

List your strengths and weaknesses:

Be sure that you are accurately assessing your strong points.

You will discover that a weakness is often nothing more than a drawback that has yet to be developed or nurtured. Develop this potential and you have eliminated the weakness!

Address your weaknesses honestly and, wherever possible, turn them into viable assets. Being in tune with your inner feelings is half the battle.

Goal-Setting

Once you have honestly assessed your strong and weak points, then you can ask yourself: "What do I really want to do with every waking moment of my life and am I willing to work for it?" The answers to this question will help you identify you life- and career-goals. These goals must include a game plan to accomplish what you have set out to do. Otherwise, you have nothing more than aimless dreams. Having a dream is okay. *But realizing a dream is the real thrill!* Making a conscious effort to be focused daily on what you really want will put you in a better position to be in control of both your lifestyle and sports career destiny.

Hopefully, you are ready to do some serious soul-searching about just what you want to do with your work life.

Once your objectives are clearly written on paper, you will need to determine how your career is a vital part of your overall dreams. In deciding a path that you want to pursue, consider such factors as family plans, physical comforts, intellectual challenges, creativity, financial security, and personal power.

The first phase of goal setting is to identify the areas of your life in which you have the greatest drive to excel. These can be either personal or career-oriented, even related to your amateur hobbies or sports.

Before you can define overall career goals, you will need to identify your personal inventory and the targeted area of sports. With this in mind, project where you would like to be 1, 5 and 10 years from now. What will your cherished achievements and personal experiences be? Where would you like to be in regards to your social affiliations and family? Don't ever forget to include the your spouse's and family's goals and desires. Many broken homes have been caused by the lack of communication between spouses as they each planned careers. Your 10 year projection cannot be considered a success, for example, you consider your career goals but not your personal and family goals as well (See Figure 4).

In developing goals, first brainstorm. Pour out all your thoughts and ideas on paper. Then, carefully cross-reference your career, personal, family and financial goals. Ask yourself: Do these goals present a composite view of your vision for the future? Are the features and qualities of this projected lifestyle consistent with the information from your personal inventory? Have you identified a realistic and feasible process to take you from your present situation, considering strengths and weaknesses, to your future goals?

Try to identify areas where you need skill development to minimize any drawbacks. As you make plans, determine your willingness to make the necessary sacrifices such as retraining, relocation to another state, and personal improvement, in order to accomplish these goals.

If you are still in school or have the opportunity to continue your education, make sure your training schedule allows for flexibility in future positions and career changes. By concentrating in only one area of study rather than having a very diverse program, you may be limiting your future options and marketability. Be your own coach: have a secondary strategy for a sure success.

Goals need to be as specific as possible. When crystallizing your thinking, keep the following suggestions in mind:

- Broaden your thinking. Don't assume what you can or can't do without allowing yourself to realistically want it.
- Be realistic about your background but don't limit yourself.
- Be creative and expand your horizons to fit your potential.
- Make your goals measurable otherwise it will be very difficult to gauge your success. For example, stating that you a want a master's degree in Sports Administration by 1989 makes this condition measurable.
- The more specific a goal becomes, the easier it will be to visualize and achieve. A good way to put your goal into perspective is to distinguish between short-range (immediate to one year) and long-range (one year and beyond) objectives. Your 10 year projections represent your long-range goals and therefore will not be as detailed as your immediate short-range plans.

- Learn to balance goals when conflicts arise between two areas, especially when both have an equal amount of desire attached to them.

  As your priorities and values change, you will be confronted with such conflict. You will need to weigh benefits gained against possible loss and risk involved with each conflict. For example, if you have saved money for a trip to Europe but realistically cannot afford both this endeavor and tuition for specialized sports administration training. The benefits for each are obvious, but the real difference is realized when comparing the loss of not attending a specialized school, which can serve a more long-term need as opposed to a three-week trip.

Not all of us would make the same decision in the above example since priorities and values will differ among individuals.

The following decision-making steps provide a framework for formulating goals:

Planning Stage
1. Define the problem or situation
2. Propose the options and alternatives
3. Gather information on the options
4. Evaluate the options
5. Make a decision

Action Stage
6. Set goals based on your decision(s).
7. Establish an action plan
8. Designate target dates
9. Evaluate, balance, and continually reassess goals, making any changes deemed necessary

Obstacles are part of the process. Don't avoid obstacles – they pose important problem-solving opportunities. Overcoming your obstacles helps develop confidence in your abilities. If your obstacles do not have a viable solution, then possibly your present expectations are set too high and need to be re-evaluated. Remember your goals and plans need to remain flexible.

Keep track of your goals and progress. This is important for your long-term success. Expect some setbacks — but don't be overwhelmed. Look back on your past success, look at where you are today, and keep an eye on your next goal. All things are possible when you have a plan, and the dedication to see it through!

The Fantasy Career Model

To help you determine what specific sports career you want to pursue, it's important that you carefully assess your own skills and abilities. Personality tests and general aptitude surveys provide one means of assessing your interests and potential. These can be administered by either your high school counselor, college career or placement office, your employer's human resources department, or possibly a university psychology department. Professionals can interpret such personality test results and point out areas of interest and qualities that you may never have recognized in yourself.

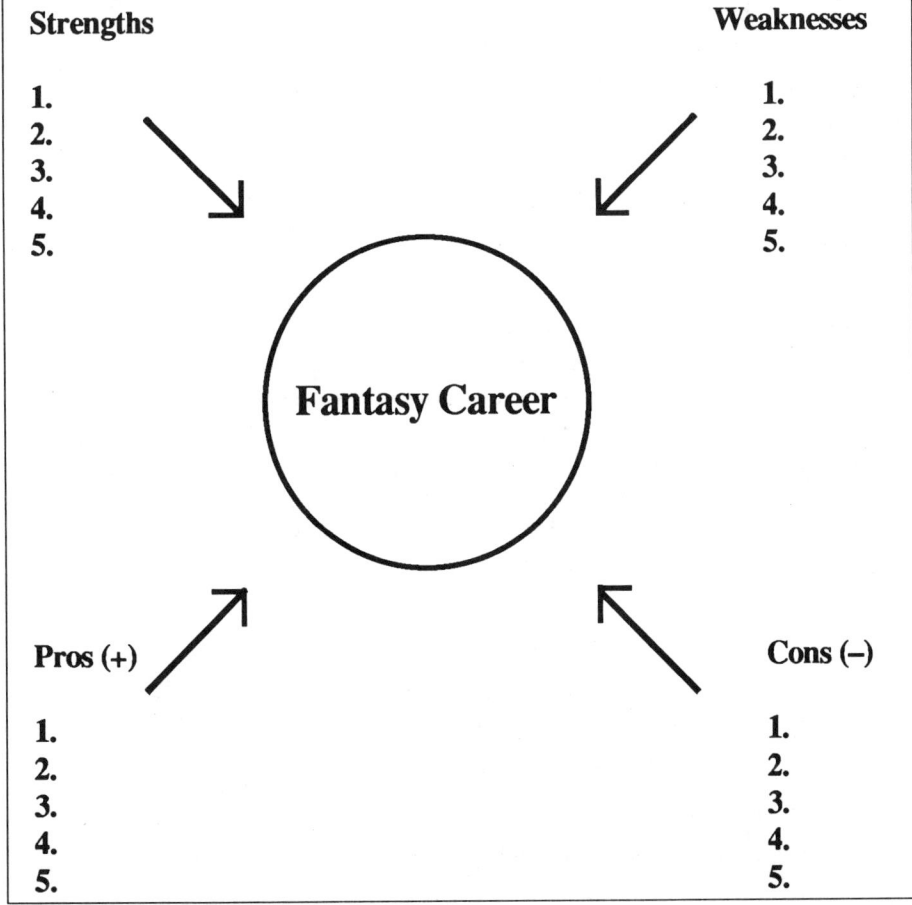

Figure 5. **Fantasy Career Model**

The Fantasy Career Model (See Figure 5) is another self-help tool to help you identify a viable career path. Start with the idea that you have all your family, financial and personal needs met. Now ask yourself how you would spend each day and still remain motivated and self-actualized. This model is based on the premise that you need to be pursuing a career that you enjoy regardless of finances.

At the beginning of this process, your goal is to identify as many interest areas as possible. Do not focus on details yet — just brainstorm.

Next, realistically consider the strengths and weaknesses you bring to each particular career option. Ask friends and significant others for their objective perspectives regarding your strengths and weaknesses as well. It is important to include others' observations as well as your own in this process. Compare your own observations to those of others.

Finally, identify the pros and cons of each fantasy career. Here again, include input from others to help you create as complete a picture as possible.

Prioritize both your strengths and weaknesses and the pros and cons as each relates to a particular fantasy career.

Be creative and imaginative in this process. Let your thoughts flow no matter what ideas come.

Finally, compare and cross-reference the information from your fantasy model with the characteristics you identified in worksheets from earlier sections of this chapter, and any personality tests you have taken.

Define Your Career Direction

Start by creating a list of all possible career avenues you would like to explore. Then, rank the list according to which you are most likely to succeed based on:
- Your personal job interests
- Your knowledge and experience compared to your job interests
- Your preferred work environment
- Your likes and dislikes in past positions
- Your weaknesses and strengths
- Your ambitions today and in the future

Be sure to use the insights you gathered in your self-evaluation to help you prioritize the areas where your best opportunities lie.

Job Factors Inventory

Task-Related
- **Responsibility**: Will there be enough to stimulate you?
- **Pressure**: High? Variable? Even?
- **Variety**: Are many different tasks required?
- **Decisions**: Will you make any? How important will your input be?
- **Creativity**: Do you have an opportunity to implement your own ideas?
- **Product**: Is there a concrete product or intangible service?
- **Expertise**: Ability to use your special skills/knowledge?

Environment-Related
- **Salary Structure**: Low or high wages? Fixed? Incentive? Commission?
- **Opportunity**: Can you be promoted easily from this position?
- **Hours and Time**: Structured? Flexible? More than 40 hours? More than 5 days weekly?
- **Dress**: Casual? Professional? Uniform?
- **Parking and Transportation**: Is parking costly? Free? Is much time spent in transportation to and from work?
- **Work Atmosphere**: Privacy adequate? Pleasant colors? Comfortable furnishings? Comfortable temperature? How noisy?
- **Work Space**: Confined? Free to move from area to area? Any windows?
- **Travel Opportunities**: What percent of work week?

Relationship-Related?
- **Supervision**: How closely supervised will you be? Will your supervisor be supportive?
- **Helpful**: Is the management conservative or liberal?
- **Status**: Is the position one that conveys the respect of others?
- **Teamwork**: Do you enjoy working closely with others?
- **Co-workers**: Do they appear friendly? Likeable? Closed? Open?
- **Service to Others**: Do your responsibilities include helping others?

Figure 6. Job Factors Inventory
Use this form to help you identify pros and cons of your previous work experiences, as well as the things you need in future employment opportunities.

Based on your prioritized list, you can then identify career areas which you will research in greater depth.

Be sure to include careful notations about:
- Where your highest (and lowest) level of interest is
- What are your strongest (and weakest) knowledge and skill areas
- What are your strongest (and weakest) experience areas

To help focus on the areas of highest interest to you, ask yourself the following questions:
- What personal sacrifices am I prepared to make to achieve success?
- What skills do I have now that will apply to the job?
- What additional skills will I have to develop for the job?
- Are these kinds of jobs available in my immediate market?

Analyze Your Work Environment Experiences

Write down past job experiences you liked/disliked to help you evaluate what kinds of situations you should be seeking. Use the Job Factors Inventory in Figure 6 to help you assess your past experiences. For example, note if you prefer a large company with a structured work environment. It will help single out specific companies for your target list. Be sure to list all the things you did not like in your previous jobs so as to avoid similar experiences in the future. Rank your likes and dislikes. These are important factors to be aware of during your career development process.

Gather Career Information

Once you've identified crucial information about yourself, your next objective is to gather as much information as possible about as many different sports careers as you wish to explore.

Create an Occupational Research Worksheet for each career area you decided to investigate (See Figure 7). That should help you narrow your alternatives to specific markets.

Occupational Research Worksheet

Career Area to Investigate _____

Positions Related to Career Area _____

Sources of Information _____

Type of Work Involved in This Field (List tasks and duties) _____

Environment/Places Where Work is Done _____

Background & Qualifications For This Work:
- Education/Training _____
- Experience _____
- Skills _____
- Personal Strengths _____

Practical Factors to Consider:
- Salary _____
- Benefits _____
- Hours _____
- Location _____

Means to Advancement: _____

Special Concerns and/or Needs, Minorities: _____

Employment Outlook for This Career Area:
- Present _____
- Future _____

Figure 7.   Career Assessment Worksheet

Action Plans for Long-Term Success

Even if you know you are qualified and would enjoy a particular position today, would you really want to continue that routine for the next 20 years? Will the pros and cons of your lifestyle inventory be the same in the 1990s as they were in the 1980s? and are simply looking for new positions.

Good examples of this are the coaches in both the college and high school ranks who have little training outside their athletic endeavors and now, due to budget cutbacks, age, or changing curricula, have few employment alternatives. A limited educational background restricts opportunities for upward mobility or job enhancement. Many coaches and physical educators are going back to school to diversify their background for future career options.

Too many career planners forget about a long-term action plan. To be successful in athletics today, you must look beyond the 1990s and recognize future issues and challenges. The last 10 years alone have witnessed more controversial issues and changes in both the collegiate and professional ranks than have been seen the last 50 years. Those who have prepared themselves to meet future challenges will be ready to capitalize on tomorrow's opportunities and benefits. Sports medicine practitioners, sports psychologists and strength coaches provide a few excellent examples of such forward-thinking career planning. Not long ago these fields were virtually unheard of, but the individuals who perceived upcoming needs and struggled with the developing stages are now reaping the rewards of their efforts.

NFL Oakland/Los Angeles **Raiders** player Al Davis is one such sports pioneer. From his involvement with the infant AFL in the early 60s to his recent franchise move from Oakland to Los Angeles for television marketing purposes, controversial Al Davis realized his dreams despite much skepticism and opposition.

Analyze any great athlete or businessperson and you will realize that talent alone did not breed his/her success. Self-direction and carefully devised and executed plan lead to fulfillment of goals.

Validating a Career Choice

To get a precise picture of your chosen career, visit a professional on the job. By actually getting out on the field, you will get a thorough firsthand look at the day-to-day realities of your chosen career: the required on-the-job skills, the personal demands, the hours, the environment. If possible, visit more than one professional in different settings to provide you with even more details. Many times local professional franchises, collegiate teams, athletic organizations, or consulting firms are willing to allow on-site observation.

Important parts of your professional network will be professionals whom you can call upon either for on-site interviews, or assistance in obtaining on-site visits.

On-site visits and information-gathering interviews are an important part of your career research. Don't underestimate the value of the contacts you make at this point in the process.

After completing my undergraduate studies, I approached a local professional hockey club with an internship proposal. I was directed to the president of the organization, but was quite frustrated by never being able to reach him on the telephone. I did not give up, however, and my tenacity finally paid off when we eventually made a connection. Even though he didn't have any opportunities available, the president invited me to meet with him and present my ideas because he was impressed with my persistence and professional manner. In fact, he tried to find a position for me within the organization!

This demonstrates that every contact is important. You never know who will be able to open a door for you by referring you to another opportunity or individual. Contacts are crucial in your job search!

Once you have identified the position(s) you want to research and have established a contact(s) for informational interviews, prepare a set of questions that will enable you to research aspects which you deem important.

The Occupational Research Worksheet provides a guide for gathering the most pertinent information regarding a new position. Feel free to add or delete targeted skills or values that you consider to be a priority in your situation. Your purpose at this stage is to gather all the information you can so you can determine whether or not you want to pursue a specific career area. Don't be concerned with making career decisions at this point. But do remember that contacts made at this stage could turn into life-long mentors. Treat every contact as if they hold the key to your future.

For Further Reading:

Career Futures Magazine
This quarterly publication is regarded as one of the most invaluable resource journals in the career search process. Its feature articles identify the latest job hiring trends from industry forecasts, geographic and economic conditions, dress for success advice and hidden job markets.

Though most college career centers provide personal copies of this publication, subscriptions can be obtained by contacting:

Career Futures Magazine
21 Charles Street
Westport, CT 06880

(203) 227-1775

What Color is Your Parachute?
A Practical Manual for Job Hunters & Career Changers
   by Richard Nelson Bolles (Ten Speed Press)
   ISBN 0898151570

This annually revised publication is considered by those in the career counseling field to be the number one tool for a career transition, job search, or basic professional soul-searching. By for the most comprehensive resource guide in the market.

Wishcraft: how to get what you really want
   by Barbara Sher with Annie Gottlieb
   ISBN 0670776084

Team work is the name of the game for a successful career in sports just as it is in producing a national television event. Photo: **Athletic Achievements.**

2
The Networking Process

How to Identify Your Network

Everyone has a network. Your network consists of individuals with whom you interact regularly and who influence your behavior, including your spouse, neighbors, your boss, fellow workers, professional colleagues, friends and acquaintances. You know their characteristics, how they behave and what degree they relate to you. Many of these individuals may play critical roles during certain times of your life. This is one network.

In the sports marketplace, your contacts may be your most vital resource. *Who you know* is equally as important as *what you know* when seeking opportunities in any marketplace including sports.

You need to develop your own sports network — even if you are just beginning your career search process and not even sure what area you will pursue. Then, as your career plans become clearer, or even change, you can further expand your network.

Develop a Contact List

Start identifying your network by developing a contact list. Begin by making two lists. The first should contain about 250 people you know. This may sound like more people than you think you've ever met, but just sit back, relax and think about it, you'll be surprised at how many influential people you *really* do know right now. The second list should contain another 250 people or organizations in sports you don't know, but want to know. You may need to do some research to develop this list, especially if you are just beginning your career search.

List #1

The first list will most likely include relatives, neighbors, fellow workers, former employers, alumni, friends, acquaintances, bankers, doctors, lawyers, ministers and professional colleagues. Refresh your memory with the following checklist of categories:

Friends *(refer to your Christmas card list)*
Neighbors *(past and present)*
Social acquaintances *(group and club members)*
Classmates *(high school and college)*
Local alumni
People you consulted or wrote a check to during the past 12 months:
Tradespeople, drugstore owner, etc.
Doctors, dentists, opticians, therapists, etc.
Lawyer, accountants, stock brokers, etc.
Insurance, real estate or travel agents, etc.

Financial services people
Relatives *(immediate and distant)*
Politicians *(local, state, national)*
Chamber of Commerce members
Church members
Students
Teachers
University officials
Trade association members
Professional organization executives and other members
People you meet at conferences or conventions
Customers
Speakers at meetings you've attended
Business club members
Salespeople
Others

List #2

The second list should represent people and organizations you *want* in your network. Brainstorming will be an important part of this list's development. Whether you are exploring career options, or changing career direction, be sure not to limit this list now because you'll be prioritizing this list later. For right now just get the names down.

As a guide, include the following on the second list:

- The top 50 companies/organizations you would like to work for
- The top 50 individuals you would love to work with.
- List 50 other highly respected companies/organizations in your interest area(s).
- List 50 other highly respected individuals in your interest area(s)
- List 50 top employees from the above-named companies/organizations.

After developing your comprehensive lists of contacts, classify the names on each list into four different categories:

- Those influential positions or who have hiring authority.
- Those with job leads.
- Those most likely to refer you to others.
- Those with long-distance contacts.

Select at least 50 individuals from each list for initiating your first round of contacts. Create 5 personal or professional links to each name for credibility. Being "godfathered" into a meeting with a personal reference is invaluable in developing relationships. You are now ready to begin an active prospecting and networking campaign which will enable you to expand your present network considerably, linking it to others' networks. This campaign should lead to informational interviews, formal job interviews and job offers.

Building Your Network

A successful career and job search includes three important techniques: prospecting, networking, and informational interviewing. These techniques are closely linked to one another. Usually, you start by prospecting, which helps you find contacts and information. Networking involves active communication with contacts, and hopefully leads to informational interview, which in turn may lead to further contact prospects, career and job information and potentially even job offers.

Prospecting

Prospecting involves seeking out contacts as well as information you need about careers and ultimately job interviews and offers, through telephone calls, letters, and face-to-face meetings.

Telephone calls are quick, easy and efficient. But, cold calls are least effective. The degree of effectiveness with telephone contacts depends on the strength of your referral.

Letters should always be well-written, and may require follow-up by phone to be effective.

Face-to-face contacts are considered the most effective, but also can be the most time consuming, and therefore the least efficient means of reaching many people.

Prospecting, like networking, is an on-going processes. You will be able to greatly increase the number of names on your contact lists by just getting the word out (by phone, letter and personal contact) that you are seeking information.

Don't overlook research. Your public library provides a wealth of information including books on virtually everything. Source listings with company names, addresses and phone numbers are also available. Many libraries today have computerized search facilities.

Approach

Your approach to prospects must be subtle, honest and professional. You are seeking information, advice and referrals in several areas:

- Career information and job opportunities
- Job search approach
- Resume
- Other contacts

Recognize this person as an expert and advisor - flattery will get you *everywhere.*

Networking

Prospecting for contacts is the all-important first step, yet networking is the essential follow-up with the contacts. Once you've identified the people to contact, you need to get out and do it. Developing your list was just the beginning — that list is not worth anything to you *until you start using it.*

The Numbers Game

The number of successful contacts you make is directly proportional to your efforts. Shoot for a 10% success ratio: for every 10 people you contact, 9 will not be of use to you and 1 will be invaluable.

Nobody wants to be turned down or rejected. Realize that *rejection* or *disappointment* are part of the process of developing any successful career. Failure is the stepping stone to success! Prepare yourself to be resilient - reminding yourself that people are not rejecting *you* personally. Knowing this, you will be in a better mindset to focus on *gathering information* rather than making sales. Accept rejections as part of the process and go on: don't let rejections halt your prospecting and networking. Make two new contacts each day. Spend 20 minutes each day initiating phone contacts, or allow a longer time for letter correspondence. Persist with this system, developing at least 15 new contacts each week.

At this pace, your odds of uncovering career information and job opportunities, being invited to formal job interviews and receiving job offers will increase dramatically. Remember to continue nurturing and managing this network so it performs well, generating information and job leads.

Do What Works

In using this system, you will seldom be turned down for an informational interview. Remember to develop personal and professional links to each contact. Getting to know your contact's secretary on a first name basis can prove to be invaluable. You should uncover vacancies on the critical *hidden* job market as well as place yourself in a positive position to take advantage of such opportunities. **Basic Principle:** The best way to get a job is to never ask for job directly. Always ask for information, advice and referrals.

Informational Interviewing: Putting Your Network to Work

While prospecting is essential for expanding your network, the informational interview is invaluable to your sports career search. Your goal is to acquire information: receive advice on your career plans, training, and resume; gather referrals to other individuals, companies, and other sources; and gain personal rapport with more people. You want to become a known commodity. This is accomplished by developing a very effective informational interviewing style. Remember informational interviews are not job interviews, even though they may lead directly to job offers.

Advantages of Informational Interviews
- You are less likely to encounter rejections since you are not asking for a job Rather, you are seeking information, advice, referrals and to get noticed.
- You can pursue higher level positions.
- You will invariably encounter little competition.
- You have the opportunity to go directly to the people who are the decision makers in the hiring process.
- You are likely to be invited to a future job interview based upon the referrals you receive.

This approach to both your career and job search has a much higher probability of generating job interviews and subsequent offers than the traditional job search strategies. Individuals in your network will become your eyes and ears for locating opportunities that are appropriate to your goals and skills. You are actually helping human resources personnel by giving them a chance to look you over without the constraints that a job interview situation presents.

The Hidden Job Market

Regardless of what you hear about affirmative action, equal opportunity and the need to advertise positions, the unadvertised or hidden job market dominates the sports industry.

Department heads, managers and directors are the people who do the hiring, not the personnel office.

Approach the Right People

Ideally, you should contact people who are busy, who have the power to hire and who are knowledgeable about the organization. From a practical standpoint, you may have to take whomever you can schedule. Sometimes people who are not busy can be helpful. You will gain the easiest access to people you already know or people to whom you have a personal or professional link.

Using Approach Letters and the Telephone

You should use a more formal approach to access referrals and new contacts. Write a letter and follow it up with a phone call. Do not enclose a copy of your resume with an approach letter. All this will do is give the contact a reason *not* to talk to you.

Keep in mind that the purpose of this letter is to make an appointment for an interview where you will seek job and career information, advice and referrals.

Key Elements in the Approach Letter

- **Use appropriate openers.**
  If you have a referral, tell the individual you are considering a sports career and state a particular interest area, if you have one. Tell who referred you to this person, stating that it was suggested he or she might be a good person to give you useful information about careers
- **Make the request.**
- **Demonstrate the courtesy rather than aggressiveness.**
  Mention you realize they are busy. Flatter them by requesting an appointment based on their most convenient time and place.
- **Close with a professional touch.**
  In closing the letter, mention that you will call the person to see if an appointment can be arranged. Be specific and follow-up. It is your responsibility to schedule a meeting.

Informational Interview Questions

The informational interview is your opportunity to find out about a certain career area: what are the duties and responsibilities of the various different positions; what knowledge, skills, abilities and qualifications are needed to hold the various positions, and what is the work environment like. In addition, it is your opportunity to test your resume on a prospective employer. Prepare for this opportunity by making yourself an interview guide: a list of the questions for which you want answers. An interview guide will help you organize your material both before and after the interview, and it will show the person you are meeting with that you are seriously searching for career information, and not just rambling and wasting their time. Use the following list of information interview questions to help you create your own interview guides:

Career Questions
- What skills and knowledge does one need to perform this job?
- How would I best acquire the necessary skills to perform the job?
- What are some advantages and disadvantages in this line of work?
- What advancement opportunities are there?
- What are the future trends of the industry?
- What is a typical work day?
- What do you like about your work?
- What do you dislike about your work?
- What are normal salary ranges?
- How did you go about finding this job?

Job Search Questions
- Where do I go to find a job related to this field?
- How can I identify both advertised and unadvertised job vacancies?
- How do I develop new job leads?
- What might be the best way to approach prospective employers?
- How do I overcome employer's objections to me?

Resume Review Questions
- Is this resume tailored for the job I am seeking?
- If an employer received this resume in the mail, how do you think he or she would react to it?
- What are possible weaknesses or areas that need to be improved?
- What specific things can I do to improve the form and content of the resume?
- How attractive and appropriate is it (length, paper quality, color, layout and typing)?

Seven Rules for Networking Success

As you conduct informational interviews and network, keep these seven rules in mind:

1. Look for a career and a job that fits you rather than try to fit yourself into an available career or position.

2. Target your career and job search toward specific positions, organizations and individuals. Most shotgun approaches tend to be ineffective.
3. Conduct a persistent prospecting campaign to continually expand your network and replenish contacts that can lead to more contacts and informational interviews.
4. Conduct many informational interviews. When you ask for information, advice and referrals, surprisingly few people will turn you down. In fact, most will be flattered and eager to assist you.
5. If your job search gets bogged down, you need to substantially increase your daily prospecting activities as well as the number of informational interviews you conduct each week. Persistence, based on an understanding of probability, pays off in the long run.
6. Always send a thank you letter to those who take the time to talk with you. Thoughtful people tend to be *remembered people*.
7. Your success is directly related to how well you network.

Expanding Your Network

Networking must be an ongoing part of your sports career and job search rather than something that is turned on and off. *You need to continue networking even after you land a job*. It should play an important role in advancing your career and can only continue to play a role if you keep abreast of the details of maintaining and expanding your network.

Follow-up and Feedback

Know the importance of follow-up and feedback both during the job search and after you accept a job offer.

When you receive a referral from a networking contact, be sure to follow-up with two phone calls: Call the referral contact and also call the source of your contact to let him/her know you have made an initial contact. Chances are your source has already talked to the referral and indicated that you would be in contact soon. If you fail to follow-up on referral efforts, your source and referral contacts may quickly dismiss you as someone who is wasting their time not to mention being inconsiderate.

After conducting an informational interview with a referral, contact the *source* of the referral to express thanks the useful contact. You need to do this to emphasize the fact that you indeed did follow-up on the referral and to emphasize your continuing interest in receiving additional referrals. This is also a good time to give your contact feedback on your job search progress. People like to know their personal efforts produce results. They will remember you for giving them this feedback.

Keep records on your network. Upon accepting a job offer, be sure to contact individuals in your network who assisted you with information, advice and referrals. Send them a thoughtful letter in which you inform them of your new position and thank them for their assistance.

Individuals who played the most important role in your job search should also receive a phone call from you to again inform them of your new position and express your gratitude for their assistance. Sending flowers or a small gift to the most important individuals can provide that additional touch!

By providing feedback to members of your network you will most likely be remembered for future reference. If in three to five years you decide it is time to conduct another job search, you should have in place a well developed network of individuals who are willing and able to assist you. If you fail to provide members of your present network with follow-up and feedback, they are less likely to assist you in the future.

Network on the Job

Once you begin your new job, remember that your organization is made up of many people who can help advance your career. Learn who is the decision maker as well as who you may want to avoid or who might make a useful mentor, advisor or friend.

Refocus your informational interviewing techniques for the career advancement process:

- What are the major criteria for getting ahead in this organization?
- How important is *whom you associate with* to advancing in this organization?
- Are you associating with the right people and clearly communicating your competence, honesty, trustworthiness, enthusiasm and likability to these individuals?

The sooner you learn the interpersonal structure of your organization, the sooner you can begin networking with the right people.

Developing Personal and Professional Associations

Regardless of how happy you may be with your present job, there will come a time when you may decide it's time to make a change. Keep in mind that you could also find yourself on the *outs* with your present employer, lose a job or simply become unhappy with your present job.

The probability is 90% that you will change jobs and careers again within the next 10 years.

Quite often, people suddenly discontinue the networking process once they find employment. They are no longer concerned with reaffirming career goals, conducting research on other organizations, updating resume material, and networking to broaden their interest base. Such complacency can make it difficult to get back into the job search process. Networking should be the one job search skill that should be kept active even while an individual is employed. At some point in the future you may be looking for another job. Maintaining your network is imperative for exchanging information, advice and referrals.

Maximize the Job Search Process by Being in Demand

Joining professional trade associations in your special interest group provides networking experiences that often lead to future job opportunities. This is the very essence of excellent networking. You no longer need to market yourself for a job since you have put yourself in demand. Using their own networking activities, employers and headhunters will recruit from within trade associations and special interest groups, thus increasing your options.

Professional and trade associations are some of the most important networks for securing jobs and advancing your career in the sports marketplace. All organizations provide services to their members which can include such benefits as: monthly magazines and newsletters, insurance, travel, training and placement counseling. More important for those seeking employment and career advancement is that professional and trade associations link individuals who work for other sports employers. In so doing, they provide a critical communication and networking bridge between organizations that assist members in making career moves from one sports organization to another. Networking via such association works best when you become noticed by other members because of your participation and involvement in furthering the goals of the organization.

Resources

You will discover hundreds of sports organizations and associations that perform this linking function as well as provide networking opportunities relevant to finding jobs and advancing careers. Most of these organizations can be easily accessed by surveying a few key directories:

National Trade & Professional Associations

(202) 737-3777

The Sports Address Bible
A directory of Who's Who in sports-related industries

(612) 484-8299

Encyclopedia of Business & Trade Associations

(313) 961-2242

Creating a Personal Advisory Team

Career decisions can be some of the toughest decisions you may deal with in a lifetime. One way to cope with these difficult considerations is by turning to others for advice, allowing them to become a support group of sorts by listening to your concerns and giving you their advice in return. In a sense, they constitute your personal board of directors.

Everybody's advisory group is different. Yours may include friends, relatives, or even the lady next door. In any case, all of these opinion-givers usually have two things in common: they care about your well-being and you value their thoughts. Though the composition of your board will change over time, there are categories from which you are almost certain to draw helpful advisors at some point in your life.

Family

Throughout college, parents typically act as both sounding boards and inquisitors in terms of your career direction. During senior year, however, the frequency and quality of your conversations with Mom and Dad can become paramount.

A former intern indicated that she spoke frequently with her parents about her senior year job search. "Your family knows your strengths and weaknesses," she told me. "They know how your personality would fit into a position."

But parental advice does have its limits. "Your parents are just not involved enough to know the intricate details," contends John Jay, a graduate of Washington University of Missouri.

Joshua Haims, another Washington University graduate, understands the reservations but feels that parents are able to give good advice regardless of whether they're involved in one's particular field. "They might not know exactly what you're getting into," says Haims, "but they can ask the right questions." In fact, Haims' parents went to some lengths to ensure that they could give their son solid counsel. "They came to campus and tapped one of the business school deans for advice," Haims says. As a result of their interest, Haims readily involves his parents in his career decisions.

Older brothers and sisters also are in a great position to provide knowledgeable career advice, particularly if they experienced not too long ago what you are going through. Linda Razor, a pre-law major from The Ohio State University, had her lifelong career goals decimated when steep tuition put law school out of reach. Her sister's suggestions to work in a law-allied field led Razor to her current position as a paralegal.

Faculty

Faculty members receive mixed reviews as career counselors, but they're an important source of information for students heading into the working world. If you're going to use professors, make sure you know them well. Get acquainted with them. Ask questions about their subject area. When they know you personally, they'll give you more attention than they give to students they only see once in a great while.

Charles Davis sought career advice from faculty members in his area of specialization when he was taking a sports marketing course at New York University. "Most gave me OK advice, but one or two were so far removed from the business world that they just gave me pat answers and what was there." Davis recommends faculty who consult regularly as good sources of accurate, up-to-date information. He has linked up with one such professor whom he calls his "technical consultant" because he's a heavyweight in the sponsorship field. He also has added an outside voice to his advisory group a consultant who guest lectured in one of Davis's classes. "She's a good advisor," says Davis. "She's in the training/education field and we frequently discuss my career directions. Her people skills are a good balance to those of my technical consultant."

Some faculty members offer more than just insight. When Jay was chatting with his advisor about his career plans, the professor offered to make a call. The call was to the president of McCann-Erickson, where Jay is still employed.

Career Planning and Placement Officers

Another readily available resource is the career planning and placement sector. While some people tap this office for library information and listings only, many successfully add the office's career counselors to their pool of helpful career coaches.

Talk with the counselors in the office. Even though you may think you know what you want, consider career counselors a good sounding board. They can tell you what to do and what resources are there.

Volunteering to work in your school's career services office is another way to develop a network of influence for yourself. In this case, the career services staff will usually be more interested in you making the right decision than in your just getting a job.

Co-Workers and Bosses

As you gain more work experience, you'll find additional career advisors on the job. When you look at career possibilities, call your previous boss, department, or the director for advice. These working coaches can be especially helpful thanks to their up-to-date knowledge and current contacts. "Not only do they serve as sounding boards, but they can give out contact names as resources." A young marketer was in the process of resigning from Anheuser-Busch when he got some unexpected but very helpful counsel from one of the managers at that firm. "The manager said, 'What I think you want to do is gain a management position. Why start over elsewhere?' That really made me think. He directed me to the right people to talk to at Anheuser-Busch." After being shown that the company was willing to let him go "anywhere in the special events business," the marketer decided to stay.

Friends

Friends can be your most consistent and sometimes most unsupportive source of career advisors. Friends will help strike a balance in the early stages of your job search but rarely are they a key element of help. In a competitive and still growing marketplace such as sports, friends usually have an extremely limited perspective.

Employment Professionals

Executive search and employment professionals bear careful watching. The employment agency types often are encountered early in the job search process; the headhunters pop into view later. Students note that agencies with jobs to fill have referred them without regard to the students' interests or abilities.

While not all agency experiences will be so negative, it's not a bad idea to exhaust your other options before turning to paid advisors. There are plenty of people out there willing to help you for free. You'll find that members of your personal advisory board will come and go and that you won't need to consult every one of them on each decision. Your team will probably be made up of some generalists and some specialists, whose expertise is tapped only when the issue is appropriate to their orientation. One role that will not change, however, is the role that you play: you are your own decision maker. It will always be your job for life. After all is said and done, you've got to weigh all the advice you've collected, evaluate the merits of each opinion, and reach a final conclusion of yourself. It's your career that's at stake. Only you will fully experience the highs and lows associated with your decision.

There is no substitute for polished people skills both as a sports practitioner or in the job search process. Photo: courtesy of **Steichen's Sporting Goods.**

3

Job Acquisition Strategies

Developing a Game Plan That Maximizes Your Efforts

Finding the motivation to launch a sports job search can be extremely difficult. It isn't unusual for job seekers to move in as many unrelated directions as possible to avoid resume writing, phone calling and interviewing. Previously bad work experiences can damage your self-confidence, causing a retreat into activities that feel secure.

A focused objective and the determination to achieve are necessary on the road to a challenging new position. Use the following commandments of job hunting to help you proceed with your search within a reasonable amount of time:

1. **Don't Procrastinate.**
   Make your time work for you; don't be a slave to each passing hour, anxiously awaiting the end of the workday.
2. **Make The Job Search Process A Game.**
   Establish your own rules. Decide what constitutes success and failure. Don't view your search as a struggle, but rather as an opportunity to enhance your standard of living and your self-esteem. Make the most of this fresh opportunity as a time to soul search.
3. **If You've Lost A Job, Accept The Realities.**
   This is a stressful period in which you've likely lost a long-standing set of personal relationships. You will likely experience anxiety,

anger, guilt, the same emotions people feel after the death of a family member or close friend. Allow yourself a few days to mourn, then move on. And remember, the loss of a job doesn't mean the loss of your dignity, no matter how poorly you might have been treated. When you've been told in your outgoing interview that "this could be the best thing to happen to you," believe that it's probably true!

4. Review Your Financial Situation.

Develop a financial strategy. Consider advising your creditors of your unemployed status and your sincere interest in maintaining your credit-worthiness.

Determine how much cash you have available if needed. Many people panic when they realize their salary will stop on a certain date. Remember that you might have IRAs you could tap. There may be a cash-surrender value available from your insurance policies. You could take out loans from a credit union. You could cash in savings bonds.

You could redirect some of your other savings programs on a temporary basis. Seldom are people forced to dip heavily into their savings if they take time to develop a financial plan.

5. Set a Target Date For The Acceptance And Start Of Your New Job.

Based on an evaluation of your marketable skills and your perception of the job market, choose a reasonable date. Then direct your efforts toward reaching that goal. Outline the elements of your ideal job. Include job title, salary, office size and location. Be specific and visualize yourself in the new job. If you don't know what you're looking for, how will you know when you find it? A realistic time frame is six to nine months.

6. Review Your Wardrobe and Image.

That abused and somewhat outdated suit that you used to wear every Friday just doesn't make the grade anymore. First impressions are important, and a worn cuff or scuffed shoe may send the wrong message. It's amazing how many job seekers wear $300 suits and $60 shirts or blouses, yet fail to shine their shoes.

7. Set A Daily Schedule and Stick To It.

Destructive habits can be easily acquired, but extremely difficult to break. Get up and take charge. The process of finding a job is a

contact sport. *The more people you contact, the faster you'll find a new position.* It can be uncomfortable explaining to people that you're out of work, but unless you meet with networking contacts and potential employers on a daily basis, your search will drag on endlessly.

Richard Bolles, author of ***What Color Is Your Parachute?*** says that about two-thirds of all job hunters spend less than five hours a week actively looking for new positions. How long would you last in any job by working actively just one hour each day? Your career deserves a full time effort.

8. Resist The Temptation To Become House-Bound.
Your time should be focused on landing a new job. It's inevitable: You'll find a job and develop a career path in sports. The question is how long will it take? By demonstrating a focused direction and making yourself accessible to employers and networking contacts, you'll shorten the time between paychecks.

9. Organize and Sequence Your Job Search.
Make sure our past is well integrated into the process of finding a job or changing your career to sports. Be sure you feel comfortable conducting your job search. Remember, it represents the best of what you are in terms of your past and present accomplishments as they relate to your present and future goals. If you follow this type of job search, you will communicate your best self to employers.

The Job Acquisition Process

Step 1   **Self-Analysis**
　　　　　Identify Goals & Objectives
　　　　　Identify Accomplishments
　　　　　Identify Interests, Knowledge & Experience
　　　　　Identify Personal Inventory

Step 2   **Career Exploration**
　　　　　Identify Industry Sources
　　　　　Identify Personal Network
　　　　　Link Information
　　　　　Define Career Direction

Step 3   **Presentation Package**
- Developing A Winning Resume
- Creating Practical Job Search Letters
- Creating Personal Value
- Having Three Unique Marginal Differences

Step 4.   **Build Your Network**
- Develop Contact Lists
- Prospect, Approach, Interview
- Access Hiring Authorities
- Create Relationships

Step 5.   **Develop Job Search Skills**
- Self-Analysis Skills
- Research Skills
- Self-Marketing Skills
- Communication Skills
- Interviewing Skills

Step 6.   **Have a Firm Action Plan**
- Implement Your Interest, Knowledge & Skills
- Chase Your Direction
- Market The Package
- Find Hidden Job Market
- Develop Job Search Skills
- Create Time Table

Since the individual job search steps are interrelated, they should be followed in sequence. If you fail to properly complete the initial self-assessment steps, your job search may become haphazard, aimless and costly. For example, you should never write a resume (Step 3) before first assessing your skills (Step 1) and identifying your career direction (Step 2). You normally network (Step 4) after assessing your skills (Step 1), identifying your career direction (Step 2) writing a resume (Step 3). Indeed, relating Step 1 to Step 2 is critical to the successful implementation of all other job search steps. You must complete Steps 1 and 2 before continuing to the other Steps. Steps 3 to 6 can be conducted simultaneously because they compliment and reinforce one another.

Try to sequence your job search as close to these steps as possible. The true value of this sequencing will become very apparent as you implement your game plan.

Chapter 2 outlined the value of ongoing networking — not just to find a job, but to maintain touch with people who can be influential in your career development. Your network is your sounding board. In the sports industry, you need to constantly review your skills to make sure they are appropriate for the changing job market. Members of your network and advisory group will help you with this self-assessment. Once you have necessary skills to perform certain jobs, you can focus your career and job search on the things you do well and enjoy doing. You will avoid the trap of trying to fit into jobs that are not conducive to your particular mix of skills, motivations and abilities; the number one temptation and mistake while changing into a sports careers.

Taking Matters Into Your Own Hands

A well run, self-placement campaign can cut your job search time in half or better. More importantly, a well prepared job search will keep you focused on what you really want: career advancement in lieu of just a slot to fill.

Behind every great job offer are great interviews! By following this system, you will be better equipped to generate and conduct interviews that produce winning jobs.

Countless numbers of people change jobs every year, so you are not embarking on *Mission: Impossible*. However, your mission will be to identify the position you really want, mobilize your personal resources and sell yourself in a way that achieves your objective. Sound simple? It is if you follow each of the steps outlined for your personal placement.

Before You Begin

Success is rarely an accident. Luck or chance certainly affect changes in life. Preparation balances chance so it is more in your favor. Remember the old saying: "The harder I work, the luckier I get." Better yet, "Preparation creates the opportunity for luck." You make your own breaks. Job searching is a full time job. This means five days a week with no less than six hours of work per day. Less than this and you are only fooling yourself into thinking that you are looking for a new job.

You are embarking on a self-marketing program. While many of the ideas may be new, give them a chance to succeed. What makes the difference between success and failure? Consider the following story:

> Jill had a good job in a promising sports marketing company. During a general lay-off, her position was terminated. It was the first time she had ever been laid off, and aside from the severe blow to her ego, she was worried that she would not get settled quickly and in a job where she could develop her career.
>
> Since her entire department was let go, she had four competitors from her own company all with the approximately the same qualifications and all looking for similar work.

Getting on the Horse Again After You've Fallen

Jill reassessed her career goals and identified her strongest skills and interests. After redoing her resume, she began to research her target companies. This all took place within one week after the lay-off. Jill was on the phone, calling people who could act as referrals to the companies she wanted to approach. She had an interview with one of her target companies.

Three weeks later, after considerable networking, she had an offer from her second choice company, and they want an answer in one week. She didn't want to lose this opportunity, but thought another interview could produce a better job for her with her first choice company. What should she tell the second choice company especially since the first choice company was not in a hurry to make a decision?

The second choice company did not have a job description and their offer was based on a verbal outline of the job. They were tailoring the job to Jill's skills—which represents the true power of networking! Jill recommended that she help them write a job description so everyone would be sure of the position's responsibilities, authority and expected results. The company agreed and became even more enamored of Jill as a result. Meanwhile, Jill was able to meet again with choice number one. At last they made her an offer. The salary was slightly less than the other company and lower than her previous job, but the potential was much more promising. Jill accepted the offer from her first choice, six weeks after she had started her job acquisition process. She was now happy and successful. Choice number two made a standing offer: If her new job did not work, they would find a spot for her.

Keys to Success:

- Spend full time on your search — 40 hours per week, if possible.
- Become tenacious and committed.
- Do your job search exercises in detail and take the time to think about the consequences on your life and career goals.
- Become aware of your strong points and how they can benefit your target companies.
- Research information about the companies and people you want to meet.
- Take the initiative in calling people to make appointments.
- Write thank-you letters after each meeting.
- Keep in shape mentally and physically.
- Be smart enough to ask for advice when a decision is needed.
- Practice with your mentor and other members of your advisory team.

Application Techniques

In most situations, you never really apply for an athletics-related position because sports organizations — especially professional franchises — literally never publicize an opening. Since openings are scarce, those who arrive at the right time, whose personalities and qualifications are well suited to the organization, are the ones who are offered positions. Timing is the key factor in nailing down a sports job. Many years may pass before key individuals retire or move on to another team. If you, your letter of application, or your resume happen to be sitting on the general manager's desk at that time, you may get the break you've been waiting for. That's why it is so important to continually follow up on leads. Even if you make an infrequent call to an organization for only a few minutes, you can keep your name in the back of your contact's mind.

Always read the sports sections carefully. Sometimes there will be a hint that an administrator is accepting another position or is ready to retire. Another hint about timing: most jobs are filed before the season begins since changes are usually made at the end of the schedule. Therefore, the best time to contact any team or league office would be just before the season's end. Also, all intercollegiate athletic openings are circulated to all institutions throughout the country, and many can be found posted in athletic business offices. The *NCAA Weekly* newsletter and *Education Week* are two publications that contain articles concerning current issues in sports and list job openings from around the country in numerous sports-related fields. Though many of these positions may have a replacement already designated, it never hurts to pursue them. However, be wary of new opportunity listings that have deadline application dates close to the posting date of the position. These vacancies more than likely are already filled and are advertised merely to meet mandated hiring policies. Still, remember, "Nothing ventured, nothing gained."

By now you have the picture: anyone with developed contracts has the best chance of landing a position. Only 18% of all professional, managerial, and executive jobs are advertised or listed with agencies, search firms, or newspapers. It makes sense: The more good contacts you make; the more and better the opportunities you will have to explore. Never underestimate the value of developing contacts through part-time occupations, social/civic activities, local influentials, past athletic acquaintances, or even during major sporting events.

Designing a #1 Draft Choice Cover Letter

Once you have decided where to apply for a sports-related position, you need to develop a cover letter and prepare a resume for the job you are pursuing.

The cover letter is very important and should accompany all resumes. Its main purpose is to introduce you to your potential employer and to get him/her to read your resume. It is important that you adhere to the following guidelines:

- It must be neat, grammatically correct, and it should be typed. Check it carefully for typos. Your objective is to make your first impression a good one. Never use mimeographed form letters, and, if possible, select paper and letterhead that adds a professional touch.
- Address the letter to a specific person. A letter is more likely to be taken seriously when it is addressed to an individual. This is why we have included in our directory (if possible) the name of either the general manager or the owner of a team. If you are applying to an organization not listed in the directory, call its office and ask the secretary for the name of the man or woman in charge of personnel.

- The first paragraph of your letter should explain your purpose. In these few words you must make the reader want to continue reading. Try to get the reader's attention, but don't use a cute expression or cliche. Never abbreviate. Since you are applying for a serious position, a light approach will not be appreciated

- Highlight your educational and business background. You can refer to your resume, if appropriate.

- Let the organization know that you are willing to work and all you want is a chance. Be sincere. Enthusiasm for the industry and the field is vital.

- Always ask for a personal interview. If it is a local organization, you may even suggest that you will telephone for an interview.

- Focus on their needs. Above all, you must impress the reader that you have something to offer the organization. All organizations are looking for someone above average who can make a positive contribution.

- Do not mention salary in your letter.

- Keep your letter brief and to the point. You are just summarizing your career. Let your resume provide the necessary details.

- Sign your letter.

- Keep accurate records of your mailing for follow-up.

Following is a sample letter from a typical student. Take a close look at the opening and closing paragraphs as well as the words that have been used as a means of persuasion. While you shouldn't just copy these samples, you might borrow words, phrases, sentences, and paragraphs and creatively adapt them to your own background.

Though you will usually accompany your letter with a resume, the combination of the two will rarely produce as many interviews as a well-written letter by itself. In a letter you can tailor your presentation, discuss

1983 Opportunity Street
Philadelphia, PA 19104

June 30, 1982

Mr. George Washington, President
Philadelphia Freedom
1 Liberty Square
Philadelphia, PA 19104

Dear Mr. Washington:

Philadelphia Freedom's reputation as a first class organization has inspired me to contact you regarding possible employment opportunities. I feel I have the potential, the enthusiasm and the training to step in and immediately make a positive contribution to your organization.

I am a recent graduate of **Biscayne College** where I have taken specialized courses in sports administration. I have also worked for the past two years on a part-time basis, as assistant to the public relations director at **Sporting Goods International**. My earnings from that position enabled me not only to finance my education, but also to gain valuable experience in communications and in dealing with the sports public.

Through my job, I have been exposed to a variety of public relations problems, and have learned how to deal creatively with them. In the absence of a senior executive, I was given complete responsibility for company relations with local recreational groups.

The field of sports has always fascinated me and I want very much to make it my lifetime occupation. I am willing to take any available position or project in order to break into your organization.

Enclosed is a copy of my resume. I look forward to meeting you personally at your convenience.

Thank you for your consideration.

Sincerely,

Paul Revere

Enclosure

Figure 8.   Sample Letter from Student Contacting Employer.

what you can do, or arouse curiosity. Besides, resumes, if not designed well, make it easier for readers to discover a reason for disqualifying you. (See Figure 8).

Creating an MVP Resume

The concept of a resume is a myth. Without it, job searchers feel insecure because there is nothing to validate their existence. Without it, the interviewer feels insecure because there is nothing to verify and no script to follow especially if the interviewer does not know how to interview!

Fact: The resume is used more often to eliminate than to hire. Consider the sports classified ad that draws 400 resumes. What is the first task of the hiring authority? To cut the pile down to as few as possible! Why? Because many applicants are not qualified but send a resume anyway, hoping it will attract attention. Second, many applicants who *do* qualify, do not know how to market themselves correctly. Third, no one has time to interview 400 candidates. Finally, resumes do not get jobs—people do.

What a Resume Does

- Fix in your mind your skills, accomplishments, work history and education.
- Assist you in networking and getting referrals.
- Provoke interest and get an interview.
- Facilitate a face-to-face presentation.
- Prospect outside your geographic area and generate interviews.

The resume is above all a calling card after the fact to remind the interviewer who you are. You must create something you hope will be little used, but create it in such a way that if it is used, it will help your campaign.

Suppose you had to select your resume out of a field of 400. How would it stack up? What can be done to put the odds more in your favor?

Assess Your Work Experience and Accomplishments

Begin by making a detailed chronological list of your total work experience. This is for your own reference. As simple as it may seem, this list will keep you from forgetting something important in your professional history just when you need it.

Working backwards from the present, complete the following:

1. **Employment History** *(list for each job you've held)*
   Dates
   Company name & main address
   Work location (if different from above)
   Your title
   Your superior, name and title
   You responsibilities
   Your key accomplishments
   Starting and ending salary
   Extra benefits
   What attracted you to this job
   Reason for leaving
   Who can be a good reference for you

2. **Summary of Education**

   Elementary school *(year graduated)*
   High school *(year graduated and certificate or diploma received)*
   College(s) or trade school(s) (dates attended)
   Course of study
   Degree(s) or certificate(s) received (date)
   Honors
   Any licenses you possess (name specialty and date of license)
   Any other relevant training (workshops, certifications, etc.).

3. **Special Talents**
   Languages (degree of written and spoken fluency, reading comprehension)

4. **Other Skills** (writing, programming, word processing, etc.)

5. **Associations** (professional , social)

Format a Resume

Three formats are widely used today: functional, chronological, and a mixture of the two called the performance resume. Choose a format that is flexible enough to allow for modification in addition to custom tailoring depending on the job you are targeting.

The Functional Resume

The functional resume presents accomplishments and work experience arranged according to function or responsibilities without real attention to chronological order.

The 20 Second Resume

Most people who read resumes simply *DO NOT*! Most resume *readers* skim over the resume and quickly grab onto one or two items of interest and, if the candidate is present, use these items to break into the interview. Most resumes which are boring for the reader, more than likely will be for the poor candidate as well.

The average attention given to scanning a resume is *20 seconds!* That is not a long time, especially if you have given the reader a two-page resume. Therefore, a "to the point" resume includes the following:

> Your name, address and telephone number — but no date
>
> An opening statement that gives a summary of your overall professional capabilities.
>
> Two to four major accomplishments.
>
> A statement that describes the way you like to work and what kind of person you are.
>
> Employment History
>
> Prior Experience (if pertinent).
>
> Education (if pertinent)
>
> Affiliations (if pertinent).

Advantages	*Disadvantages*
If you have had a number of jobs in a short period of time, a functional style can help by highlighting skills and accomplishments rather than focusing on changes.	Employers and personnel managers are used to a chronological presentation of work history. Deviation from this format can arouse suspicion, if not confusion.
If your most recent experience *does not relate* to the position for which you are applying, a functional resume will focus more on your past strengths.	It is not an easy resume to prepare and it must change to match each job objective.

The Chronological Resume

The chronological resume lists positions by date, beginning with the most recent. Emphasis is placed on recent experience rather than past history, and usually a progression in responsibility is indicated. Each job listing should show: company name and location, dates of employment, job title(s), main responsibilities and key accomplishments.

Advantages

This is an easy resume to organize and for many years this has been the standard format and consequently it is the most familiar.

It shows progress made in your field of specialization as well as increasing responsibility.

Disadvantages

If you have changed jobs frequently, it shows instability and will require explanation, especially if there are any gaps in employment.

If you have changed professions or career direction, it may raise questions about your real goals.

The Performance Resume

A mixed chronological-functional format incorporating a powerful upfront section, designed to attract the reader's attention immediately. It combines accomplishments into functional areas and places your greatest accomplishments up front in relation to the position you are targeting.

Advantage

It immediately highlights your strengths and is extremely flexible.

It maximizes your chances of catching a reader's interest.

You can adapt the resume to suit the job you are going after without sacrificing quality.

It permits you to display originality in your ideas and manner of presentation which will lead the reader in the direction you want to go by noticing your skills and accomplishments.

Disadvantages

Putting together this resume takes know-how.

Some Basic Guidelines

Follow these rules to create a winning resume:
- Focus on accomplishments, skills and results.
- Never include statements or accomplishments that cannot be proven.
- Keep sentences short and punchy.
- Your resume should be attractive and easy to read: good spacing, margins and bold printing, Avoid overcrowding.
- Do not use abbreviations when there could be doubt as to meaning. Be clear and precise.
- Keep it short. A good resume will be as short as possible, certainly not longer than two pages and, if possible, one page.
- Do not use personal pronouns.
- Use *Action words* to describe each accomplishment.
- Whenever possible, show results in numbers.
- Be original.
- If you have a sense of humor, let it show a little in your resume. A resume that can reflect your real personality is a wonder.
- Show only the year you started or terminated the position. If there have been promotions during the period of employment, dates can be shown in parentheses next to each job title.
- There should be only enough information to provoke the reader's interest.
- The resume has to convey a certain level of competence in the employer's area of interest, or there will be no invitation to interview. The employer should ask, "Does this person have the kind of talent I am seeking?"
- Candidates without much work experience, or who are tackling their first job search, must change the *Accomplishments* heading to *Skills*.
- Test your resume before launching it on the market!

Accomplishments: The key to what's in it for the Employer

The word *accomplishment* is becoming part of our everyday language. When someone does something exceptional, people take note. Getting a new job requires ammunition, and this ammunition will come from your prior experiences and *accomplishments*.

Accomplishments are the key to your resume, interview and ultimate job offer. Your ability to show what you have done and what you can do for a prospective employer determines his interest in hiring you over someone else. What is an accomplishment? It is something you personally did that improved a situation, solved a problem and/or made a contribution either in value or substance. *Remember this:* Potential is nothing more than talent that has yet to prove anything.

You need to first identify your skills. Then list what you accomplished with those skills in your resume. Finally, you will need to draw upon your reservoir of successful experiences during the interview process.

Think back over your first job experiences. You may have been in school or have had a summer job or contributed to a school project. Ask yourself the following questions to help you identify your accomplishments.

What was one problem you encountered?
What did you do to solve the problem?
What skills did you use?
What was the benefit for you?
How did your company benefit?

Your accomplishments come from:
- Performance
- Profits
- Efficiency
- Handling an emergency
- Excellence
- Finding
- Teaching
- Savings
- Sales
- New business
- Creativity
- Inventing
- Expanding
- Restructuring

Your list of accomplishments should include instances in which:
You solved a problem or handled an emergency situation.
You created or built something.
You developed an idea.
You demonstrated leadership in the face of challenge.
You followed instructions and realized a goal.
You identified a need and satisfied it.
You contributed actively to a decision or a change.

You increased sales or profit or reduced costs.
You helped somebody realize his objectives.
You saved time and/or money.
You received an award or special commendation.

Assign numbers or values to the accomplishment and state explicitly what happened as a result of your action. If sales increased by $1 million, or costs came down by 18 percent, or efficiency improved by 33 percent, saving $575,000 over two years make sure everyone knows it!

Types of Accomplishments

Sales	Financial
Manufacturing	Service
General Management	Personnel Relations

A *good* accomplishment will do one or more of the following:

- Increase performance
- Decrease costs
- Increase profits and/or sales
- Reduce time
- Increase efficiency
- Expand client base
- Lower unit costs
- Provide better controls
- Permit better decision making
- Introduce new talent through recruitment
- Provide service where it did not exist before
- Improve employee relations
- Improve reliability
- Streamline operations
- Improve strategic planning
- Turn around losing operations
- Eliminate waste
- Improve working conditions
- Identify and solve problems
- Solve emergency situations.
- Make things more beautiful or functional
- Help management to manage better than it did before

Look over these past few pages about accomplishments, then identify at least 20 of your own accomplishments and describe them in terms of what problem you dealt with in each case, and what skills you used to solve each particular situation.

Paul A. Revere

1983 Opportunity Street　　　　　　　　　　Phone:　(404) 377-0247
Philadelphia, PA 19104　　　　　　　　　　　　　　　(404) 624-7301

Employment Objective

Position in sports administration leading to a franchise administration in public relations or promotions.

Summary of Qualifications

Educational background concentrated in business administration with emphasis in personnel psychology and relations. Sports administration minor specializing in public relations, sports psychology, and wellness fitness programs.

Familiarity gained through promotional and fund raising procedures gained with experience as program coordinator with a major university.

My strongest personal assets are self-discipline, strong communication skills, aggressiveness, and a personable disposition. My main attributes are the ability to organize, innovate, and deal with the public, while at the same time being very influential.

Education

1990 graduate of Freedom College, Philadelphia, Pennsylvania.

Received a Bachelor of Science in Personnel Administration and a minor in Sports Administration. Electives have been predominately in industrial relations with emphasis in psychology/sociology departments. Scholastic record: 3.0 (out of 4.0) in major field: 3.7 in minor field.

1989 graduate of St. Thomas University, Miami, Florida.

Considered one of the best sports administration programs in the country. Completed 24 credits toward my minor in sports administration at Biscayne College, Miami, Fla. Earned recognition on the Dean's list.

1985 graduate of Valley Forge High School, Boston, Massachusetts

Graduated 25th out of 250 in college preparatory, military school. Member of the concert and marching bands as well as received the rank of officer in the R.O.T.C. junior program.

Figure 9.　　　Sample Resume

Broadcast Letter in Reply to an Ad

A broadcast letter is your resume in letter form designed to address a very specifically targeted company or opportunity. A well-written broadcast letter — like the 20 second resume — should highlight your key accomplishments. It has a much better chance of being read by the person you addressed and getting a reply.

Great broadcast letters can still be rerouted, but these still stand a fair chance of getting you an interview.

If your resume does not meet all the criteria of the job but your skills are in line, this letter can omit chronological employment data and concentrate directly on accomplishments paralleling the company's needs. Remember, your primary objective is an interview. Well-written broadcast letters or letter/resume combinations have done their job if these get you an interview.

Writing a Broadcast Letter

To create a broadcast letter, use elements from your resume:

- Salutation - always verify correct spelling of name and title unless you are addressing a blind ad; then use "Dear Sir/Madam" or "Gentlemen."
- Introduce yourself, adapting sentences from your 20 second Resume.
- Lead into key accomplishments taken from your resume either in support of the ad you are answering or backing up the position you are trying to approach.
- Include a very brief indication of your education and focus the reader on what you feel you can do for this company.
- Close your letter a suggested meeting time: When you write a specific person, indicate that you will be calling him for an appointment within a few days. When addressing a box number, suggest an early meeting.
- Your letter should only be one page.

Your 20 second resume statements may need to be rewritten to conform to the stated needs. You can include a full resume, but the extra information it contains could be on the screener's eliminate list.

Making it Happen with a Game-Winning Interview

If your introductory letter and resume do their job, you may be called for a personal interview. The first personal contact will be extremely important in promoting chances for employment.

Before the interview, form a strategy that will allow you a partial lead in the meeting (see the Interview Strategy Checklist, below).

Begin by making sure that you are on time. Sports professionals are busy people and if you are late, it will cut into your allotted time or even force cancellation of your interview all together. It will definitely be a strike against you if you are late.

Dress conservatively, but comfortably in clothes that are clean and fit properly. While you often see professional athletes wearing the most outrageous clothes, owners and administrators are usually conservative. Remember, conservative attire will not offend anyone while a gaudy outfit may leave someone with the wrong impression. John T. Malloy's *Dress For Success* books for both men and women are packed full of attire and grooming guidelines. Try to maintain an athletic, healthy physical image.

As for the interview itself, try to be at ease. Everyone will be a little nervous at first, but realize that the General Manager, or whoever is doing the interview, is human too and must be interested in you or he/she wouldn't be seeing you. Questions will be based on your letter and resume, so it's a good idea to study these documents before your interview so the details are fresh in your mind. Try to be as informed and as educated as possible about the interviewing organization especially in regard to its current issues as well as and the position you are applying for. Since each interview and its subsequent interviewer will be different, the following checklist should assist you in preparing for any interview situation.

Interview Strategy Checklist

- **Research the Position.**
  Research and attempt to be as knowledgeable as much as possible regarding the position that you are pursuing. If possible, request that a job description be sent to you. Talk to your contacts within in the organization for additional inside information.

- **Research the organization.**
  Learn about the organization, its history and track record and philosophy. Talk with your contacts who work with the company or who are familiar with it.

- **Research yourself.**
  Remember, it's not what you know but who you know that matters and that *who is you*! Based on what you know about the opening and the organization, make a list of strengths and skills needed for the job. Now consider your sports background with its relating job specific skills and strengths. Identify specific examples of activities or work experiences where you used or gained the skills or knowledge you listed as necessary for the position. Write down 34 major points that you want the employer to know about you and why you should be hired.

- **Anticipate the possible questions.**
  Formulate answers to these questions. If possible, find a contact or mentor to guide you through a practice interview.

- **Prepare questions to ask the employer.**
  Consider what you want to know about the position and the company. Write the questions down and bring them with you to the interview. A well-known interviewing strategy is to ask an open-ended question in an attempt to see how much control the interviewer will assert.

- Bring with you to the interview:
    Extra copies of your resume
    Typed list of references
    Portfolio your work (if relevant)
    Your questions for the employer
    A notepad to remember pertinent names and information

- Consider what you will wear. Choose comfortable, businesslike clothes appropriate for the position.

During the Interview

- Be polite, present a sincere nature, wear a quick smile, and display an interesting and enthusiastic personality. Keep in mind that the purpose of the interview is to exchange information, not to conduct an inquisition.

- Arrive 5-10 minutes early.

- Have a firm grip when shaking hands and always maintain direct eye contact.

- Be frank and answer all questions asked. If you do not know the answer to a particular question, say so; don't try to fake it.

- Be alert and eager. Never appeared bored or disinterested. Try to keep the conversation concentrated on your positive achievements and how you can help the organization.

- Don't exaggerate your achievements. It's easy to check any extraordinary claims you make.

- Be a good listener and, if time permits, ask intelligent questions about the organization.

- If your strategy about leading your interview does not work, don't fight it. Let the interviewer lead. You must be a good listener as well as a talker. Don't fall into the trap of formulating answers or rebuttals in your mind while the interviewer is talking.

- Don't rush your answers. After a question is posed, it is not necessary to give an instant answer. Take a few seconds to organize your thoughts and then give a direct answer.

- Be consistent and truthful. Don't agree with an interviewer just because he/she says something. You don't have to agree with everything. On the other hand, don't go out of your way to disagree with everything just to show your independence.

- Don't dwell on your past experience. Find out what the new position requires and point out how you can apply your know-how to it.

- Don't try to snow your interviewer with your sport knowledge or name dropping. He/she probably knows more than you and is looking for a worker, not a fan.

- Never beg for a position. Organizations are looking for individuals who are in demand and have something unique to offer.

- Speak well of your present employer. If you speak poorly about him/her, then your potential employers may feel you will do the same to them.

- Always follow-up with a thank you letter to show your appreciation and concern for the organization. It could be the touch that makes the difference.

- Remember that there are many people looking for jobs in sports and you must show the interviewer that you are more eager, sincere, and serious than the others, and that you are willing to start anywhere just for the chance to make a positive contribution to the organization.

If You Get the Job

Notify your contacts and references that you have taken a new job and thank them for their assistance.

If You Don't Get the Job

Contact the person who interviewed you and ask him/her to give you feedback about your experience and interviewing skills to improve your job search.

If you are still interested in the organization, send a letter stating your interest and maintain contact to learn of future openings.

Becoming Your Own Marketing Agent

A fully developed marketing strategy will insure that your sports job search will be efficient and quick,. Two factors will make this plan a reality:

- Be prepared to spend at least six hours daily on your search. Four of these hours should be spent networking.
- Make sure your target company list is complete, up-to-date, and realistic according to your qualifications and geographic interest.

Where is Your Next Job Coming From?

Your first priority is to create as many interviews as you can. This will lead you to someone who has a need for your skills.

Where are the best sources of leads for a sports career?

Networking	75%
Other	14%
Ads	6%
Agencies	5%

In addition, of those who find jobs through personal contacts, 45% have new positions created for them.

Looking at the above figures, the logical conclusion is that seven out of ten jobs come from personal contact. Pursue all job search techniques but spend proportionate amounts of time and effort on the activities that produce interviews.

Classified Ads

If you are spending more than 10 percent of your job search time looking at classified ads, you are wasting energy that should be applied to more productive methods like networking.

For the average job searcher, getting a job through and ad is like winning a beauty contest. If you go after an advertised job, keep in mind the odds, which can be as high as 400 or 500 to one. Weigh those odds against running into a job opportunity every 12 to 16 interviews through networking, where there are not as many competitors, if any!

Should you answer ads? Of course, but selectively, so that it does not take you away from your number one priority: networking.

Blind Ads

A blind ad that looks like a dream job may be just that: a dream concocted by someone just fishing. It could also be a recruiter who simply

needs to fill his data base with a number of people from a given special interest group. The reasons for legitimate blind ads placed by firms are:
- To maintain secrecy from both competitors and employees
- To shield companies with questionable reputations
- To help companies test the market
- To protect companies from job seekers who do not meet all their specifications

Be suspicious of any blind advertisement. If a post office box is used rather than a newspaper box, call the post office to get the name of the box holder (use the zip code to help you get a phone number). Once you have the company name and their newspaper ad, you can devise an approach.

Complete Ads

When you have a specific ad, with the company name, does this mean you want to reply? Not always.

If your resume or letter contains one of their criteria for elimination, it may never get to the hiring authority. They've developed methods of evaluating candidates as quickly as possible. In addition, part of any screening process is to eliminate the poorly written resumes.

You can avoid being screened out in the preliminaries if you bypass the ad completely. For example, if the ad is for a sales rep, research the company and get the name of its sales manager. Figure out your best approach through networking. If you cannot locate a referral who can introduce you to someone in the organization, you can still make an approach, either by direct phone call or a letter.

Should your letter to the sales manager include a resume? Not necessarily. What the letter should do is address the qualifications described in the ad without making reference to an advertised opening.

Hints for Answering Ads
- Sources for advertisements: *The Wall Street Journal* especially Tuesday and Wednesday. Los Angeles *Sunday Times*, *The Chicago Tribune*, Sunday **New York** *Times*. Sports industry trade magazines and special publications, all other big city Sunday newspapers in areas in which you are interested. Check your library for the Standard Periodical Directory. This has addresses for all sports publications and trade magazines.

- If you answer, do it right or not at all. Tossing a resume in an envelope with just a few words or without a letter will not get you where you want to go.
- Make a list of all the requirements the ad specifies. Next to each item, write your specific accomplishments that addresses that need. If you do not meet the most important job requirements, you should think twice before investing the time for a proper answer.
- You risk exposure by replying to a blind ad; it may not be worth it.
- Be sure to update your 20 second resume to conform to the needs stated in the advertisement. Matching your most important accomplishments to the specifications maximizes your chances of a response.
- The higher your salary objective, the less chance you have of finding a job through an advertisement. High-level jobs are secured through networking and recruiters. Salary levels under $50,000 will have a much better response rate.
- In most cases, the person who writes the ad is not the person who has requested the search. Do not spend time worrying about the reason if you do not hear back.

Job Hot Lines

Many large sporting goods companies, universities, and non-profit sports organizations maintain 24-hour job hot lines with recorded messages listing current openings.

These usually include brief job descriptions, requirements and salary ranges along with closing dates for applications. These messages are normally updated weekly and, if you keep up on the changes as they occur, you may be able to target a position before it reaches the classified section of your trade journal.

Utilizing Recruiting & Search Firms

There are two types of executive recruiters: Contingency recruiters and Retained recruiters.

Contingency recruiters sometimes help the client define the position, but usually work to fill a particular company's job specification. They conduct searches and receive payment only if their candidate is chosen. The company only pays a fee if a contingency recruiter's candidate is hired. There is no charge to the candidate.

Contingency recruiters work on lower to middle management assignments. They can work months on an assignment, submit good candidates, only to lose the placement to another firm that has presented a more acceptable candidate. Since contingency recruiters do not have exclusive searches, submitting your resume to more than one could mean that competing firms my present the same company with your resume.

Retained recruiters usually have an exclusive arrangement with their clients and work on middle management to senior executive levels. They receive fees for their searches and will continue to submit candidates until their client either is satisfied or calls off the search. Part of their work is to help the client create the job description, define the salary package and review the responsibilities of the position.

Working with Recruiters

Here are some basic concepts for working with recruiters that will save you a lot of time and perhaps anxiety:

- Recruiters work for *their clients* — not for the candidates. A recruiter will only submit you as a candidate if he feels he can make a sale.
- When accepting an assignment, recruiters sometimes will submit different sample candidates to find out what their client really wants, which may be completely different from the written job specification.
- When a recruiter tells you that you are a selected candidate, remember you are probably one of at least three others and the recruiter may be only in the testing stage.
- Your chances of landing a job through a recruiter are slim. Under the best conditions, recruiters fill less than 5 percent of all jobs. A successful recruiter fills 10 or more positions a year.
- You do not need to send references to recruiters until requested.
- Most recruiters maintain resumes in data bases.
  You need to ask four questions:
    1. Under what heading will you, as a candidate, be listed?
    2. How current is the data base?
    3. How many candidates are in the files with the same qualifications you have?
    4. When sending your resume to a recruiter, what certainty is there you will be placed in their data base at all?

Employment Agencies

Employment agencies differ from recruiters in several ways:

- They work within specific regions, although they may be linked together by computer to furnish candidates from other geographic areas.
- Employment agencies move more quickly than recruiters.
- Some agencies have their fees paid by the employer. Some will insist that you sign an agreement giving them up to 15 percent of your starting annual salary.
- Agencies work on all types of jobs, from entry level to middle management. Many are specialists in certain special interest groups, functional areas and types of positions.

Employment agencies only make money when they place people. You must be careful that they stick to your agenda.

Some agencies may send your resume to a large number of companies, just to test the water. Some of these companies may be on your target list of planned contacts, so be careful to limit the information you give an agency. Try to insist that they let you know beforehand which organizations they are contacting so you can avoid any duplication.

Some agencies guarantee the most placements, so if a candidate does not work out in one or two months, the agency may refund the fee.

Placing an Advertisement

Almost every day, job searchers place ads in *The Wall Street Journal*, local newspapers or trade publications. The better choice is a trade publication rather than a regular newspaper.

Registering with a Computer Service

Someday this will be a powerful means of placement, but at the moment it is only beginning. Do not lose sight of a very important point: resumes do not get jobs, people do. Networking is the preferred method for finding your next position.

Applying in Person

For middle management and above jobs, you cannot just pop in and hope for an interview. People who hire the decision makers make appointments.

Generally, you should find out who is hiring. That information may come through your network of contacts, telemarketing calls or even watching the classifieds.

School Placement Bureaus

For new entries in the sports industry, school placement bureaus are at least a start. Unless you are in a sports management program, you will never know about the opportunities. This does not mean, however, that you can put aside preparing a top-notch resume and perfecting interviewing and negotiating techniques.

The Mail Campaign to Target Companies

It is now time to select a list of target companies. Your target list could include competitors, suppliers, former employers, new sports organizations you have discovered, or opportunities from related fields. You have to research companies and their management. Factors such as size, products and/or services, position in their industry, corporate policies, opportunity for advancement, attitude with respect to hiring your age group (including entry level), location, sales and profits are easy to research and will help you know better what you want and where to find it. One of the most important parts of your research will be to identify the people you would be working for and the decision makers regarding your hiring. These people should be part of your research, and your approach to them, whether by mail or through personal contacts, is essential.

The time invested in research will make you a better networker because you will know more about the companies and people you will be seeing. Once you have a list of target organizations, the next step is to find the person most likely to respond to your skills and potential. It may be anyone from the president on down. Finding your contact requires effort, and this is where research pays off. Networking is the surest method, but a good reference book can help. When your information comes from a directory or other reference, call the company to verify that the person still is in that job.

Reaching Your Target Companies

Try a limited mail campaign consisting of 15 organizations at a time from your target list, with carefully researched contacts. The reason for a limited mailing is that you must follow-up each mailing with a phone call (instead of waiting for a reply) and try to complete the contact with a personal interview. Your letters should conclude with a statement such as, "I will be calling your office in a few days to set a mutually convenient time for an appointment."

What kind of mailing should you do?

If your salary is less than $30,000 per year, your letter should be sent to the hiring authority of your specific interest, not the personnel department. You should send a good cover letter and a resume.

If your salary is more than $35,000, your letter approach should be either to the president or hiring authority. Do not send your resume but a well-constructed broadcast letter.

If you are addressing a small or medium-size sports group, write to the president regardless of your salary level. In this case, use a broadcast letter without a resume if your salary is in excess of $50,000. If your salary is less than $50,000, use a cover letter and resume.

Hazards of a Mail Campaign

Many times your broadcast letter or cover letter and resume will not reach the person you address and will be sent to the personnel manager or vice president of human resources.

If they are not looking for someone with your exact experience, you will get a computer letter thanking you for your inquiry, saying you have a most interesting background but they have nothing at the moment. This does not mean you should drop your target company. It means you must find a better way of reaching your key person within that company. This brings you back to networking and finding a bridge to that person. The challenge at this point is to find a bridge.

Strategically, it is only by personal contact that you can get the information you need. The mail approach cannot provide this detail.

A few words of encouragement...

Realistically your success in the sports profession depends on your diligence. Don't let letters of rejection get you down: you will receive many of them. If a team tells you that there are no openings at the present time, but someone will talk to you in person if you like, by all means do it. Follow up all leads and if someone in sports does see you, be sure and write a letter of thanks for his or her time. Your chances really depend on you.

Are you willing to write to all these organizations? Are you willing to work anywhere, doing anything? Are you willing to start out at a modest salary? Are you willing to keep trying when the odds are against you and the rejections are piling up?

Career Steps: Summing It All Up

- **Evaluate yourself.** You know you love sports, but are you ready to devote yourself to a sports career? Make sure you are not transforming a fun, energizing part of your life into a daily grind
- **Set your goals.** You must decide what you want to be. Then let this aspiration guide you in a general direction as you follow through with the information you learned here. Write to the professional organizations in the fields that interest you, talk to people who are already in the field, head for the library and read applicable journals and other publications. Think about what you want in terms of salary, responsibilities, location, and advancement opportunities, and think about what talents you have to offer and what interests you want to pursue. Career planning is a process you may not know exactly what you want right away, but the better defined your goal, the easier the rest of the process becomes.
- **Continually update your personal inventory.** Stay in touch with your personal, family, and career goals. Revert back to the dream career model and constantly evaluate your needs and priorities. Soul search now before you leap into an adventure that may not be right for you. If in doubt, visit a career counselor. Seeing a counselor now, who you trust, is advantageous and more efficient than seeing him/her later when the consequences are much more expensive in all respects.
- **Get the education you need.** No matter where you are in your education — high school junior, college freshman or schooling far behind you — you'll need to meet an employer's bottomline educational requirements. If you're still in high school, now's the time to start planning. If you've already graduated from college, you may have to backtrack or supplement your education with additional schooling. As this guide makes clear, some careers have firm educational prerequisites; for others, there are recommended courses of study. Your career research and the advice of guidance counselors can help you construct a program to fit your needs. Keep your career goal in mind when you choose your electives and extracurricular activities.

- **Get experience.** Internships, workstudy, part-time and summer jobs are all good sources of experience that can help you prepare for a career. Almost any real world job experience will gain you points by showing that you can tackle projects, take on responsibility, and deal with people and deadlines. But like your education, the more directed this type of experience is and the more connected it is to your goals, the more impressive it will be on a job application or resume. You can also use work experiences as a laboratory to test your career goals and add information to your job research files.

Remember that sports experience helps. If your competitive speciality jives with your career goals, so much the better. The value of hands-on experience can never be underestimated whether it be sports-related or not. But even the general lessons you learn in sports teamwork, how to win and lose, the value of competition will be among your best selling points no matter what career or line of work you choose

Get into the job market. Once your diploma is in hand and you've buttressed it with experience, you're ready to attack the job market. Again, the first step is research. Look for entry level positions that can be paths to your career goal. Update the research you did before (and this time let the groups and individuals know that you are looking for work) and check the standard job listings newspapers, magazines, placement services. Don't forget word of mouth. Once you decide what jobs you want to aim for, prepare a resume a listing of your educational and work experience designed to emphasize your best attributes. Keep it short, simple, appealing, and directed as specifically as possible toward the job or jobs you want.

Be aggressive. There is a long-standing job-hunting dictum: follow every lead no matter what direction it takes you and stop only if you are convinced that it has reached a dead end. Send your resume to all the possible job sources from your research whether or not you know a job is available. Getting a job is sometimes just a matter of being in the right place at the right time, and you should do everything you can to make sure you're the *lucky* one. Try to get in to talk to people, briefly, even if there is no specific job available. At least, it's another form of research. At most, the impression you make now may pay off when an opening does occur later. Present yourself to a prospective employer positively and with a cooperative, *I'm willing to work hard* attitude.

Don't be afraid to ask questions. Stress your strongest qualifications and let the interviewer know why you think you'd be good at the job.

The field of professional athletics is fiercely competitive, and yet the number of goods jobs, unlimited. Be prepared for disappointments and be prepared to keep trying. Keep a positive attitude. Don't allow yourself to be discouraged over small failures. Nothing significant has ever been achieved easily.

And by the way, good luck.

Broad Employment Category	Job In the Field	Sports Related Occupation
Advertising	Account Executive	Sports Promoter
	Copywriter	Business Executive
College Student Administrator	Dean of Students Director of Student Affairs	Athletic Advisor
Education	School Counselor Administrator	Physical Education Teacher Athletic Coach
Health & Leisure Administration	Hotel Manager	Health Club Manager
Journalism	News Reporter Correspondent	Sports Reporter
Nutrition	Community Dietitian	Sports Nutritionist
Personnel	Employment Interviewer Labor Relations Specialist Training Specialist	Sports Team Manager Coach
Photography	Photojournalist Still Photographer	Sports Photographer
Physical Therapy	Physical Therapist	Athletic Trainer
Psychology	Clinical; Counseling;	Sports Psychologist Industrial; Organizational
Public Relations	PR Representative Public Information Officer	Sports Information Director Sports Promotion Director
Radio & TV	News Analyst Commentator	Sports Announcer
Recreation	Recreation Leader Director	Sports Recreation Leader
Selling/Retail Buying	Buyer; Manufacturer's Rep.	Sporting Goods Rep.
Statistics	Financial Analyst	Sports Statistician
Writing and Editing	Writer; Editor	Editor of Sports Books

Figure 10. Comparison of Broader Employment areas and Sports Career Area Qualifications.

4

Increasing Your Marketability

Sports performance on the playing field is predicated by two basic concepts: control and momentum. Every job seeker needs to have these same goals to put him/herself in the best position to gain the competitive edge in securing that dream job. There are many intangibles that a prospective employer will be evaluating in the quest to hire the most qualified applicant. It is generally agreed by those who hire individuals in all walks of life "that there is no substitute for experience." The business of sport is no exception. In addition to acquiring the know how necessary to make an impact in a progressive market, it is equally important to learn the "tricks of the trade" which will maximize one's time and effort especially in a competitive job search.

Acquiring Experience: A Key Job Seeking Attribute

Job seekers with proven experience and refined contacts set themselves apart from the rest. Don't pass up opportunities to acquire that much needed experience through volunteer work, internships, or salaried experiences. It's never too soon to start acquiring practical skills and nurturing developing contacts for future employment. Due to the large number of organized athletic activities that preside for nearly every segment of the population, there undoubtedly will be less competition for those positions in the more non-traditional sports such as women's basketball and men's softball as there will be in the major professional organizations or franchises. It's not the size of the firm or the particular sport that will make your credentials more marketable, but rather the quality of the experience you gain.

You may be surprised at how - with the proper approach - top sports executives will be receptive to discussing particular positions and possibly even put you on a volunteer project to get your feet wet. Being professional and assertive with your contacts makes an impression on the team's management. And if the occasion should arise where a vacancy does open, you may be in the right place at the right time to fill that vacancy. Remember that you must be more innovative and aggressive than the next person if you are going to crack into a tough job market.

Some top administrators have entered into the field in novel ways. Take, for example, these story, printed in The National Sports Marketing Bureau's publication:

> While in college, Ron Wolf, a former Vice President of the **NFL**'s Tampa Bay franchise, subscribed to a popular football magazine and often wrote to the editor to correct errors and make suggestions. The editor was so impressed with Wolf's suggestions and corrections that he offered him a job. He later recommended Wolf to Al Davis of then, the Oakland **Raiders**. Davis took Wolf on as an assistant, and when Davis became Commissioner of the American Football League, Wolf went with him. When Davis returned to the **Raiders**, Wolf returned as a personnel director and did a brilliant job of drafting. He landed the Tampa job without even applying for it.

◆ ◆ ◆

> Two brothers from New York, Pete and Carl Marasco, also took a unique route into the sports profession. Since they both loved football, they began gather statistics on college seniors. They wrote to practically every collegiate football program to attain vital player profile data on select individuals and consequently watched as many college games as they could to track each player's progress. With the huge amount of material they collected, they proceeded to rate college seniors' professional playing potential. They even predicted the order in which players would be selected in the National League draft. To create an awareness of their avocation, they leaked their predictions to a major football magazine. After seven years of accurately forecasting the draft, they become recognized talent experts. With this new-found notoriety, they left their jobs to take positions in sports administration: Pete Marasco became a scout for the New York **Jets** and Carl

Marasco landed the position of personnel director for the Chicago **Bears**.

These men really entered the sports marketplace via left field, but they prove opportunities exist for aspiring individuals with imagination, initiative, and determination.

A majority of front office personnel with major league franchises received their training in the minor leagues. Most would agree that they didn't care who they worked for or how much they made. They just wanted a chance to prove themselves and learn the idiosyncrasies of sports from the bottom up. A good example is Pat Williams, former general manager of the Philadelphia **76er**s. After playing minor league baseball, Mr. Williams went to work for the Spartanburg **Phillies**, a minor league team in South Carolina. At Spartanburg, he created a promotion for every one of the **Phillies** 63 home games. The year before Mr. Williams arrived, Spartanburg drew only 46,000 for the entire season. By the time he was ready to move on, attendance had soared to a record 173,000 in a county with a population of only 145,000! Pat Williams went on to become business manager of the Philadelphia **76ers** and general manager of the Chicago **Bulls**. Not everyone has the promotional genius of Pat Williams, but the point to be made is that his reputation was formulated in the minor leagues.

As you read the daily sports pages in your local newspaper or magazine, be aware of recent administration changes or the formation of expansion franchises and developing leagues. Newly established teams and conferences will have smaller budgets, and depending on the nature of the sport, experienced sports practitioners will either be hard to come by or not willing to accept the low pay indicative of an upstart entity. Also, be alert for athletic departments that are expanding and creating first-time positions. Universities are always seeking cost saving measures to cut back on higher salaried positions by hiring several entry level positions.

Keep an eye out for opportunities like the preceding ones. Especially at the beginning of your career, when you will not be competing for positions in established franchises who already have experienced staff people. The key to your future is getting your foot in the door.

The Value of an Internship

Another excellent opportunity to gain valuable experience is to pursue an internship. An internship is part audition, part test, part question, part answer. Internships can last for a summer, quarter or semester and are usually — but not always — earmarked for college students to try out their career by working in a professional capacity. Sports internships can be attained by soliciting organizations and firms directly. Some internships, while not paid, can be contracted through your school's curriculum advisor for possible course credit. An internship allows a limited time experience without the fear of choosing the wrong career. Interns are able to learn firsthand about the industry, company, even the specific job function they may be seeking after graduation. Though not all internships are paid, they still afford you an excellent opportunity to test drive your future career.

Internships should be good for your and for the company that hires you. White you get the chance to wield a copywriter's mighty pen or learn how leaders maintain their marketing clout, the companies get the chance to take a look at you. Not surprisingly, many firms hire interns after graduation or at least give them precedence over other candidates for entry level jobs. Why not? They've had upwards of three months to test drive you, which has certainly told them whether they want you around for more than just a summer. Internships are not meant to convince you that a particular sports area is the right one for you, but they do provide you the opportunity to try out different career areas while gaining valuable experience. Many of today's executives were offered permanent positions due to the exceptional performance they displayed during their internship.

If you wish to solicit an internship on your own, consult the directory of this publication for the names and addresses of potential contacts. It can never hurt to pursue a field of interest or a particular team that you would like to work for. You never know what could happen during that trial period. Don't just sent a letter; rather, make an appointment in person at the convenience of the director or department head. If the franchise or organization is not sold on the idea on your first try, be persistent and restate your proposal on another occasion. Your aggressiveness and tenacity alone could sell your proposal.

If you aren't sure and want to get a better feel for the specializations within each field, access the library for resources and directories. They feature articles by top professionals in each field covering every speciality.

With detailed information about salaries, career paths, recommended courses and majors and what you'll be doing as an entry level person in each field and/or department, these articles will surely help you gain a broader understanding of each field and provide the detailed information you need to decide exactly what you want to do.

Why Employers Want Interns

Student internship programs have proven to be a valuable, win-win experiences for both the students and participating organizations. Interns are career-oriented, undergraduate and graduate college students who are seeking to gain experience that will enhance their professional development. The internship site provides an opportunity for the students to get hands-on experience that cannot be duplicated in the classroom. The students are anxious to put theory into practice in a true business setting. Participating organizations can expect a great many benefits in exchange for providing this working education.

Internship Benefits:
- Provides significant savings by decreasing monthly payroll expenses
- Places career-oriented, young professionals on the staff
- Keeps employer up-to-date on the most current industry information
- Provides fresh enthusiasm and creative ideas each year
- Attracts high quality, permanent employees
- Motivates existing staff to perform at peak capacity
- Provides national exposure for employer's facility and programs.

Other Avenues to Pursue for Practical Know-How

Don't ever rule out obvious potential sources such as your local high school or recreation department when developing your plan of action for acquiring experience. If coaching is your forte, then check out the possibility of student coaching in the public school sector for college credit or supervising an athletic program on a volunteer basis in the private school system. Private schools may not as stringent about hiring. However, what the schools are seeking are individuals who have a sincere interest in the goals of that institution.

For those who have collegiate athletic playing experience, numerous graduate assistantships are available for each intercollegiate team. Unfortunately, no salary is involved, but the training and contacts to be gained by being an integral part of the collegiate ranks will prove invaluable in your future endeavors. Even though these initial years may seem financially straining, in the long run it will be much easier to be promoted once you are within a system than to make a move from the outside.

If you are still in high school or college, numerous opportunities already exist right before your eyes. From positions as yearbook coordinator and newspaper editor, to those as equipment manager and athletic trainer, the chance to learn or try something new is readily available without having to obtain formalized training. Also, with the budget cuts becoming more and more prevalent and positions being abolished, many athletic directors would welcome your services and may even provide you with some form of compensation.

Sports information directors can always use editors, statisticians, and publication specialists. Trainers and managers are continually in short supply in both the high school and collegiate circle. Many universities are now offering scholarships for students who work in these areas, which very much resemble the aid granted to student athletes.

Numerous part time and full time entry level positions are available at major arenas as well as golf and tennis country clubs and recreation centers. Not only are you being paid for a job that you enjoy doing, but you will also be able to possibly meet significant individuals in your field. Most of these positions can be obtained without ever giving up your regular source of income or while you are still completing your education. Don't overlook volunteering your services during national golf or tennis tournaments, or possibly spending your free time around the local race track. By just being helpful and asking questions of the right people, eventually you will be noticed by someone. Cream always rises to the top!

A gutsy yet determined approach is to attend one of the many national conferences and league meetings. Vince Naus, a 1980 Biscayne College graduate, attended the 1979 Major League Baseball's winter meetings in Toronto, Canada, to learn more about the sport and develop contacts for future employment. Though the adventure was costly, his efforts were not in vain. By *smoozing* with the many franchise representatives and by promoting his career objectives, he was able to land an internship with the

Amarillo **Gold Sox** of the Texas Baseball League. Soon after his appointment, his success led him to be named general manager of the club for the remainder of the summer season. His ongoing accomplishments were so profound that the club's owner made a recommendation to then Baseball Commissioner Bowie Kuhn, indicating that Naus was an aspiring administrator with definite potential. Shortly before graduation, at the age 23, Naus was offered an administrative position in which he reported directly to the Commissioner. He was the youngest individual to ever hold such a position!

Success stories like these are rare. But with determination, you can succeed. For Naus, succeeding came at a great sacrifice in the form of time, money and effort. He persevered and ultimately reached his goal in spite of the odds.

Whenever you come upon a contact or lead, follow it up completely until you are sure it's a dead end. Many letters and long distance telephone calls will only lead to more of the same, but follow through even if you think you are on a wild goose chase. As long as there is another lead or contract to be made check it out. Nothing in life is accomplished without a sincere commitment and sacrifice.

Unfortunately, openings in sports related positions are probably the least publicized of any occupation. However, one of the most common means of finding job leads in any career is through the process of networking. *Review the tips on Networking from Chapter 2.*

As you set out to market your skills, keep in mind that thousands of aspiring enthusiasts like you are also developing dreams. That's why you need to be creative in your career marketing.

Bruce Jenner said it so well when a reporter asked him how it felt to be "best in the world" after his decathlon victory. His response was "the 'best in the world' is somewhere out there and doesn't even know it. He's probably sitting behind an office desk right now. The difference is either he doesn't know it or didn't care enough to do anything about his talent. I'm really not the best in the world, I simply wanted it more than anyone else in the world."

Switching Careers to a Sports Related Occupation

To this point, the emphasis has been on students seeking sport related careers. But what are the possibilities for the individual with years of experience in a non-athletic career? Can someone with no specific sports

Broad Employment Category	Job In the Field	Sports Related Occupation
Advertising	Account Executive	Sports Promoter
	Copywriter	
College Student Administrator	Dean of Students Director of Student Affairs	Athletic Advisor
Education	School Counselor Administrator	Physical Education Teacher Athletic Coach
Health & Leisure Administration	Hotel Manager	Health Club Manager
Journalism	News Reporter Correspondent	Sports Reporter
Nutrition	Community Dietitian	Sports Nutritionist
Personnel/ Relations	Employment Interviewer Labor Relations Specialist Training Specialist	Sports Team Manager Coach
Photography	Photojournalist Still Photographer	Sports Photographer
Physical Therapy	Physical Therapist	Athletic Trainer
Psychology	Clinical; Counseling;	Sports Psychologist Industrial; Organizational
Public Relations	PR Representative Public Information Officer	Sports Information Director Sports Promotion Director
Radio & TV	News Analyst or Commentator	Sports Announcer
Recreation	Recreation Leader/ Director	Sports Recreation Leader
Selling/Retail Buying	Buyer, Manufacturer's Rep.	Sporting Goods Rep.
Statistics	Financial Analyst	Sports Statistician
Writing and Editing	Writer; Editor	Editor of Sports Books

Figure 10.   Comparison of Broader Employment areas and Sports Career Area Qualifications.

training make a new start in the world of sports? Actually, depending upon the field you choose, your other professional experience can be viewed as an advantage. Earlier it was mentioned that it is important to begin developing a career at a youthful age. This has been proven to be the most effective route since usually a minimum of responsibilities and liabilities exist in one's early 20s, which should allow for more extensive soul-searching and risk-taking. Unfortunately, even though a recent graduate may discover his/her true career endeavor, the greatest drawback to youth is lack of experience and unproven potential. Though individuals in their mid-life or later years may not be as easily retrained or as willing to pay dues like their younger counterparts, what they do possess is established work experience which can't be taught in books. For this reason, a public relations director will not recruit young interns fresh out of school, but usually seek administrators with 20 years or more experience from the corporate world. Figure 10 illustrates how experience gained in broader career areas can be comparable to qualifications for specific sports careers. This is not to say that an intern or graduate may not be approached to be an assistant or possibly a protege, but when push comes to shove, experience conquers all.

Characteristically, sports-specific occupations require a more specialized knowledge and, many times, a certain type of personality. This is why in such fields as sports medicine and sports psychology, practicing physicians and clinical psychologists without higher training in these specialized areas would be doing an injustice to patients and clients who would request such services. Partaking in symposiums, clinics, and workshops in addition to attending seminars and taking coursework at institutions that offer specialized curricula will provide meaningful insight and application techniques.

For those who are hesitant about making a complete switch into a sports career, use the informational interviewing techniques outlined in Chapter 2 to explore other career options. Then acquire the necessary experience to break into your area of interest either on a part time or volunteer basis. This will enable you to make slow career transition while still maintaining the security of an income. Whenever an individual chooses to switch careers, sports-related or otherwise, it is imperative to have a plan of action for a smooth turnover. Briefly stated, never quit an established job just on a whim, much less dive into a lifestyle change without having a course of action outlined that will facilitate your personal, family, and career goals.

Accountants, business managers, marketing specialists, or for that matter any of several other sports related occupations, perform basically the same functions as similar positions in education, government, or private business. However, the one distinct difference is that the world of sports careers may be viewed as more glamorous and enjoyable. The flip side to this mystique is the supply and demand principle. Since so many members of the workforce are willing to take a sports position no matter what the sacrifice, usually the salary and benefits will be less than those of comparable positions elsewhere. The possible exceptions to this rule are the highly technical fields such as physical therapy, exercise physiology, or sports nutrition, which may demand higher salary figures due to their relative uniqueness and scarcity.

When applying for a sports position for the first time, review the section in this book on resume writing. In the cover letter, market your existing skills and emphasize your enthusiasm and commitment to athletics by noting your involvement with applicable coursework and seminars to further your training. When interviewing, make it a point in your strategy to express how your sports knowledge of current issues coupled with your past experience will be an additional asset and provide a new dimension to the organization. Throughout the cover letter and functional resume, employ sports terminology and buzz words which give the application an athletic flavor. This may be accomplished by using terms such as sports information instead of statistics, or sports studies rather than physical education. This technique may provide the touch that attracts the interviewer.

A solid and successful non-sports background is a much greater value and attraction to an employer than a resume that is very sports oriented but lacks a successful work. Being around athletics all your life isn't as important as associating yourself with accomplishment and established work principles. When approaching a vacancy the question to be asked is not "what can the employer do for me," but "what can I offer to the employer?"

Do You Need a Mentor?

The benefits of a mentor-protégé relationship can be invaluable in preparation for your professional sports career.

As you undoubtedly realize, no matter how determined, talented, and knowledgeable you are, making a career transition can be a difficult task.

However, after spending a year in the career endeavor of your choice, hopefully learning the ropes and evaluating the workings of the organization, it's time to develop your game plan for moving up into a permanent position. No doubt having a mentor could enhance your chances of getting there. The trick is finding the right one.

Choosing the Right Mentor

Choosing the right person to cultivate as your mentor is extremely important. According to Annie Moldafsky, a consumer and communications specialist, "A mentor is someone who is genuinely interested in helping you move ahead in your career; someone who is supportive, non-judgmental, can help build your knowledge and abilities through creative discussion, and can provide encouragement at critical points in your career." The ideal situation would be for a mentor to seek you out. More than likely, that will not happen; therefore, you must begin your search process.

Know What you Want

A mentor may be able to teach, advise, and help shape your career. But he or she should not be expected to know what you want. You need to have in mind some short-range goals and objectives.

Identify Possible Mentors

Having one mentor, possibly your boss or another influential person within your chosen organization, is great. However, changes do occur. A mentor may move on to another franchise or relocate to a different city and you may be left feeling powerless. Therefore, be on the lookout for mentors inside and outside your organization as well as your career field.

Develop a list of suitable mentors. Study the list, considering the pros and cons of what each person can offer. Then, identify one or more possible mentors you want to begin cultivating.

Grab the Attention of Potential Mentors

If you want potential mentors to notice you, work at getting their attention in the following ways:

- Gain a reputation as someone who can get results
- Develop expertise in a particular area of the company and tackle tough assignments
- Discuss your career goals and expectations with your boss and talk about your desire to have a mentor, possibly within him or her. If you get negative vibes during the discussion, don't pursue the issue. He or she may not want to assume that role.
- Maintain a professional attitude and develop the image of a would-be manager.

Finally, don't jeopardize your mentor-protégé relationship by expecting your mentor to fulfill all of your career development needs. Mentors have their own career ambitions and work problems. So be considerate of your mentor's time. Express your gratitude for the help you receive, and be willing to the extra mile.

More and more women are making inroads in the sports marketplace, most notably in the area of the mass media. Photo: courtesy of the **University of Minnesota.**

5
Women in Sports

Watching and participating in sports has become a major interest for many of the women in the 90s. In fact, you may be one of those enthusiasts who fantasizes about earning a living on the playing field or working for an athletic organization. You may be discouraged by comments like "only ex-athletes get front office jobs," or "sports is a man's world." Although women have more opportunities now to participate in sport, they have fewer chances and administer high school and collegiate athletic programs. In sports, women have *lost*—not gained—ground. A nationwide study by Vivian Acosta and Linda Carpenter of Brooklyn College reveals that women coached more than 90 percent of all female teams in 1972, compared with only 48 percent in 1988. It is the same in athletic administration, where only 16 percent of all women's programs are headed by women in 1988 as opposed to more than 90 percent in 1972. A number of related events of the early 1970s, including the passage of Title IX, the founding of the Association for Intercollegiate Athletics for Women (AIAW), and rising expectations for women's rights, launched an auspicious era for women in college sport. The end of the era came only a decade after its beginning. Failure to ratify the ERA, the negative impact of the Grove City decision on Title IX, and the death in 1982 of the AIAW combined to temporarily cripple or hinder forward progress made in the sports marketplace up to this point. Presently, women in sports are caught between the end of an age and the discovery of that end.

Despite the widespread belief that women have arrived in sacrosanct bastions of athletic power and privilege within the university, the reality is otherwise. In no area of higher education are women so noticeably absent from the most prestigious positions of decision making as in sports. A woman may even aspire more realistically to become chief executive officer or a member of a governing board, than to become a director of athletics of an NCAA Division I institution. Opportunities for women athletes have improved, but total participation slots available for women have declined. As the economic crunch is confronted in athletics, women are expected to share equally in the cuts. Since women never achieved anything close to parity (participation is less than 1:2 ratio), participation would still be less than equitable even if all cuts came from men's athletics.

Part of the inequity rises from the very fact that more sports are offered for men than for women. In 1990, the NCAA sponsored 76 national championships; 41 for men, 33 for women, and two for both. In 1980-81, AIAW sponsored 39 national championships for women in 17 different sports. If a Division I institution offered the maximum scholarship limits in the maximum number of sports available for women, it would award 135 full awards in 13 sports. Football alone permits 95 awards, and other Division I men's sports allow an additional 150 full scholarships.

While the NAIA offers championships for women in ten sports, these are not additional opportunities beyond those already available through the NCAA. Sports that have been strong interest areas for women in the past (badminton, slow-pitch softball, and synchronized swimming— all sports that men have not pursued at the collegiate level) have experienced drastic cuts. The popular women's sport of gymnastics is declining at such a rate that the NCAA Division II championship has already been eliminated.

The Need for Role Models in Coaching

Considering that a coaching position usually represents the first step to future administrative and leadership roles, it is no wonder that a red flag has been raised with the declining number of women now in the coaching ranks. Becoming a coach of a women's team used to be simple: you majored in physical education, lettered in varsity sport, got a teaching job, and raised your hand when the athletic director asked, "Who would like to coach softball?" Now it's tougher. Getting your foot in the door is a complex process that requires training, education, commitment professional connections and, more often than not, being male.

When Brooklyn College professors Vivian Acosta and Linda Carpenter surveyed 350 NCAA women's sports program heads in 1992, the overwhelming explanation of female respondents for the diminished role of women in the management of women's sports programs was the success of the old boys' club and not the lack of an effective old girls' club. "Whether it's intentional or not, the male athletic director knows males and hires them," contends Acosta. Jean Perry, chair of the San Jose University physical education department and one of the rare women at the top of the athletic administration ladder, explains the situation this way: "If I'm looking for a football coach, I can't tell you how many men call me and say they have the hottest thing in the world and that I really need to hire him. When I hire a women's basketball coach I don't get those kinds of calls. Women are so busy trying to get their own jobs or do well in them that they don't have the time, or take the time, to help other women. Because of their socialization, men expect to be leaders. Our problem as women is that we're convinced that we're not as competent as men, and therefore we're not humble when applying for a job. We don't get on the phone and toot our own horns like men do."

The men in women's sports administration don't agree that they run a special club, say Acosta and Carpenter. Men in their survey listed "lack of qualified women coaches and administrators" and "unwillingness of women to recruit and travel" as the top reasons for the dearth of women in leadership ranks.

Coaching involves night competition, traveling with the teams, and being away from home on weekends, which places different demands on women than men. "Whether anyone wants to admit it or not, women still have the chief responsibility for the kids and home," says Kathy Francis, who oversees 50 coaches as athletic director and assistant principal for Gateway High School, in Aurora, Colorado.

Regardless of the disparity in female and male reasoning as to why the number of women coaches are dwindling, there is a small but steady movement to reverse the tide.

The National Association for Girls and Women in Sport has written a position paper that suggests steps schools should take to increase the female staff. These include affirmative action hiring; courses and internships in coaching, officiating, athletic training, and administration; hiring women to officiate scrimmages and non-conference games to gain experience; and hiring women as assistant coaches and trainers when the head coach is male.

Another successful strategy has seen representatives from 25 organizations create the Coaches Advisory Roundtable (CAR) of the Women's Sports Foundation. Among their objectives is the recent publishing of a booklet for women who want to enter the field of coaching, creating a national job vacancy service, providing a speakers' bureau, grants to develop and train coaches, officials and administrators, and honoring women coaches. Because the world of sports is often considered a glamour field, another hurdle exists in that there are often more people than vacancies for many of the more visible positions. Hence, salaries are often low when compared to similar positions in private industry. Due to the enormous supply of potential employees, there will always be someone who is willing to work twice as hard at half the money just to get a foot in the door.

However, in other areas there is a shortage of qualified personnel. The best strategy would be to pursue positions that are not in relative demand. Examples include the ever growing need for fund-raisers in collegiate sports as well as promotions and marketing specialists.

Positions as accountants, traveling administrative assistants, and public relations agents on the other hand are less in demand and are much more competitive. Job descriptions for sports administration positions are basically the same as their corresponding positions in the corporate sector. The skills and training involved in sports finance, marketing, and public relations are no different from those in any other business vying for the public's dollar.

Education and Training

After you've read about all the available opportunities and completed your career analysis process, what might you look for in choosing a college program? Even though this publication can direct you to schools and institutions that offer sport specific programs, it is not paramount that you acquire a specialized degree in the field of your choice. However, an advantage in attending an institution that has a national reputation in your chosen endeavor is that it will present you with the ability to attain internships, as well as possible job leads. When seeking educational training, check for

- Reciprocal programs with other departments within the university. Health, physical education and recreation (HPER) majors should, if

needed, be able to take business courses from the school of management or enroll in science classes from the physical sciences faculty.
- Specialized sports courses within the department. Since the area of sports has unique problems and requirements, the HPER program should include departmental courses on sports management, sports law, and sports physiology.
- Opportunities for internships and other forms of interaction with resources in the area. Students should be allowed to pursue real world experiences with local sports facilities, athletic administrators, and to work with sports school coaches.
- Specialized course packages. Someone interested in school athletic administration should be able to take classes different from those of a student looking for a career in arena management.

Above all, select a school with a program that will allow you to reach your career goals or one where you can design your own degree program. With the right combination of education and training, you could be batting 1,000 in a dream sports career!

Going For It

Women sports enthusiasts should approach the sports job market much in the same way that males would. Be aware, however, that many sports organizations continue to believe that key sports positions should be awarded strictly to the white male. Women—like many other minorities—must understand *but not accept* that the professional sports hierarchy is currently represented by a very traditional and conservative mode of thinking. Securing employment in the sports arena presents some unique but not insurmountable obstacles for the female job seeker. The following tips should provide assistance in pursuing a career endeavor:
- Network with as many students and professionals that you know who are employed in sports at both the profit and nonprofit levels. Don't, on the other hand, shy away from groups and organizations which are male-dominated since it may be your continued diligence that may provide the impetus to break the established pattern. Review the networking tips in Chapter 2.
- Volunteer to work with people you respect or those who have jobs that appeal to you. Find out what qualifications are needed for those jobs.

- Arrange meetings with other professionals. Go to sports conferences and meetings with local and state associations; introduce yourself to other coaches and administrators and make sure that you have an updated resume with you.
- Contact local sports professionals and let them know your availability; follow your conversation by sending a resume. If they have no openings, they may refer you to other jobs that they may have heard of through the grapevine or give you suggestions about whom to contact.
- Become involved and learn more about female sports organizations. When contemplating an entry level position, these groups will usually provide your first line of employment opportunity.
- Become knowledgeable in all aspects of sports issues and current trends in both women and men's activities. Never limit your expertise to one topic or sport.
- Acquire some fund-raising experience. Considering that most female events and non-profit groups operate on a limited budget, this will prove to be an invaluable asset.
- Attend different types of females sports activities. Be assertive and introduce yourself to the key people, such as the organizers and performing athletes. This type of contact which may be able to supply you with a recommendation in the future.

There's More to Television Than A Pretty Face

Television is a powerful shaper of American values. Women working in highly visible roles in TV sports make the suggestion, though subtle, that women belong in any arena men do. *PERIOD.*

ESPN decided from its inception 10 years ago to hire women for on-air roles. This was considered risky in light of CBS' failed experiment several years before with former beauty queens Phyllis George and Jayne Kennedy. Convinced women couldn't cut it in sports, the networks shied away until cable TV proved them wrong.

"A women's presence in a newsmaking operation adds a dimension that wouldn't be there," said John Walsh, managing editor of ESPN's **SportsCenter**. "Women have an insight on certain things that men don't have." In the fall of 1991, Visser became the first woman since George to be part of CBS's **NFL Today** cast. She will do both studio work and reporting. She came to the job after a long career as a sportswriter for the

Boston *Globe*. "The difference between women on TV sports 10 years ago and today is we're no longer window dressing," Visser said. "It's really hard core. You stick your nose in the basketball huddle, digest it and deliver a synopsis. You have to know what you're talking about."

The front offices of professional sports opened up to women for one reason, say the women who work in them: Money.

The New Wave Sports Executives

The good ol' boy had an idea, and he couldn't let go of it. The year was 1972. The idea was from the Paleozoic Era. We can only imagine the look that must have been on Sandy Knapp's face.

The American Basketball Association—starved for credibility and exposure—was holding a league meeting in Virginia Beach, VA. The attendees included a full roster of men and Knapp, who was director of promotions for the Indiana **Pacers** and the first woman executive in any professional sport. Suddenly, up steps this guy, who was quite enthused. "He had this brilliant promotional scheme," Knapp said. "He said it would get us all kinds of nationwide publicity. He wanted me to wear a bikini to the meetings." Sandy Knapp manages a chuckle as she tells the story. These days, she is outgoing president of the Indiana Sports Corporation. and among the most accomplished executives in the country, no matter the gender. Launched in 1979 to attract big sports events in Indianapolis, her program has become a model for using sports for economic development. Knapp has lured 250 major competitions to the city in 12 years, turning a decaying downtown into a mecca of amateur sports. "She has done an absolutely outstanding job," Mayor William Hudnut said.

Nobody ever asked Paula Hanson to model swimwear at a business meeting, but she has a story, too. Hanson is the NBA's vice president for team services. In 1979, she was named VP and assistant general manager of the Denver **Nuggets**. One of her first meetings after the **Nuggets** joined the NBA was in Washington, D.C. She and her male counterparts went to a club one evening.

"When we got back to the hotel, they wanted to see my room key before they let me up. They thought these guys were bringing back a hooker."

"Why don't you ask *them* to show you their keys?" Hanson replied.

Sandy Knapp and Paula Hanson are bona fide pioneers, the Sally Rides of the sports world. They can make light of affronts now, because their tenure as front office novelties is history. They have a lot of female company—and they're getting more all the time.

Not long ago, the world of sports management and administration was right up there with the Loyal Order of Moose in the all-male enclave department. Occasionally, a woman owner would slip into the fraternity, though typically the connection would trace to a husband or father, which made it OK. Those days have gone the way of the doubleheader, the two-hand set shot and the notion that nice girls shouldn't get sweaty.

Susie Mathieu is a VP with the St. Louis **Blues**, and a pioneer herself. In 1977, she became the first woman PR director in pro sports, prompting one sportscaster to howl to Emile Francis, who hired her, "What are you, crazy?" Said Mathieu, who got her start as an assistant in public relations with the Minnesota **North Stars**, said "The change is very dramatic. In today's world, in the marketing side and in general, it's not even questioned if you're a woman. There are no problems."

"It's a really positive feeling," said Frann Vettor, baseball's retail marketing supervisor. "I really believe, at least in this sector, that it is totally nonsexist."

Washington **Bullets** owner Abe Pollin named a new president. Her name is Susan O'Malley. She is 29, weighs 92 pounds, and has already proven herself a heavyweight in her former job as executive VP.

"It's sort of like there's this mantle I'm carrying. I feel very watched, and that part is a little uncomfortable. For a while I thought I was just working for Abe Pollin. Now it seems it's bigger than that." O'Malley joined the **Bullets** in 1986, after a 3-year stint in advertising. She was named Executive VP in 1988, in charge of all off-court matters. That season the team had its biggest ticket sales year in its history. A year later the **Bullets** topped the NBA with a 36 percent increase in attendance.

"I love coming to work every day," O'Malley said. "I always wanted to run a pro sports team, ever since I was 11."

That was when she started rooting around the offices of the Washington **Capitals**, then owned by her father, Peter O'Malley (not the Peter O'Malley of **Dodgers** fame).

The New York **Knicks** have named Pam Harris director of marketing. The NCAA has elected its first female president, Judith Sweet of the University of California-San Diego. Two of the top four movers in the Big East office are Linda Bruno and Christine Plonsky.

The list goes on. The NBA has four female VPs The National League has two.
- 13 of the 23 people at the manager level or higher in Major League baseball's properties division are women.
- Seven of the NHL's 26 team PR directors are women.
- Three of the NBA's four licensing directors are women.

None of this means that women are about to throw the ol' boys out. The overwhelming concentration of power still belongs to males, as do the fattest salaries.

Don't expect to see a commissioner named Faye Vincent anytime soon nor a general manager named Ernestine Grunfeld. Very few women are involved in the games themselves much less in the game behind the scenes evaluating and trading the players. "The playing field is still a bit tilted in as far as talking about firsts and milestones," says Deborah Anderson, former executive director of the Women's Sports Foundation.

There are some areas where the influx of women is not much more than rumor. Of the 28 NFL teams, 20 have either one woman or none in their executive lineups. But the NFL is trying. In 1990, a Women's Sports Foundation report showed that 147 of 149 league-wide management positions were held by men. Now there are 30 women executives around the league.

Nowhere is the women-in-sports movement more pronounced than in the NBA. Commissioner David Stern draws high praise from women, in and out of his league, for his progressive approach.

Said Stern, "It's just intelligent business. As enterprises, they're under enormous pressure to deliver the best. In order to do that, you hire the best. The old boy network is not consistent with that."

Carol Blazejowski, former Montclair State All-American, is one of the NBA's directors of licensing. Though she doubts females ever will be on truly equal footing with the males in the sports world, she is gratified by the progress.

The Prototype Sports Agent - And YES, She Is A Woman!

If ever a young and aspiring female sports enthusiast needed a role model who epitomizes the formula to personal and professional success, there could be no better example than Ellen Zavian. Though young by industry standards at 30, Zavian so far represents NFL players and one coach as an attorney-agent. Her legal work runs the gamut from the personal (wills, house closings, car agreements, insurance) to the professional (employment contracts, promotional contracts, endorsement agreements).

There is another issue: being a woman in a male-dominated profession. Some moments are awkward for her. But she says: "I'm up to par with other agents, and whatever I bring to my job as a female is a bonus." Zavian brings her own stamp of athleticism to her job. She was a competitive bodybuilder and is a participant in runs, biathlons and triathlons, When asked what she likes best about a triathlon, she answers: "the competition."

But football is not second nature. So she plies her clients with questions about the sport. "In a sense I try to overcompensate for anything I may lose for the fact I am female. I study film, I study play books, I ask tons of technical questions," she says. Zavian is not necessarily trying to become the ultimate football fan. She wants to understand just how her client sees himself fitting in with the team so she can best represent him.

After getting a B.S. in business management from the University of Maryland, she added a law degree from American University at 24. An internship with the NFL Players Association convinced Zavian to combine her degrees with her interest in sports.

Her work, she says, never ends. "I'm their friend, attorney, their representative, their sister and their mother sometimes," says Zavian.

Buffalo Bills defensive line coach Chuck Dickerson, one of Zavian's clients, agrees. "She does more than a normal agent. She's my counselor, my organizer and my confidante and she's all those things for my wife as well," he said. Zavian takes pride in her relationship with her clients: "I have a great relationship with each of my players. I can give them advice. We're open about drugs and steroids, too."

Philadelphia **Eagles** defensive back John Booty says, "She's like a sister to me. She helped me when I needed it the most," referring to Zavian's help cleaning up his finances after problems with another agent. Zavian stretches the conventional limits of being an attorney/agent. She sends clients care packages, filled with treats. "I spoil my players," she says. If need be, she'll help find housing when they move. And, of course, she is constantly on-call. That, she says, is never a problem.

"If you love what you do, you can have unlimited energy."

More Success Stories: Women in Sports Administration, TV

The front offices of pro teams and the sports playing fields were once considered male domains. One of the few ways for a woman to get to the front offices was to buy the team. And, to get into sports, a woman had to win the Miss America pageant. Now, women are making slow but steady progress into both these areas without having to use money or looks as their hammers.

In television, Lesley Visser's career at CBS has skyrocketed. Since her hiring 18 months ago, she has become the network's leading sports reporter. Also at CBS are reporter Andrea Joyce and tennis commentator Mary Carillo. Four women either anchor or report full-time ESPN's **SportsCenter**. ABC Sports has Donna DeVarona and Beth Ruyak. And NBC has Gayle Gardner, who became the dean of women sportscasters when she rose to stardom at ESPN. Diana Nyad and Cheryl Miller have also joined the ranks of sportscasters who have enjoyed national prominence.

The importance of women in both the front offices and television is twofold. Pro sport is a deep-rooted cultural institution, and women must have a voice in its direction if it is to belong to all people. "Teams now are more business-oriented. It's not just an owner's hobby, so there's not much of the old boy network," said Laurie Albrect, director of marketing and promotions for the **49ers**. "Teams need to hire the most qualified person, male or female."

The **Oakland As** are among the most progressive franchises in hiring women. Sharon Jones is director of outreach activities. Kathy Jacobson is media relations director. The directors of ticket sales, group sales, promotion and advertising are women.

Women took a long step in breaking into the baseball side of the business when the **Red Sox** hired 26-year-old attorney Elaine Weddington as assistant general manager in January. She is the first woman in that position. Unlike most her female colleagues, Weddington always planned on a career in sports. After law school, she worked as an intern in then-baseball commissioner Peter Ueberroth's office, concentrating on legal issues. Two years ago, the **Red Sox** hired her as assistant to general counsel. She was promoted in January to assistant general manager, primarily to advise general manager Lou Gormon on contracts and rules regarding waivers and free agency. But don't despair if you don't possess either a jock background or formal training in a sports-related field. Quite frankly, most sports administrators and support staffs today have non-athletic backgrounds and have marketed themselves mostly through work experience in non-sports settings. In fact, the better the career track record an individual can present to an employer regardless of where it was attained, the better the chances are for securing employment See Figure 10 in the preceding chapter for examples of non-sports experience that can be applied to sports careers.

Areas of Growth for Women: Sports Broadcasting

The growth in sports journalism is presently phenomenal, and many women have aligned their career paths accordingly. How does one prepare a career in sportswriting or broadcasting? While preparation tips are identical for men and women, this answer will be directed to females interested in sportswriting or broadcasting careers. **Start early** is the best advice. Participate in every sport available to you. Be a well-informed spectator to those you cannot participate in. Start writing or broadcasting as early as possible. A sportswriting position on the school newspaper is a good first experience. Many schools have broadcasting facilities. Work you way into the sports side of these broadcast programs.

Develop a relationship with coaches. Learn what makes them tick. Learn to talk their language. Learn something about them personally, their background, coaching records, etc.

Be a sports authority in sports in your school and competitive area. On a regular basis, read sports sections of all newspapers in your area. Listen to sportscasts on radio and television. Read the sports sections from area high school newspapers.

Read extensively on sports in national publications. Listen to national sportscasts.

Don't let your editors and professors channel you into covering only women and women's events.

Take advantage of every opportunity to associate with professional sportswriters. They may help you get a full-time job when you're ready. Try to get an apprenticeship in sportswriting and sportscasting. Coaches or publication advisers may be able to help you do this. Research reports. Know the history of each sport, the names of the greats in sport, the names of famous coaches.

Try to be a walking encyclopedia of sports information, even sports trivia.

Unless you are writing opinion in a column, write as objectively and fairly as you possibly can. This will establish a reputation for you that will help you get the inside story from coaches and athletes when the occasion arises, because they will trust you.

Check part time jobs with professional media. In smaller communities, a one-person sports staff cannot cover all sports in heavy seasons and may use high school or college sports writers as interns or part time staff. Keep a scrapbook, called a *stringbook,* of your published writing, or keep tapes of the on the air broadcasting. These are your most examples of your experience when you seek a full time job.

Where to Look for your First Job

If you have really been involved as a high school student and college student in sportswriting or sportscasting, you will have developed numerous contacts in the media. They are the best sources for help with a job. Let them know you are looking; tell them what you are interested in and when you will be available; ask them to contact you if they hear of openings. Apply at newspapers or broadcast stations in your area. Write requesting an application, or including a copy of your well-prepared resume. Ask for an opportunity to discuss possible openings now or in the future with the editor, news director or appropriate person. Be sure to say your willing to come for an interview at the employer's convenience. Offer to supply references and samples of your work. Check with faculty members in your schools. Many journalism professors receive calls from employers asking for names of prospective employees. Talk with your instructors about possibilities.

Read professional publications for job openings: writer, editor, reporter; publisher's auxiliary, announcer or broadcaster. Ask you journalism school adviser or the administration for sources and addresses. Advertise in state press association publications or broadcast publications. Some take ads without charge for graduating journalism or mass communication majors. Ask your school administration for other possible resources.

Don't Get Discouraged

Rejections usually are not personal rejection. There are usually logical explanations for rejection, that do not reflect on you personally: the employer may not have an opening, someone with more experience may have applied, someone on the staff may be chosen to move up. If this happens, inquire about the vacated position. Some employers do not acknowledge letters of application when they do not have an opening, and some do not acknowledge if they are not interested in the applicant. Don't be afraid to follow-up, asking if your application has been received and if you are being considered for a position.

To a smaller degree, women have made great strides in the areas of officiating, physical education and health teaching, and in aerobic and fitness instruction. Though more often than not, these occupations are relegated to part-time status, they can, open the doors to other opportunities as well as provide excellent side income.

In any case, whatever sports endeavor you may choose to pursue as a career or part-time vocation, remember what women's sports as a whole needs more role models. Girls need women in strong decision-making positions to learn that they, too, can become effective leaders whether it be in sport or some other aspect of their lives. Even if you choose not to make sports a lifelong occupation, your involvement could inspire a young woman to make the difference for the future generations of women sports enthusiasts.

Career Steps: Summing it All Up

Realistically, your success in any sports-related profession depends on your diligence. Are you willing to write or call organizations all over the country? Are you willing to work anywhere, do anything? Are you willing to start out at a modest salary? Are you willing to keep trying when the odds are against you and the rejections are piling up?

- **Evaluate yourself.** You know you love sports, but are you ready to devote yourself to them in connection with a career or is this nothing more than a fleeting whim? Make sure you are not transforming a fun, energizing part of your life into a daily grind.
- **Set your goals.** You must decide what you want to be. Then let this aspiration guide you in a general direction following through with the information you acquired. Write to professional organizations in the fields that interest you, talk to people who are already in the field, head for the library and read applicable journals and other publications. Think about what you want in terms of salary, responsibilities, location, and advancement opportunities, and think about what talents

you have to offer and what interests you want to pursue: Do they coincide with your chosen field? Career planning is a process you may not know what you want right away, but the better defined the goal, the easier the rest of the process becomes.

- **Continually update an inventory of your personal interests.** Stay in touch with your personal, family and career goals and constantly evaluate your needs and priorities. Soul search now before you leap into an adventure that may not be right for you. If in doubt, visit a career counselor. Seeing a counselor now, who you trust is advantageous and more efficient than seeing him/her later when the consequences are much more expensive in all respects.
- **Get the education you need.** No matter where you are in education high school or college you'll need to meet an employer's bottomline educational requirements. High school is the time to start planning.
- **Get experience.** It's never too early to begin acquiring internships, workstudy, part-time and summer jobs. They are all good sources of experience that you can put on your resume. Almost any real world job experience will gain you points by showing that you can tackle projects, take on responsibility, and deal with people and deadlines. But like your education, the more directed this type of experience is and the more connected it is to your goals, the more impressive it will be on a job application or resume. You can also use work experiences as a laboratory to test your career goals and add information to your job research files.
- **Be aggressive.** There is a long-standing, soul-searching dictum: follow every lead no matter what direction it takes you and stop only if you are convinced it has reached a dead end.

  Try to get in to talk to people briefly, even if there is no specific job available. At the least, it's another forum of research. At the most, the in-person impression you make now may pay off when an opening does occur later. Present yourself positively and with a cooperative, *I'm willing to work hard* attitude. Never be afraid to ask questions.

It can't be stressed enough: the field of professional athletics is fiercely competitive, and the number of good jobs limited. Be prepared for disappointments and be prepared to keep trying just like you would during athletic competition. Keep a positive attitude. Don't allow yourself to be discouraged over small failures. Nothing significant has been achieved easily.

Women's Sports Resources

National Association for Girls and Women in Sports

This professional group provides information on events, issues, and developments for women in sports. The membership is composed of both young and old alike in numerous areas including coaching, physical education, officiating, athletic training and administration. For more information, contact:

National Association for Girls & Women in Sports
1900 Association Drive
Reston, VA 22091

(516) 542-4700

Women's Sports Foundation

The Women's Sports Foundation is America's foremost organization for the promotion and future development of women in sports. To accomplish its goal of providing females of all ages the benefits of a physically active lifestyle, the WSF provides referral services, quarterly newsletters, conferences, and serves as a support group to further legislation that affects women in sport. For information, contact:

Womens Sports Foundation
Eisenhower Park
East Meadow, NY 11554

1-800-227-3988 or (212) 972-9170

Women in Sports Promotions & Marketing, Inc.

WSP is a women's sports promotions and marketing company specializing in positive marketing avenues for women in sports. They provide expertise in marketing and promoting women nationwide for

- Planning, developing and organizing of special sports events for women.
- Targeting women in order to raise the level of participation of women in a specific sport or special event.
- Planning and developing sport marketing strategies for the women consumer.
- Marketing educational seminars and clinics for women in health and sports fields.

In Addition, WSP provides resources through a network of professional women in sports health care, training, sports marketing, and advertising, sports media, sports medicine, education and coaching. For more information, contact:

Women in Sports Promotions and Marketing, Inc.
2100 N. Sepulveda Ste. 34
Manhattan Beach, CA 90266

(310) 546-7887

Association for the Advancement of Career Opportunities for Women in the Business of Sports (AACOWBS)
This non-profit special interest group has a prestigious advisory board comprised of the foremost leaders in the sports marketplace. This organization's mission to allow women to network and expand their career opportunities in sports.

Ocean Pacific
Pam McGee, Director of Marketing
3 Studebaker
Irvine, CA 92718
(714) 580-1888

American Women's Economic Development, Inc.
This group is comprised of women entrepreneurs and provides support and information to women business owners and women contemplating business ownership. Member services include: product and service discounts, networking and referral service, conferences, training programs, national newsletter subscription. Non-member services include consulting sessions-in office or by phone (one to one and a half hours: $35). Hotline mini-counseling sessions ($10), training programs. For more information, contact:

American Women's Economic Development, Inc.
60 E. 42nd Street
New York, NY 10165
(212) 692-9100

Association of Women in Sports Media
This group, comprised of men and women in sports media supports and promotes women in sports media. Services include: networking; a directory of women in sports media and a quarterly newsletter. For more information, contact:

Association of Women in Sports Media
Mary Schmit
St. Paul Pioneer Press
345 Cedar Ave.
St. Paul, MN 55101
(612) 228-5520

National Association of Women Artists
This group of active female artists promotes production and exhibition of the work in women artists. Membership services include: information regarding the planning of exhibits of women's work and a newsletter. For information, contact:

National Association of Women Artists
41 Union Square W.
New York, NY 10003
(212) 675-1616

Society of Professional Journalists, Sigma Delta Chi

This society of media professionals strives to ensures freedom of information for the press, and promotes professional development of journalists. Membership is open to student and professionals. Services include: referral to local chapters, networking systems, workshops and seminars; *The Quill* monthly magazine, annual publications *Freedom of Information Report*, *Annual Ethics Report*. For more information, contact:

Society of Professional Journalists, Sigma Delta Chi
53 W. Jackson Blvd.
Suite 731
Chicago, IL 60604

Women's Sports Advocates of Wisconsin

WSAW encourages, promotes, supports and recognizes Wisconsin girls and women who participate in sports. Its newsletter, *ARENA*, includes a calendar of women's sports events, feature articles on teams and athletes, and physical fitness and sports medicine information. *ARENA* is permanently archived at the State Historical Society of Wisconsin in Madison, Wisconsin. For information, contact:

Wendy L. Young
Chicago Area Women's Sports Association
3645 E. Allerton Ave.
Cudahy, WI 53110 - 1107

(414) 229-4673 (work)

Melpomene Institute

Melpomene Institute is a non-profit resource center to study the impact of physical activity of girls and women throughout their lives. The primary areas of study are physical activity and osteosporosis, exercise and menstrual function, exercise and pregnancy, and issues relating to body image. For information, contact:

Melpomene Institute
Judy Mahler Lutter
2125 E. Hennepin Avenue
Minneapolis, MN 55413

(612) 378-0545

International Association of Physical Education and Sports for Girls and Women

This multi-national association has the aim to bring together women of many countries by working in the fields of physical education and sport to promote the exchange of persons and ideas as well as research into problems affecting physical participation for girls and women. I.A.P.E.S.G.W. shares their findings with other international associations at rotating conference sites.

Barbara J. Kelly
Carpenter Sports Building.
University of Deleware
Newark, DE 19716-1910
(302) 831-2261

Publications

Women's Sports & Fitness Magazine

The magazine covers every aspect of the sports participation from personal features and performance to advancements in sports psychology and sports medicine. For more information, contact:

Women's Sports Publications, Inc.
1919 14th Street, S421
Boulder, CO 80302

(303) 440-5111

A/V Learning Materials

Aspire Higher: Careers in Sports for Women

This new video from the Women's Sports Foundation introduces a variety of sports career options, including some that may not be familiar. The video, which was made possible by **Avia** athletic footwear, was narrated by Olympic figure skater Debi Thomas.

Most of our information requests are for sports career opportunities, according to former Women's Sports Foundation Executive Director Deborah Anderson. "Many young women have enjoyed participating in sports and want to make it their career. They may only know about being a coach or a physical education teacher and wonder what other options are open to them. This video expands their horizons." The 40-minute video is especially appropriate for use in high school or college sport classes, libraries, or career centers. To purchase a personal VHS copy, send $24.95 plus $3.00 postage and handling to:

Athletic Achievements
3036 Ontario Road
Little Canada, MN 55117

(612) 484-8299

Reference Guides

The Comprehensive Women's Sports Bible

This 1992 edition will encompass every aspect of women in sports as well as who's who in the industry. In addition to a listing of every imaginable organization and athletic activity, a directory of over 2000 names of women who are involved with sport is included. To purchase this invaluable resource guide, send $17.95 plus $3.00 postage and handling to:

Athletic Achievements
3036 Ontario Road
Little Canada, MN 55117

(612) 484-8299

Turning a sports avocation into a career vocation not only provides enormous self-satisfaction but may also require a lifestyle and work ethic shift that few sports enthusiasts are willing to sacrifice. Photo: courtesy of the **1991 U.S. Open.**

6

Is the Professional Athlete's Lifestyle for You?

"I'm proud of them and happy that they don't have to work for a living," said Phil Niekro, Sr., the ageless pitcher for the New York Yankees, when speaking about his sons, Phil Jr. and Joe, both professional baseball players.

Professional sports is an entertainment industry, complete with its cast of uniquely talented stars — athletes. Sports careers are considered fast-paced, exciting and challenging. Yet people who involve themselves in the highly visible sports environment as a life-long career endeavor should also learn to accept their chosen field's peculiar nuances, the structure of its rules, and its sometimes overly egotistical and demanding players.

Individuals entering athletic fields should be prepared to work for more than just monetary compensation. Sports practitioners should be willing to put something of themselves into their chosen profession for the preservation and enhancement of sport itself. This career area demands work on weekends and holidays, and often endless hours of attention to tedious details which go unnoticed by a public whose only interest is in winners and losers. The field of professional athletics demand that players be their physical and mental best. The adage success is directly proportional to the amount of time invested is as true in the sports arena as any other area. The American society continues to place a premium on the competition and the entertainment value of sport, insuring that there will be new and developing opportunities in sports and athletics.

Professional Athletes

The most visible and glamourous positions in the sports world are those held by professional athletes. Take away the athletes and the entire sports marketplace, and all its supporting industries cease to be necessary. Never has there been a society where athletes possess the notoriety and acquire the prosperity as they do in the United States today. The desire to compete in the United States becomes apparent, considering the growing number of international athletes who continually seek professional contracts in soccer, hockey and tennis. What other country can offer its athletically gifted people the opportunity to obtain at no charge a college education which could also result with a multi-million dollar contract at a young age? And that does not include the many business propositions that may evolve following a playing career. Since the professional athlete has become the number one American hero, it is no wonder that youngsters emulate every move of the athletes they see on television and in person. Socially disadvantaged youths view professional sports as a quick route to easy street, mistaking the wealth and fame of a select few athletes as a representation of the norm for all professional athletes. The insatiable quest to become a professional performer is usually pursued at the expense of formal education and normal career development.

Dr. Harry Edwards, a California sports sociologist, believes socially deprived youths would benefit more by emulating and following the career paths of doctors and lawyers. His belief is based on the premise that these fields are readily more attainable, especially for minorities. Arthur Ashe wrote this provocative statement to black parents:

> There must be some way to assure that the 999 who try but don't make it to pro sports don't wind up on the street corners or in the unemployment lines. Unfortunately, our most widely recognized role models are athletes and entertainers "runnin" and "jumpin" and "singin" and "dancin." While we are 60 percent of the National Basketball Association, we are less than 4 percent of the doctors and

lawyers. While we are about 35 percent of major league baseball, we are less than 2 percent of the engineers. While we are about 40 percent of the National Football League, we are less than 11 percent of construction workers such as carpenters and bricklayers. Our greatest heroes of the century have been athletes - Jack Johnson, Joe Lewis, and Muhammad Ali. Racial and economic discrimination forced us to channel our energies into athletics and entertainment. These are the ways out of the ghetto, the ways to the Cadillac, those alligator shoes, the cashmere sport coat. Somehow, parents must instill a desire for learning alongside the desire to be Walt Frazier. Why not start by sending black professional athletes into high schools to explain the facts of life. I have often addressed high school audiences and my message is always the same. For every hour you spend on the athletic field spend two in the library. Even if you make it as a pro athlete, your career will be over by the time you are 35. You will need a diploma. To further delude the picture of professional playing careers, it is possible that with a mere stroke of a pen, an unproven 22-year-old without even a college degree has the possibility of becoming an instant millionaire with fringe benefits comparable to any tenured corporate executive!

Can playing professionally truly be regarded as a viable career considering that the average longevity of a professional sports career is only four and a half years? Put into simpler terms, by the time a young person has reached age 25, the individual's professional playing days may be winding down, many times without possessing a legitimate career alternative.

Pro sports were once looked upon as nothing more than an opportunity to continue competing as well as establish a financial base before entering a permanent occupation. Now competition has given way to the emphasis placed on extravagant wealth and high living. Unfortunately, financial security, with the ability to retire early, can rarely be accomplished in most pro playing careers.

Athletes aspiring for pro status should keep such goals in perspective and remain realistic about their individual talents. In football and basketball, drafted college players must either make it during their first season or forget about any future considerations. Comparing the professional systems utilized in baseball and hockey, young enthusiasts must be prepared to spend developmental time in the minor leagues which on the average usually amounts to 5 years. The longer one remains in the junior circuits, the smaller the chance of reaching the major leagues with the parent franchise. To even complicate matters, sports such as golf, tennis, or bowling have success barometers that are not as well-defined. These sports have career development processes that involve apprenticeship programs to nurture their professional abilities.

Realize this: regardless of the sports playing career you may be seeking, the odds are against you. To be more specific, the ratio for making it to the *Big Show* is approximately 140,000 to 1 when computing the number of sports participants to the actual total of athletes who are performing at the professional level. Granted, the odds will vary immensely from sport to sport, but the fact still remains that during a normal season, only 1,400 players are rostered in the NFL, 650 in the MLB, 425 in the NHL, and 400 in the NBA.

What It Takes To Be A Pro

Without a doubt, the major prerequisite to attaining professional playing status is physical ability. If an individual has the tools to compete professionally at the highest level of a specific sport, then he/she will play somewhere-period. If natural ability is present, athletes could in all likelihood be drafted in a sport in which they have had little playing experience. Dave Winfield, former outfielder for the New York **Yankees** and California **Angels**, was selected during both baseball's and basketball's professional draft due to his natural ability and illustrious collegiate career at the University of Minnesota. What has rarely been publicized is the fact that Dave was also chosen in the 17th round in the NFL's draft despite never playing a down of football in college. An NFL personnel director sums it up best by stating,

"You can accomplish a great deal with a burning desire to play and by working as an overachiever, but the first step to success is inevitably possessing the ability to compete proficiently at the professional level."

Another key element sought by team scouts in evaluating pro prospects is the intangible of instinct, better known as street sense. Athletes who exhibit this trait are characterized as having the feel for a given game situation: they can recognize and act accordingly without the need to be overly analytical. Many times the physical skill required becomes a reflex response to a mental trigger. Athletes possessing this talent are known as the *big play* people who seem to have the uncanny knack to turn a game around with a nose to make it happen. Some of sports' all time greatest clutch players didn't possess the on paper statistics representative of an overachiever. Brooks Robinson, former third baseman for the Baltimore **Orioles**, exemplifies such an individual. He never possessed an extraordinarily high life-time batting average or fielding percentage. But with runners in scoring position when his team was behind, or if the situation called for a double play to be turned in order to squelch a rally, the person you wanted the ball hit to was Brooks. It was his *give me the ball* take charge attitude rather than his overall batting average that will long be remembered as his trademark. The instinctive intelligence that has been documented to this point cannot be learned or even coached.

Intelligence, in a sports context, may also be viewed as the knowledge and understanding of what it takes to be a winner. Key factors include: accepting roles that may be for the betterment of the team as opposed to self, the importance of respecting one's own body through proper conditioning and nutrition, and *giving it all* each time the clock starts or the umpire calls "play ball."

This sports intelligence concept has become the cornerstone of the mindset for those veterans who yet in their 40s are still able to continue to find a way to win while others with more natural ability have fallen victim to that elusive statistic of a four and a half year playing career. It is also important to realize at an early age which sport best fits your personality style and physical capacities. Many athletes find themselves excelling at one sport, and at times, floundering in another. This is why the emergence of sports psychologists and biomechanists have become so valuable. Practitioners in these fields can provide insights to which athletic activities are best suited to attain optimal performance.

Playing Professionally For the Wrong Reasons

Professional athletes who compete only for the financial rewards and recognition will rarely perform consistently over the long run, much less experience an extended career. In the eyes of the sports fan, the most admired professional athletes are those who are not only skilled, but who are equally committed to utilizing every ounce of ability to better themselves. To establish the proper mindset from the start, aspiring pros should study the lifestyles of athletes who exhibit a passion for the game they play. Discover what has made these athletes successful and emulate their qualities in your own personal and professional development.

Adjusting from amateur to professional playing status will be one of the biggest transitions encountered by most young athletes. The professional game does not propose preferential treatment among its athletes like so many have become accustomed to in high school and college. Professional organizations, unlike interscholastic programs, don't need to be concerned with keeping their people academically eligible, much less get involved in personal issues. Since the bottom line at the professional level is results at any cost, student-athlete rights – with the individual's concerns placed as a priority – are now replaced with a business contract that mandates performance despite the physical, personal, or emotional state that may preside at game time. A former professional athlete compares the pro frame of mind to that of the amateur athlete or collegiate ranks: "one must learn to accept and play with physical pain and personal adversity for the good of a higher force -the team."

Comparably speaking, the professional seasons are longer, the stakes become higher, and the travel is more extensive. Performing a skill to perfection is not the only attribute necessary to achieving excellence. Performing successfully in the face of obstacles day in and day out will eventually separate the haves from the have nots. The emotional and mental burnout so prominent today in sports has been the catalyst in the termination of what could have been potentially prosperous careers. Remember, it is not whether an athlete can kick a 63-yard field goal in practice or land a triple jump during a skating routine, but whether or not the same feat can be duplicated time and time again under the most trying of situations?

Consider this statement made by 1984 Olympic medalist Mary Lou Retton:

> "Here's what it takes to be an elite performer. Someone should be able to sneak up and drag you out of bed in the middle of the night, push you out on some strange floor and have you perform your entire routine in your pajamas, without even one mistake, when you can attain such a level of proficiency in an instinctive, natural reaction- that's the secret."

While it may appear premature to discuss life after sports especially since a playing career has yet to materialize, still it is equally important to prepare for the inevitable. The sports pages are full of stories reporting how ex-jocks are unable to rejoin the real world upon retirement. In retrospect, this behavior is to be expected since the better share of an athlete's life has been spent being coddled by a public that has a thirst to worship heroes and sports celebrities. This lack of a normal lifestyle is compounded by an almost cult-like relationship developed among fellow teammates who together have survived unique and stressful situations that are rarely experienced in other walks of life. It can be much like a retiring combat veteran. Letting go of this shared camaraderie is a difficult adjustment especially when it has represented the one support group that proved to be so invaluable when things went wrong or others outside of the group could not understand the idiosyncrasies of a sports life.

Even though it is not easy to recreate or duplicate an experience such as competing in front of millions in the quest of a world championship, there is much more involved in becoming a *complete* person than having played pro sports for a few years. Those athletes who can not grasp this concept are only short-changing themselves of a fulfilling existence. The inability to cope may leave these individuals vulnerable to various forms of addictions or quick fix schemes in order to compensate the need to be in the spotlight.

Any chance of a successful professional playing career demands the utmost intensity and personal focus. But this dream, even if attained, will definitely come to an end. And it will probably end, at an age when others are just formulating their careers. You need a plan of action to realize your secondary personal and professional goals which represent the remainder of your life after your playing days are over.

Resources

The following resources offer information about planning your entire career - both in the pros and after, and making a smooth career transition.

Athletic Career Connection (ACC)
The ACC is a non-profit organization whose mission is:
- To support the efforts of student-athletes to graduate with practical degrees
- To expose student-athletes to suitable career alternatives upon graduation
- To encourage corporate mentors to support the progress of ACC participants after being hired

The ACC was established to orient more student-athletes toward quality degrees and career oriented jobs. The four phases of the ACC program are designed to support the efforts of student athletes at virtually all colleges.
- The ACC holds on campus presentations to student athletes.
- The ACC arranges on campus corporate sponsor panel discussions.
- The ACC provides career search workshops for student athletes.
- The ACC "recirculates" student athletes who receive jobs back to their campus so they can be role models for student athletes who follow them.

Athlete Career Connection
4201 Cathedral Avenue, NW, Suite 102E
Washington, D.C. 20016

(202) 966-1490

Center for the Study of Sport in Society
Northeastern University
360 Huntington Avenue
Boston, MA 02115

(617) 437-5815

PACE Sports, Inc.
9625 Black Mountain Road, Suite 305
San Diego, CA 92126

(619) 530-0700

Athletic Achievements
Performance and Career Consultants
3036 Ontario Road
St. Paul, MN 55117

(612) 484-8299

Publications

Going The Distance:
The Athlete's Game Plan for Excellence on the Field and in the Classroom,
by Stephen Figler and Howard Figler
Peterson Publishing
Princeton, NJ
1991 ISBN 0878669523

A career as a professional athlete is one of the most high profile and glamourous of sports occupations, however it has the shortest longevity of any sports careers. Photo: courtesy of **Triumph Sports Counseling.**

7

Playing the Professional Game

Professional Baseball

The road to professional baseball includes considerations other than just playing ability.

In professional football or basketball, prospects are directly assigned to a team in the major circuit. However, the majority of pro baseball will nurture their talents in the minor leagues. Without a doubt, life there will test a player's character and desire to make it to the *Big Show*. For many, such a "gut check" will result in having them forego their dreams of fame and notoriety.

Life for the young baseball player can be extremely boring and at times, unfulfilling in the junior leagues. Most minor league franchises are located in small remote communities that require extensive travel for league play. The daily per diem allowances for travel and living accommodations are kept to a minimum so the franchise be able to remain financially solvent. In fact, most minor league teams operate on the revenue generated by spring training's increased attendance while the parent club play exhibition contests in their home ball parks.

George Brett of the Kansas City **Royals** recalls the most valuable lesson he learned in the minor leagues:

"Baseball was the most important thing in my life and I was determined not to spend too many years in the minors. You have to keep yourself motivated by setting goals higher than what you are currently doing. As soon as you get too satisfied, you're ripe for another trip down to the minors."

The outlook for baseball salaries remains competitive, with salaries ranging from $750 a month for a minor leaguer to a yearly scale of over $4 million a year in major league baseball.

Since there is little money to be made in the minors, young players are encouraged to wait until their skills are better developed and are in greater demand before entering the professional ranks. Securing a contract several years out of high school will ultimately result in a higher overall salary as opposed to signing at a young age even though a *Bonus Baby* signing incentive could be offered.

Collegiate baseball is fast becoming the more recommended route in which to enter the professional market considering that it presents an additional dimension in the opportunity to receive a free education. Many colleges, especially those in the Sun Belt regions, are providing exceptional playing experience in upwards of 75 games during the season. For those pursuing baseball careers who are neither academically inclined nor feel their skills need further polishing before testing the big league market, another option would be to compete in one of the Mexican or Central American winter leagues. Many parent franchises assign their draftees or even cooperatively trade players with these foreign instructional leagues to better evaluate or nurture marginal prospects.

Resources

American League of Professional Baseball Clubs
350 Park Avenue
New York, NY 10022

(212) 371-7600

National League of Professional Baseball Clubs
350 Park Avenue
New York, NY 10022

(212) 371-7300

National Association of Professional Baseball Leagues
P.O. Box A
201 Bayshore Drive S.E.
St. Petersburg, FL 33731

(813) 822-6937

Baseball Winter Meetings
Early December
N.A.P.B.L. (813) 822-6937
Commissioner's Office

(212) 339-7800

Publications

USA Today's *Baseball Weekly*

If it happens in baseball, you'll find it in *Baseball Weekly*. The nation's most comprehensive look at our national pastime the majors, the minors, fantasy leagues, nostalgia, collectible features, commentary and much more. On sale at newsstands every Friday weekly throughout the year. For information, call:

1-800-USA-1415

Baseball America

The choice of amateur coaches and serious baseball buffs, collegiate baseball provides in-depth information regarding the collegiate scene that no other publication provides. This year-round newspaper gives first hand data on who's who and just what they're doing en route to the College World Series. For information, contact:

Baseball America
Tom Llewelyn
P.O. Box 2089
Durham, NC 27702

(904) 386-6668 or (800) 8452726

Professional Basketball

Pro basketball franchises often draft players based on the needs and coaching philosophy of each individual team. However, the one main difference with basketball, in comparison to other sports, is that physical size is nearly irreplaceable. It's a given that all basketball players be good shooters. But even though scorers and slam-dunk artists sell tickets, it is the player who will play both ends of the court, offense and defense with equal intensity, who will be awarded a college scholarship and signed to a professional contract. Red Auerbach, former Boston **Celtic** coach, has this to offer young players:

> Teams are successful when their players excel defensively. Therefore, let it be a lesson to young players to emphasize and develop defensive skills from the very beginning. Scoring is important, but the player who plays tough defense, despite not scoring as much or being recognized for flamboyant play, will find a spot in the NBA if the other skills are there.

Currently, professional basketball has many financial opportunities for both the sport and the player. Roster sizes are limited, but average playing salaries are nearing $1.5 million per year, while attendance figures to rise. Amazingly enough, the expansion franchises beginning play in 1988 were purchased for a record $32.5 million each. It appears that the escalating costs associated with the NBA have yet to reach a ceiling! However, keep in mind that only 2 of every 100 college basketball players make it in the pros with an average career span of only 3 years.

Resources

National Basketball Association
645 Fifth Avenue
New York, NY 10022

(212) 826-7000

Continental Basketball Association
425 S. Cherry St., Suite 230
Denver, CO 80222

(303) 331-0404

World Basketball League
3767 New Getwell Road
Memphis, TN 38118

(901) 795-9334

U.S. Basketball League
P.O. Box 211
117 N. Broad St.
Milford, CT 06460

Publications

Overseas Basketball Newsletter
The *Global Village Hoop Update* is the official word on inside basketball news from Europe, Asia, Australia and the United States. Sold worldwide, it features a classified section on playing and coaching jobs, stats, Americans overseas, educated rumors and more.

Pro Management and Overseas Basketball Services
P.O. Box 66041
West Des Moines, Iowa 50265

(515) 277-4313

Professional Football

Professional football is considered a national pastime in America, so it is no wonder that the overwhelming dream of most young athletes is to play someday in the Super Bowl.

Despite the emergence of the now defunct USFL, the newly established WLAF and expanded roster limits in the NFL, the outlook for playing professional football has not changed drastically in the past few years. This is because the salaries of these additional players are marginal when compared to the overall player compensation structure. First year players in the NFL can expect an annual starting salary of no less than $100,000 which includes an excellent retirement plan after 5 years. Playing in the CFL in Canada has always remained an option, but better salaries and prestige reside in the U.S. market. With the recent crackdown on anabolic steroids, the now disproportionate size of football players may return to the once smaller and agile athlete. This will allow for a more *rounded* athlete to succeed at positions that have more recently been restricted to the *biggest of the big*. Even though much can be said for the player who is able to compensate for a lack of playing ability with the aforementioned performance factors, the fact remains that there is no substitute for talent.

Due to the larger roster sizes, professional football has the luxury of adding 200 new rookies from the college ranks each year which is higher than any other professional sport. Keep in mind, however, that the average playing career in football is around 4 years, as compared to higher levels of longevity experienced in other sports.

Resources

Arena Football
2200 East Devon, Suite 247
Des Plaines, IL 60018

(312) 297-7600

Canadian Football League
1100 Eglinton Avenue W., 5th Floor
Toronto, Ontario, Canada M4R 1A3

(416) 322-9650

Minor League Football System
Noah's Ark Inn, Suite 117
1500 S. Fifth St.
St. Charles, MO 63303

(314) 949-8858

National Football League
410 Park Avenue
New York, NY 10022

(212) 758-1500

World League of American Football
P.O. Box 540218
Dallas, TX 75354

(214) 869-9437

Professional Hockey

What it takes to make it in professional hockey is summarized best by former Philadelphia **Flyer** star Bobby Clarke, "Be where the puck is. Hockey is 75 percent mental and 25 percent physical."

In other words, hockey players, much like defensive backs in football, need to have that sixth sense known as instinct. If a player lacks this ability and becomes totally dependent on his natural skills, it is doubtful that a prolonged playing career is possible.

Another key element is courage. Says Boston Bruins general manager, Harry Sinden:

> "We look for courage. The demand for good hockey players is exceeding the supply at this time. A player can come into the pros and make the parent franchise squad's within 2 years. If it doesn't happen in that time, chances are it may never happen at all on a full-time basis."

College hockey in the U.S. is turning out more professional players than ever before, with many stepping right into NHL. This trend was unheard of a decade ago when the last level of amateur competition before the pro ranks was primarily the Junior A leagues in Canada. There still remains some debate as to whether or not collegiate hockey is on the same level as Junior A. However, the advantage of pursuing hockey, like baseball, at the college level is the ability to receive an education which will be necessary for life after hockey. Minor league hockey, similar to that of minor league baseball, can be very risky and demanding of its aspiring youngsters. The financial, living, and travel accommodations will test the fortitude of any individual. This proving ground of sorts is certainly no place for the insecure or timid individual. Upon arrival into the NHL, players will receive salaries from $50,000 to as much as $1,000,000 per year based upon, of course, the round in which they were drafted. Realistically speaking, unheralded rookies can expect a salary in the neighborhood of $30,000 for the first couple of seasons in the minors, until they are promoted to the NHL.

Resources

American Hockey League
425 Union Street
West Springfield, MA 01089

(413) 781-2030

East Coast Hockey League
P.O. Box 310
Vinton, VA 24179

(703) 345-8626

National Hockey League
650 Fifth Avenue, 33rd Floor
New York, NY

(212) 298-1100

International Hockey League
3850 Priority Way, South Dr.
Suite 104
Indianapolis, IN 46240

(317) 573-3888

Publication

One of the foremost guides ever written to assist future hockey players and provide a realistic outlook on what to expect as a playing professional is as follows:

***Many Are Called... Few Are Signed* The Hard Realities of Professional Hockey**
by Rick Heinz, former NHL goalie
ISBN 0969049110
Heinz Purchasing, 1988

(612) 484-8299

Golf

To the amazement of many golf enthusiasts, there is a considerable process that one must complete before being called a golf pro. The Professional Golf Association (PGA) organizes two programs: one for those who wish to become club professionals; and another for those who will spend many of their early years on the tour.

For nearly a decade the PGA has been running an Apprenticeship Program that essentially teaches individuals how to become pro golfers. Included in the curriculum are courses in business management, practical knowledge in becoming a director of a golf club and instruction in developing a highly competitive game of golf.

Required scores:
- For men, 151 for 36 holes over a 6000 yard test course, or 163 for 36 holes over a 7200 yard course.
- For women, 161 over the 6000 yard course and 175 over the 7200 yard layout.

Upon completion of this test, golf pros have six years to become eligible for PGA membership. During this period of time, several important criteria are needed before application: credit references, golf experience, completion of an oral test, and examination on subjects such as teaching and merchandising.

Such golf specialization as is seen today was neither required nor available to young golfers in years past. Rich Williams, coordinator for the PGA's Apprenticeship Program in Palm Beach Gardens, Florida, believes the best preparation for this phase is attending a college where you can participate in a golf program and acquire an applicable educational degree. For those wishing to become part of the popular golf tour, there is a breaking-in period. Besides attending one of the approved tour schools held in a different region of the country each year, a player must qualify in a regional competition and later compete against other winners. It is not unusual for players to return three or four times before finally attaining a tour card. Even then, pros must take additional courses given under the auspices of the Association of Touring Pros (ATP), the governing body for regular tour players. If that isn't enough, even tour players must stay active in various phases of the game and must accumulate enough credits over a period of time to maintain their cards.

The process for women varies somewhat. They may attend a qualifying school in Colorado Springs for a week-long seminar which includes required execution of golf skills and completion of a written examination on the U.S. Golf Association's rules of golf. Normally only eight women a week with USGA handicaps of 3 or less are eligible to attend.

The outlook for tour pros is good, but very competitive with yearly earnings on the 10 month tour varying from $0 to $2,000,000. Personal expenses may exceed $45,000 making it nearly mandatory to have a sponsorship. Local pro golfers residing at golf clubs, the outlook remains very good for both men and women.

Famous senior PGA tour competitor Chi Chi Rodriguez puts golf into its perspective with this advice: "If an aspiring golfer cannot consistently score 66 over six months on a 6600 yard course, then that individual has no business competing with the pros on the PGA tour."

The *Game of Kings* will experience the fastest growth of any sport in the 90s with a 30% increase of participants projected in the first three years of the decade. Since 40% of all new golf enthusiasts are female, there is a need for women instructors and administrators. With this growth, it is estimated that 10,000 new courses will be needed in the next decade.

The following is a list of the personnel needed to operate a typical country club as well as a national average for each position's salary.

General Manager of Operations	$60,000 - $120,000
Club Manager	$50,000 - $65,000
Course Superintendent	$35,000 - $60,000
Food & Catering Manager	$35,000 - $65,000
Club Professional	$40,000 - $70,000
Assistant Teaching Pro	$25,000 or $60.00/hour for lessons

Caddying

They are corporate partners, psychiatrists, cheerleaders, confidants, consultants, sounding boards, friends and enemies all at the same time. And they come in generally two classes: the mega caddies and the vagabonds.

"Everybody thinks most caddies out here are toters who just say, 'Yes,' and carry the bags," says caddy Pete Bender. "But we do a lot more than carry bags. We've got to give good yardages, we've got to club 'em, read greens and keep their heads and attitudes up."

Bender, 41, is one of the elite caddies. He has worked for Jack Nicklaus and Greg Norman. He earns six figures annually, travels by jet and takes vacations when his employer takes a couple of weeks off. On the other end of the spectrum reside the vagabond caddies. They drive by the carload from PGA Tour spot to the next, sharing cheap motel rooms and hoping to find work. The numbers are against them. There are more than 170 members of the Professional Tour Caddie Association, but only 144 players usually tee it up every week and half miss the cut.

"You can't underestimate the importance of a caddie out there," says PGA pro Tim Simpson. "My caddie, Todd Brinkman, and I are very close. He knows all my moods, my strengths and weaknesses. He knows when to say something and when to say nothing.

Depending on their reputations, caddies earn between $350 and $800 a week in salary and then receive about 5 percent of their golfer's winnings. The winner of a tournament usually will give his caddie 10 percent of the prize.

Major Golf Associations

American Society of Golf Course Architects
221 LaSalle Street
Chicago, IL 60601

(312) 372-7090

Florida MiniTour
Charles Witworth, President
P.O. Box 876
Tarpon Springs, FL 34286

(813) 937-9259

French Golf Federation
69 Avenue Victor Hugo, 75783
Paris Cedex 16, France

15006220

Futures Golf Tour (for Women)
Vicki Wainwright, President
Eloise Trainor, Tournament Director
2820 SE Lakeview Drive
Sebring, FL 33870

(813) 385-3320

Golf Coaches Association of America
c/o Georgia Southern University
P.O. Box 8082
Statesboro, GA 30460

(912) 681-5522

Golf Course Superintendent Association
1617 St. Andrews Drive
Lawrence, KS 66046

(913) 841-2240

Golf Writers Association of America
1720 Section Road, Suite 210
Cincinnati, OH 45237

(513) 631-4400

International Association of Golf Administrators
c/o Jay Mattola, Secretary
125 Spruce Place
Mamaroneck, NY 10543

(914) 698-0390

Ladies Golf Union
12 The Links
St. Andrews, Fife, Scotland
KY16 9JB

03347681

Ladies Professional Golf Association
27 Volusia Avenue, Suite B
Daytona Beach, FL 32114

(904) 254-8800

National Golf Foundation
Headquarters
1150 South US Highway One
Jupiter, FL 33447

(305) 744-6006

National Golf Foundation-Midwest
1617 St. Andrews Drive
Lawrence, KS 66046

(917) 749-5334

National Golf Foundation-West
800 Las Gallinas
San Rafael, CA 94903

(415) 479-6649

National Golf Salesmen's Association
P.O. Box 275
Centerbrook, CT 06049

PGA Tour
Sawgrass
Ponte Vedra Beach, FL 32082

(904) 285-3700

United States Golf Association
Box 708
Far Hills, NJ 07931

(201) 234-2300

Professional Golfers Association of America
P.O. Box 12458
Palm Beach Gardens, FL 33410

(407) 624-8400

Space Coast Tour
P.O. Box 2125
Plant City, FL 33566

(813) 996-2361

Academic Institutions Offering Golf Programs

New Mexico State University

Professional Golf Management Program
This program has been certified by the Professional Golfer's Association of America. Upon completion of this program, graduates receive 24 credits towards the 36 credits required for Class A PGA status. The program can be completed in four and a half years and includes:
- Course work leading to a marketing major in business administration
- 20 months of coop education (on-the-job training) under the direct supervision of PGA Class A professionals at public courses, country clubs, and golf resorts
- Four PGA workshops. The academic program, which is fully accredited by the American Assembly of Collegiate Schools of Business, is housed in the Department of Marketing and General Business in the College of Business Administration.

PGA Certification Program
Upon the completion of all academic and coop work requirements, Marketing/PGM majors will be certified for 24 of the 36 credits for the Class A PGA membership. The PGA also requires passing a playing proficiency test, attendance at the PGA Business School II, and a membership interview, plus six months' experience on the job as a golf professional. For Information about either programs, contact:

New Mexico State University
Department Head Marketing/Professional Golf Management
Box 30001, Dept. 5280
Las Cruces, NM 88003-0001

(505) 646-3341

Ferris State College

The Professional Golfers' Association of America, together with Ferris State College implemented this program (the first of its kind in the nation) in 1975. Ferris offers a four and a half year program which leads to a bachelor of science degree in business, with a major in marketing. After graduation and upon completion of additional PGA requirements, the students may anticipate Class A membership in the Professional Golfers' Association. A career in this field requires not only acute golfing skills, but skills in business operations, golf course maintenance, teaching, golf club repair and organization of golfing events. Courses you will study on campus can be divided into three categories: pro golf management, business; and general studies.

The pro golf management classes include golf cart repair and maintenance, golf instruction techniques, equipment repair, rules and orientation to the game's organizations. The curriculum is comprised of 45% business courses, 30% general studies, and 25% golf management courses. For more information, contact:

Ferris State College
School of Business,
Big Rapids, MI 49307

(616) 592-2380

Mississippi State University

The four and a half year Professional Golf Management leads to a bachelor's degree in business administration with a marketing major. It includes 20 months of on the job training (coop work) with Class A PGA professionals at country clubs, public courses, and golf resorts, plus the completion of four PGA Workshops. Professional Golf Management (PGM) Graduates receive 24 credits toward the 36 required for a Class A PGA status. The academic segment of the program is administered by the Marketing Department of Mississippi State's College of Business and Industry, one of the oldest and most highly respected business schools in the South. Those who complete the program thus earn a prestigious degree and reach the threshold of PGA Class A Membership. For information about the program, contact:

Dr. S. Roland Jones, Professor of Marketing and
Coordinator of Professional Golf Management Program
P.O. Drawer N
Mississippi State, MS 39762

(601) 325-3161

Golf Academy of the South

The Golf Academy of the South is a two year accredited college offering a combined curriculum of golf education and business management. The Golf Academy has an outstanding faculty of professional business people, golfers and educators and has achieved a worldwide reputation in the field of golf education. The Academy is a unique concept in the field of education. It is dedicated to rigorous academic standards as well as excellence in golf proficiency. The Academy Program is designed to provide graduates with the business skills required to manage, or assist in the management of all golf complexes, including training in golf instruction. The Academy classrooms, club repair shop, student lounge and administrative offices are housed in a newly constructed sixty-four hundred square foot building complex.

For more information, contact:

The Golf Academy of the South
P.O. Box 3609,
Winter Springs, FL 32708

(407) 699-1990

Bowling

The Professional Bowlers Association of American (PBA) is the acknowledged major league of bowling in the world today.

Some 3,000 members strong the organization is a far cry from the 33 famous players who banded together in 1958 to start the organization. They now compete for more than $10 million in prize money annually. Armed with increasing prize monies and new television pacts, the organization appears solid.

The PBA is also popular abroad, as evidenced by the fact that tournaments have been staged in Canada, Puerto Rico, Hawaii, Japan, South American, France and England.

The Professional Bowlers' Association, like golf, has several prerequisites that must be met before joining the tour. Both women and men must be a minimum of 18 years of age, as well as being high school graduates. Men must establish an average score of 190 during the two most recent seasons in an accredited league that has at least a 66 game schedule. Women must have a similar schedule and maintain an average of 175. These scores must be verified by the American Bowling Congress (ABC).

Applicants must secure endorsements from 3 PBA members. Once an application and a fee of $75 have been accepted by the PBA commissioner, future pros will be eligible to compete in any of the 35 national tournaments with a national membership or compete in the more than 100 events regionally, with a regional membership.

The outlook for professional bowlers remains good. Financial sponsorship is advisable, considering personal expenses may run as high as $20,000 annually. The pro tour has a 10 month season with earnings ranging anywhere from $10,000 to $250,000.

Resources

American Bowling Congress
5301 South 76th Street
Greendale, WI 53129

(414) 421-06400

Ladies Pro Bowlers Tour
7171 Cherrydale Blvd.
Rockford, IL 61112

(815) 332-5756

Professional Bowlers Association
P.O. Box 5118
Akron, OH 44313

(216) 836-5568

National Amateur Bowlers Association
P.O. Box 17-1610
Kansas City, KS 66117

(913) 621-7337

National Bowling Association
377 Park Avenue South, 7th Floor
New York, NY 10016

(212) 689-8308

Bowling Publications

Bowling Digest
110 Grove Street, 3rd Floor
Evanston, IL 60201

(312) 491-6440

Bowling Magazine
5301 76th Street
Greendale, WI 53129

(414) 421-6400

Woman Bowler
5301 S. 76th Street
Greendale, WI 53129

(414) 421-9000

Tennis

The professional tennis world is divided into two career paths: touring pros and teaching pros. Tennis players can achieve pro status without intense schooling and course study. Touring pros first compete on the local or district level, then, advance to a sectional ranking, and finally, based on that ranking and their ability to win, receive a national ranking. Many players accomplish their rankings as juniors, while others develop their skills at the intercollegiate level. An educational background may make the difference in securing a club position once the playing days are over. Players are classified as professional once they accept money in tournament play.

The U.S. Pro Tennis Association governs the procedures for becoming a teaching pro. Future pro teachers must successfully complete a 2-day test, which includes demonstration of the varied tennis shots, and expertise in teaching both private and group sessions. The final phase involves a 25-page written test with the final application requiring both employment and sponsorship references.

The growing popularity of private clubs and the need for new talent on the pro tour are both indicators of continuing opportunities in this career area. Like most professional sports, however, the tennis scene is very competitive. Salaries for touring pros run as high as $1 million., yet expenses can total anywhere from $10,000 to $100,000 yearly, which makes sponsorship a must. Life at the local country club or tennis center will never be as lucrative. Administrative positions usually begin with salaries in the mid-teens, with the major portion of income being received through private lessons. These vary from $18 to $60 per hour.

Following are the foremost programs in the country for instructor certification:

Vic Braden's U.S. Tennis College
1 Coto de Caza Drive
Coto de Caza, CA 92679

800-42-COURT
(714) 581-2990

**Dennis Van Der Meer's
Tennis University**
2150 Franklin Street, Suite 580
Oakland, CA 94612

Bollettieri Tennis Academy
5500 34th Street West
Bradenton, FL 34210 80042

1-800-USA-NICK
(813) 755-1000

Resources

U.S. Tennis Association
1212 Avenue of the Americas
New York, NY 10036

(212) 302-3322

U.S. Professional Tennis Association
P.O. Box 7077
Wesley Chapel, FL 34249

(813) 973-3777

Women's Tennis Association
2665 S. Bayshore Drive
Miami, FL 33133

(305) 856-4030

Youth Tennis League
1701 Vardalia
Collinsville, IL 62234

Specialized Training/Educational Curriculums

Tyler Senior College

Since 1974, Tyler Senior College's tennis teaching program has attracted students from more than 35 states and 20 countries. As the oldest and largest tennis teaching curriculum in the world, TJC is dedicated to showing its students that being a professional in the tennis world involves more than playing tennis. Over 90 percent of the graduates in TJC's program find full-time tennis employment, in many cases, before they graduate. For more information on the Recreation Leadership/Tennis Tech Program, contact:

Paul N. Soliz, Director
Tyler Junior College
Box 9020
Tyler, TX 75711

(903) 510-2473

Methodist College

Methodist College is one of three colleges or universities in the United States which offer a program in Professional Tennis Management. This four year program results in a Bachelor of Science degree in Business Administration with a concentration in Professional Tennis Management. Students completing this degree track are prepared for professional tennis certification. The campus facilities consist of a recently constructed eight court tennis complex and a professional management office and classroom building. For more information, contact:

Mr. T. Jerry Hogge, Director
Charles Reeves School of Business
Methodist College
5400 Ramsey Street
Fayetteville, NC 28311-1499

138   *Developing a Lifelong Contract in the Sports Marketplace*

Each year, new and rising sports activities come to the forefront of professional competition. Downhill racing is one such entity that has now become a viable sports career. Photo: courtesy of the **U.S. Ski Association.**

8

Competing in Professional Sports As An Avocation

Numerous short-term, part-time opportunities exist for the athletes competing in the sports world. To become more informed about the possibilities and requirements of becoming a professional in any of these sports, contact the sport's appropriate organization.

Auto Racing

With the latest technology involving computerized testing and aerodynamic engineering, the car buff must couple driving skill with mechanical specialization. Since there always will be auto races, the outlook as a career remains somewhat bright. Personal expenses are exorbitant requiring sponsorship. Winnings and compensation may vary from merchandise as a trade-out to $1 million per year.

The National Hot Rod Association

The National Hot Rod Association is the world's largest motor sports sanctioning body. National event attendance averages over one million spectators, and more than 100 companies contribute more than $14 million in cash and merchandise awards to competitors. The organization's membership is over 59,000, and of these more than 22,000 are registered competitors, racing at more than 175 member race tracks, and a total of more than 3,000 sanctioned events. The NHRA continues to be firmly established at the top of the motor sports pyramid.

Resources

NASCAR *Stock Car*
National Headquarters
Daytona Beach, FL 32015

(904) 253-0611

NHRA *Drag Racing*
National Hot Rod Association
P.O. Box 5555
Glendora, CA 91740

(818) 914-4761

U.S. Auto Club *Indy Car*
4910 West 16th Street
Indianapolis, IN 46224

(317) 247-5151

Body Building

This very competitive sport has evolved from a fitness fad to one that could ultimately produce financial rewards. Four major national events are held each year, and are open to both men and women. At this point, the majority of all earnings in this sport come from guest lecturing and posing. Most bodybuilders need a major sponsor to cover personal expenses.

Resources

International Federation of Bodybuilders
2875 Bates Road
Montreal, Quebec H35 187

(514) 731-3783

The United States Weightlifting Federation
1750 E. Boulder Street
Colorado Springs, CO 80909-5764

(719) 578-4508

Boxing

For the past two decades boxing has sought to overcome a tarnished professional image that depleted its spectator interest. Despite such negative publicity, major title bouts will always be in demand. Most young boxers blossom in locally-sponsored club programs, which can lead to spots on the National and the Olympic teams.

Finding a sponsor to fund boxing training is difficult unless you are a national contender. Despite a growing audience, boxing is not presently financially profitable for the fighters. Since the boxing world has been associated with many unethical practices, young boxers should carefully check with the state athletic commission for the names of accredited trainers and managers before entering into any long-term contracts. Local Golden Gloves chapters are the best resources for starting a boxing career.

Resources

International Amateur Boxing Association
DRR 11337 Berlin
G.D.R. 137

(589) 229-3413

International Boxing Federation
Robert W. Lee, President
50 Commerce
Newark, NJ 07102

(201) 621-7200

Golden Gloves Association of America
Ace Miller, President
8801 Princess Jeanee N.E
Albuquerque, NM 87112

(505) 888-1176

International Boxing Writers Association
Marc A. Maturo, President
Box 610
Milwood, NY 10546

(212) 365-0226

USA Amateur Boxing Federation
Col. Dan Hull, President
1750 E. Boulder Street
Colorado Springs, CO 80909

World Boxing Council
Genova 33-DESP 503
Mexico D.F. 06600 Mexico

(905) 525-3787 or (905) 569-1911

Publications

Knockout
Stanley Weston (President)
55 Maple Street
Rockville Centre, NY 11570

(516) 764-0300

The Ring Magazine
Denis Blanck, Publisher
130 W. 37th Street
New York, NY 10018

(212) 736-7464

KO Magazine
Stanley Weston (President)
55 Maple Street
Rockville Centre, NY 11570

(516) 764-0300

Equine Sports—The Horse Industry

According to the American Horse Council, there are currently 5.25 million horses in the United States, collectively responsible for $15 billion trickling into the economy annually. The owners of these horses spend $13 billion in annual investments and maintenance expenditures. The industry is healthy and is providing job opportunities to many eager horse enthusiasts.

According to the Department of the Interior, more than 27 million individuals over the age of 12 ride horses each year. Over 50% ride on a regular basis. These 27 million riders alone require a large number of veterinarians, riding instructors, trainers, farriers, transporters, tack and clothing merchandisers. Horse events draw over 110 million spectators each year. The industry is looking for good employee prospects who can think, write well, solve problems, express themselves well, and who have good work ethics. According to Colorado Extension Horse Specialist, Dr. Ginger Rich, the equine industry has made its impact: "Right now, we have more jobs to fill than people to fill them. The best markets for horse-related jobs are on the east and west coasts. This is where the people, horses and money are concentrated."

Game Plan

Knowing where the jobs are is critical in landing a position in the horse industry, but knowing what you want to do and how to get there come first. The market is saturated with veterinarians, riders and trainers. Combination careers are currently popular: combining what you already do well with an equine specialization. Photography, art, business, computer programming, journalism, accounting, architecture and insurance brokering are just a few of the combination careers. Compensation for careers in the equine industry is as varied as the career options. A good photographer can just about name his own price. For the individual seeking a comfortable salary level, a formal education should be a part of the career plan.

Education

There are numerous colleges from which to choose, offering 2 and 4 year programs, in addition to specialized training institutes. Almost every state has several two year and junior colleges offering equine programs, some public and some private. Generally speaking, two year colleges offer some type of associate degree in sciences or arts.

Two year and Junior Colleges

Findlay College in Findlay, Ohio
Scottsdale Community College in Scottsdale, Arizona
Lamar Community College in Lamar, Colorado
Colby Community College in Colby, Kansas
Black Hawk College in Kewanee, Illinois

There are also colleges such as Connors State College which offer training certificates. These schools couple classroom learning with a great deal of on-the-job experience. Traditional four year colleges offer bachelor degrees in several different fields.

At this time, the only state-run land grant university which offers a bachelor's degree in equine science is Colorado State University in Fort Collins, Colorado.

Other four year land grant and state universities offering a bachelor's degree in animal science with a well-developed equine program:

Texas A&M University
Oklahoma State University
Louisiana State University
University of Georgia

Schools offering a bachelor's degree in equestrian studies:
William Woods College in Fulton, Missouri
Middle Tennessee State University in Murfreesboro, Tennessee
Meredith Manor International Equestrian Centre in Waverly, West Virginia

Equine Industry Program, University of Louisville

The University of Louisville School of Business offers an exciting program to develop leaders in the equine industry. The Equine Administration major is a four year program with a solid business foundation that is tailored for the equine industry. The program is designed to provide education in the finance, management, marketing, regulation, and administration of the equine industry to include breeding and racing. Special seminars with leading breeders, trainers, stewards, and track superintendents provide keener insights into the industry. Internships at race tracks and breeding farms will provide valuable practice experience. The curriculum includes a strong emphasis on economics, accounting, finance, production, marketing, quantitative methods, management information systems, legal environment of business, organizational theory and the administrative processes. This background should enhance the future management capabilities of the Equine Administration major.

"...the Program will provide the equine industry with a new breed of management who will be uniquely equipped to meet the myriad of challenges facing the industry." -Thomas H. Meeker, President Churchill Downs, Inc.

For information, contact:

Equine Industry Program
School of Business
University of Louisville
Louisville, KY 40292

(502) 588-7617

Horse Racing

This *sport of kings* is comprises of two groups of athletes: harness racers and jockeys. Both specialists will require a sound knowledge of breeding, training, and veterinary practices, along with proven riding experience. A jockey rises from the ranks of serving as stable hand, exerciser; apprentice, and finally a jockey. Jockeying is very competitive. By comparison, harness racing is still male-dominated, and more limited due to the small number of tracks as well as gambling restrictions. A maximum body weight of 110 pounds is allowed. The most important skill necessary for career success is the knack of guiding a thoroughbred around a race course. Both standard breed drivers and jockeys must be 16 years of age and pass a driver's exam. Earnings for jockeys are much more than harness racers ranging from $15,000 to $200,000 for the circuit season. Personal expenses will vary but are usually covered by the horse's owner.

Positions Available

Job Description	Compensation
Outrider	$100 a day
Chartcaller	$30,000 a year (if employed year-round)
Clocker	$90 a day
Farrier	$75 trim and shoe on all four feet
Clerk of Sales	$95 a day
Racing Secretary	$150 to $200 a day
Broodmare Foreman	$325 a week
Track Photographer	Private contract
Paramutual Manager	$195 a day
Groom	$230 a week
Horse Dentist	$33 per horse, avg. 10 horses per day
Horse Identifier	$90 a day
Horse Trainer	10% of the purse money earned by his horses
Hotwalker	$205 a week
Jockey	10% of purse money, $100 for losing mount
Nighwatchman	$275 a week
Paddock Judge	$150 a day
Patrol Judge	$150 a day
Placing Judge	$150 a day
Steward	$35,000 to $40,000 a year
Track Superintendent	$30,000 to $45,000 a year
Valet	$55 a day by track, staked $15 per horse per rider
Van Driver	$280 a week
Stud Groom	$280 a week
Racing Chemist	$35,000 to $50,000 a year

The Jockey

"Horses don't take a day off. So we can't take one either." That simple statement, from the mouth of a young jockey, identifies the biggest drawback to working with thoroughbred horses. It is a 7 days-a-week commitment, with hours that stretch from 6 a.m. to 6 p.m.

A jockey is an independent businessperson whose salary is based on success. The jockey shares in the purse, or prize money, only by riding the winning horse. Ordinarily, a meager salary for the race will range between $35 and $100 and more. From that salary, deductions must be made for retirement and benefits; fees to the agent who booked the jockey, and fees for the valet. After expenses, a jockey may clear as little as $13 for one race.

To get a good horse, a jockey must be willing to exercise the animal in the morning-without pay. It's just a service that must be performed. Jockeys make early rounds of the barns every morning, checking with the regular trainers in hopes of finding new mounts.

Weight is a major factor in most jockeys' careers. Though the average is about 110 pounds, the Jockey must be 4 pounds lighter than the horse's assigned weight for the race. The 4 pounds are taken up by the tiny saddle, pads and girths. Whether you are male or female, there is only one way to break into the business of being a jockey: hard work. Though there will always be a need for jockeys, career spans remain short due to the grueling lifestyle and meager pay scales. However, for those who make it to the top, the ride is very sweet, indeed.

Race Track Industry Program, University of Arizona

This program, which receives international support from the racing industry, is offered in conjunction with the University's bachelor's degree requirements. Students gain a working knowledge of the racing industry and at the end of the program, intern within the racing industry, thus gaining valuable experience. Placement is excellent with 7 out of every 10 graduates immediately placed in the racing industry. Undergraduate and graduate students, range in age from 18 to 50 and have come from all over the world to participate in this curriculum. Approximately 70 percent of the program's students are referred to the University of Arizona by race tracks, racing commissioners, horsemen's organizations, or former RTI students. For more information, contact:

Race Track Industry Program
University of Arizona Office of Admissions
Tucson, AZ 85721

(602) 621-5663

Resources

American Horse Council
1700 K Street, N.W
Washington, D.C. 20006

(202) 296-4031

American Association of Equine Practitioners
410 W. Vine Street
Lexington, KY 40507

(606) 233-0147

American Horse Publications
Council
201 Colorado Place
Arcadia, CA 91006

(818) 445-7800

American Horse Shows
Association
220 E. 42nd Street, 4th Floor
New York, NY 10017

(212) 972-2472

American Farriers Association
P.O. Box 695
Albuquerque, NM 87103

(505) 345-2784

American Youth Horse Council
4093 Ironworks Pike
Lexington, KY 40511

(606) 259-2742

American Veterinary Medical
Association
930 N. Meacham Road
Schaumburg, IL 60196

Harness Horse Youth Foundation
P.O. Box 266
(513) 767-1975
Provides equine school and college directory with scholarship listing

Professional Rodeo Cowboys
Association, Inc.
101 Pro Rodeo Drive
Colorado Springs, CO 80919

(719) 593-8840

Western/English Retailers of
America
2011 Eye St., N.W. #600
Washington, D.C. 20006

(202) 347-1932

United States Trotting Association
750 Michigan Avenue
Columbus, OH 43215

(614) 224-2291

Women's Jockey Association
6075 Franklin Avenue, Suite 070
Hollywood, CA 90028

(213) 705-0344

Ice Skating

No other sport will require the amount of sacrifice and commitment for such a limited number of professional opportunities as does ice skating. The serious amateur figure skater could spend an average of $6,000 a year for lessons, ice rental, equipment, and travel for competitions. Those skaters wishing to compete at the national and Olympic levels will be required to train year-round, often 4 to 6 hours per day. The outlook for show skating has not changed over the past decade—males and females have been equally in demand. Earnings for a 40-44 week professional tour, including room and board, will vary:

Line and Background Skaters	$15,000 to $25,000
Soloists	$25,000 to $100,000
Olympic Champions	$100,000 or more

With a shortage of male participants at the amateur level, professional performing opportunities for a man are much more plentiful than for a woman.

Many competitors choose to become skating pro instructors, once they have attained their highest level of amateur status. These teaching pros will receive upward of $25 to $30 for individual hourly sessions. To date, there are no prerequisites or requirements to becoming a teaching pro.

Resources

ISIA
Ice Skating Institute of America
1000 Skokie Blvd.
Wilmette, IL 60091

(312) 256-5060

USFSA
United States Figure Skating
20 1st Street
Colorado Springs, CO 80906

(303) 635-5200

PSGA
Professional Skaters Guild of America
P.O. Box 5904
Rochester, MN 55903

(507) 281-5122

Skating Shows

Ice Capades
6121 Santa Monica Blvd.
Los Angeles, CA 90038

(213) 469-2767

Holiday on Ice International

P.O. Box 9341
1006 AA Amsterdam
Holland

Walt Disney on Ice
3201 New Mexico Avenue NW
Washington, D.C. 20016

(202) 364-5000

Holiday on Ice
3201 New Mexico Avenue NW
Washington, D.C. 20016

(202) 364-5000

Racquetball

Racquetball interest peaked in the late 70s and early 80s. Keen competition continues with 15 major tournaments a year, however, most players cannot sustain the career on a full-time basis.

Earnings may vary from $1,000 to $60,000 annually and, as with many other sports, sponsorship is necessary to afford the many traveling and touring expenses.

Resources

**Women's Professional
Racquetball Association**
1001-C North Harlem
Oak Park, IL

(312) 383-9437

**American Professional
Racquetball Association**
5089 N. Granite Reef Road
Scottsdale, AZ 85253

(602) 945-0143

Rodeo

The rodeo cowboy is an athlete like no other. The risks of professional rodeo are greater and the security less than perhaps those of all other competitive sports. Physical danger is a fact of life, yet a paycheck is never guaranteed. It's a rugged road built for a special breed. Rodeo remains the only sport in the world to have developed from the skills required in a work situation. However, today's rodeo cowboy may come from almost any background. While only a few thousand cowboys rely on rodeo competition as their sole means of support, many more compete when and where their real jobs allow. While the vocational trend of America today is toward specialized education and job security, rodeo continues to attract talented young athletes. Often these future arena stars play football or wrestle throughout their school years, only to leave these traditional sports for the dust and sweat of the rodeo arena.

With a winning ride, a rodeo cowboy can make $10,000 in eight seconds. Just as easily, he can be tossed to the arena floor and seriously injured. The life of today's rodeo cowboys, champion or wide-eyed rookie, is anonymous and often lonely. Miles of highway stretch between every rodeo, and the cowboy spends much more time at the controls of a truck than in control of a bucking bronc.

The rodeo scene has recently gained popularity in several regional areas of the country with salaries rising sharply. It's not unusual for the top male riders to earn in the $100,000 a year range while female performers may exceed $60,000 a year for the over 600 events. Personal expenses may vary from $5,000 to $30,000 annually, but with a total yearly purse exceeding $2 million in both indoor and outdoor shows, the outlook for future riders remains good.

Resources

Professional Rodeo Cowboys Association
101 Pro Rodeo Drive
Colorado Springs, CO 80019

(719) 593-8840

International Professional Rodeo Association
P.O. Box 615
Pauls Valley, OK 73075

(405) 238-6488

Publications

Rodeo News
106 E. McClure
Box 645
Paul's Valley, OK 73075

(405) 238-6488

Downhill Skiing

Professional ski racing has achieved new prominence as a major winter sport. Part of its success is due to the worldwide attention it has received through the combined promotion of World Association of Pro Skiing (WAPS) members. WAPS is an international association of tournament directors established to ensure uniformity within the sport professional ski racing as a worldwide sport. Members include: U.S. Pro Ski Tour; Japan Pro Ski Tour; Women's Pro Ski; and Australian Pro Tour. All professional ski racing tours are eligible to join WAPS. Participating members feel that unity within the sport is the key to growth worldwide. Associate tours use a uniform point and seeding system which makes it easier for skiers to transition from one tour to another for competition. This key factor has increased the caliber of competition on all WAPS tours.

For men and women, professional skiing career opportunities are limited. The season is very short: only 12 events a year. Earnings will rarely exceed $50,000. Endorsements and exhibitions increase financial support.

Sponsorship by ski manufacturers is common, keeping the yearly personal expenses which range from $6,000 to $15,000 to a minimum. Many touring skiers, like tennis pros, eventually become instructors or manage their own resorts. There are lucrative business opportunities though totally dependent on annual snowfall in the west and far northeastern parts of the U.S.

Resources

North American Pro Ski, Inc.
P.O. Box 680
Bath, ME 04530

(207) 443-2743

U.S. Ski Association
1500 Kearns Blvd., Hwy. 248
Park City, UT 84060

U.S. Ski Foundation
Box 100
Park City, UT 84060

(801) 649-9090

Soccer

Soccer is currently in a state of flux in the United States., but should get a shot of popularity when the World Cup comes to America in 1994. Although competition continues to grow at the youth and high school levels, the game has not reached expectation levels in the professional market. Indoor soccer has been accepted to a certain degree, largely because its smaller surface allows for increased scoring. However, the sport is still dominated by foreign performers. Many promoters feel the American public cannot relate to supporting foreign stars while others attribute a lack of interest to television's inability to market the product on air.

The outlook remains bleak with current salaries averaging $20,000. For those who are young enough to weather the growing pains, the best route would be to play in the collegiate ranks and possibly link up with the European circuits.

Resources

U.S. Soccer Federation
1750 E. Boulder St.
Colorado Springs, CO 80909

(719) 578-4689

World Cup '94 Organizing Committee
1413 K St. N.W., Suite 900
Washington, D.C. 20005

(202) 842-1994

Surfing

There is little hope that this activity will ever reach full-time professional status. Those who have sponsors may win as much as $15,000 a year, but with little national or even local interest. Professionals or enthusiasts should view this sport as a competitive hobby.

The World Tour works with promoters from several countries to develop and sanction events which offer the greatest prize money available. Over 30 events with prize money totaling over $2.5 million are held in Australia, United States, South Africa, Japan, Brazil, New Zealand, and European coastal countries.

Women's surfing has seen a lot of growth in a short period of time. In 1982, the total prize money for the whole five events tour was just $25,000. Since that time, it has increased to over $150,000 with 13 events.

Resources

Association of Surfing Professionals
P.O. Box 309
Huntington Beach, CA 92648

(714) 842-8826

Triathalons

Even though the popularity of triathalons has blossomed immensely, only a few triathletes are making a living competing full-time. In fact, the only triathletes that have been successful at generating personal income are those highly toured competitors who receive honorariums to appear in Ironman contests and national triathalon events.

TriFed/USA estimates there are over 300,000 triathletes competing in over 1,800 events nationwide. Approximately 120,000 of these triathletes will have competed in one or more of the 350 TriFed/USA sanctioned events by the close of each season.

With the first Official Olympic Distance World Championship in 1989, and the imminent Olympic exhibition sport status in 1992, the membership base should continue a growth rate of 15 to 20% per year. There are now five races that offer over $100,000 in prize money and ten major races being covered by the networks and cable. A cautious estimate indicates that 1,500,000 triathletes will compete in 5,000 events in 50 countries around the world each year. As seen with other non-revenue producing sports, the triathlete must travel frequently to compete. Expenses can mount substantially, and sponsors and race directors do not always pick up the tab. The primary motivator for a triathalon career should be enjoyment of the activity itself.

Resources

Triathalon Federation/USA
P.O. Box 15820
Colorado Springs, CO 80901

(719) 597-9090

United States Triathalon Series
P.O. Box 1438
Davis, CA 95617

(916) 758-9868

Association of Professional Triathletes
25108B Marguerite Parkway 209
Mission Viejo, CA 92692

(714) 432-8226

Volleyball

Women's Professional Volleyball League is still struggling to become a legitimate sports entity. The Pro Beach Volleyball Series has established itself as a viable spectator sport.

The tour features over 30 stops with over $1 million in prize money. Even though sponsors are readily becoming involved due to this dream market of participants and demographics of spectators, it is still ill-advised to consider this sport for lifelong career endeavors.

Resources

Association of Volleyball Professionals
100 Corporate Pointe, Suite 195
Culver City, CA 90230

(213) 337-4842

USA Pro Beach Volleyball
P.O. Box 57
Huntington Beach, CA 92648

(714) 536-4900

Publications

Volleyball Monthly Magazine
P.O. Box 3137
San Luis Obispo, CA 93403

(805) 541-2294

Pro Beach Magazine
1875 Century Park East, Suite 1240
Los Angeles, CA 70067

(213) 284-8847

Water-skiing

Like its water counterpart, surfing, water-skiing provides excellent entertainment, but should not be considered a full-time career. Most events are invitational tournaments in which the purse size limits yearly winnings to no more than $12,000. Expenses will usually outweigh the prize money, therefore requiring a sponsor.

Resources

American Water-skiing Association
P.O. Box 191
799 Overlook Drive
Winter Haven, FL 33884

(813) 324-4341

The business of sport has taken upon a whole new mindset in the 90s. No longer do sports administrators serve as figureheads or celebrity spokespersons. Photo: courtesy of **Business Week's** *Careers*.

9

The Sports Marketplace

Scouting Report

Sports organizations are just like any other business entity. The many administrative positions within these organizations are simply business positions in an athletic setting employing many executive staff members without a long sports background.

If your dream job is in sports management, the best advice is: *Be over-prepared, be lucky and have impeccable timing.* Despite salaries that generally peak in the $40,000 to $60,000 range, the competition for jobs in the front office is fierce, with low turn-over. Even as the industry booms and becomes more sophisticated, there are over 150 qualified candidates for every opening.

Laurel Prieb, the Milwaukee **Brewers'** marketing director, says he gets at least a resume a day from applicants primarily college students with dreams of representing the team in the front office. However, openings are few and once people get in the door, they usually stay. "The business is glamorous, but the work is not," says Prieb, who rose through front office ranks as a college intern. "Working in baseball gives you dealings with contacts in business and politics, as well as sports. I guess the glamour factor is that everyone who is going into the work force wants to have a job they perceive as fun and enjoyable." If you're serious about a sports management career, it's best to lay the groundwork while you're still in school. Besides tenacity, front office people need poise self-confidence and emotional wit. You need to be able to walk up to a 260-pound all-pro NFL lineman and say, "I've got an interview at 2:30," and not blink. They can't be intimidated by celebrity status or size.

Nepotism has been particularly prevalent in the sports world. Like Minnesota **Twins** general manager Andy McPhail (son of former American League President Lee McPhail), many high level managers come from sports families. But the trend is slowly beginning to change:

"The practice for years was to hire family or kick people upstairs," says Dr. Frank Mach, athletic director at St. Thomas University. "When someone was no longer effective as a coach, they made him a front office guy. But now the tendency is to hire for competence, rather than for previous association. The industry is a lot more complex, and a lot more sophisticated." Though not identical in structure, sports-related positions are basically the same as corresponding positions in the corporate sector. The skills and training required in sports finance, marketing, or public relations are similar to those necessary for any other business that is vying for the public's entertainment dollar. To get a real feel for a specific interest or particular occupation, visit someone performing those tasks in the field you plan to pursue. By examining the position firsthand, you will be able to determine if your expectations are realistic and discover if this is truly how you want to spend your work-life. You will then be better able to assess if you are seriously committed to a chosen field. A key element in developing opportunity is utilizing the informational interview to discover where your career niche is.

The Professional Ranks

The majority of sports positions will be of an administrative nature. Professional sports administration can be divided into two areas: league or sport governing agencies (such as the Commissioner's Office) and individual team front offices. Collegiate and amateur sports place the emphasis participation and education. However, every professional team is run like a business: The bottom line is profit and winning.

Front offices will vary from sport to sport. A typical major league baseball team may staff as many as twenty positions. An NBA basketball franchise is capable of having its entire operation run by five administrative members. The number of office personnel is determined by the club's priorities and the number of support staff required for each department. Some franchises feel a greater need to bolster such areas as community relations or special events, while other organizations may split these positions under one title. An NFL football club, which faces near sell-outs each Sunday, can be content with only one ticket manager to run its sales campaigns. Since the sale of tickets represents an NBA franchise's main source of income, the basketball team may hire a marketing and a promotions specialist. However, a NFL team may be content in managing its communications department at a high level because of its television revenue contract. (Over $39 million per year for each club).

Of all facets of sports careers, sports administration is the toughest to crack into due to need to hire at a high level of professional experience.

Executives: Team Presidents & General Managers

Today, the team president is usually the person who invested the most money in the franchise or someone selected by the investors. Many of these executives have little knowledge of their respective sport. By not knowing the many idiosyncrasies of the business, they may not be doing justice to the parent franchise. Fortunately, this breed of administrator is slowly being phased out of the marketplace by trained, qualified members who are aware of each sport's nuances. The pinnacle of success for most administrators is that of general manager (GM). In the past, general managers were former players and coaches. Today, a GM's responsibilities include finance, promotions, and labor negotiations. The successful general manager is able to understand and deal with day-to-day labor problems., the complexities of television and marketing, monetary investments, and changing trends that will affect the team's success. More than likely, GMs have administrative experience. They may rise through the organizational ranks, possibly having started in a minor league team. A GM may still have past playing and coaching experience but that is certainly not the only qualification.

General managers will average approximately $250,000 per year depending upon the sport itself and the responsibilities involved.

Business Manager

In many organizations, if the general manager is not a strong business administrator, the business manager will become the general manager's major asset. A business manager rarely possesses an athletic background but must be well-versed in all aspects of operations. Some of the basic responsibilities will include: personnel staffing, concession bidding, finances and accounting, team travel, event security, and coordination of daily business transactions.

Like most higher management positions, an undergraduate degree in business administration with an emphasis in finance and accounting is necessary for this position. Business managers' salaries range from $30,000 to $40,000 annually.

Administrative Traveling Coordinator

Though many teams require their business managers to handle all out-of-town arrangements, almost all major league baseball and some professional football teams rely on specialists to handle this. Traveling coordinators must go where the team competes to coordinate all travel arrangements, transportation, and living accommodations. An outgoing and patient personality is essential in this position. A background as a travel agent would be most helpful here, but is not required. Traveling coordinators will earn approximately $18,000 to $25,000 annually and have few prospects of upward mobility within the organization.

Computer Specialists

Computers are standard business tools — the sports business is no exception. Many professional football clubs rely on their computer banks, not only in formulating team preparations, but also in establishing season ticket lists, publicity outlets, financial data and player information.

Football utilizes computers more than any other professional sport with Baseball coming in a close second. Computers are used to decipher competitive tendencies in addition to being able to scout one's own team for deficiencies. Computer programmers and analysts need not possess technical sports knowledge, but do need to be well-versed in sports terminology. Since supply overshadows current demand, technicians should expect to earn slightly below the present corporate market scale.

College Sports Administration

Though the professional administrative ranks usually have a higher employee compensation and a more prestigious work environment, the collegiate environment offers better job security and a broader experience base for individuals wishing to advance in the sports job market. Since collegiate athletics operates numerous sports programs for both men and women on limited budgets, many of these positions will integrate the responsibilities from several areas of expertise. This will ultimately benefit the young administrator, who will acquire a more varied background. The basic administrative positions and job descriptions in college sports are virtually the same as those already mentioned in comparable roles in the professional circle. However, due to the structure and needs of collegiate sports programs, many of these similar positions have specialized duties and tasks which are not necessary functions in a professional franchise.

Athletic Director

This position will vary according to the size and the athletic philosophy of the institution involved. Unlike the general manager in the professional ranks, the collegiate athletic director must also be a fund raiser, politician, personnel administrator and finance manager. The prototype Athletic Director (AD) is an individual with a post-graduate degree in education or liberal arts and an accounting or business administration track record. Though it is not mandatory, most Division I ADs will have coaching experience to establish both credibility and a common link with the coaching staffs.

An AD must serve the coaches and athletes first, while also taking on the role of liaison between the student body and faculty. The AD is responsible for the department's financial status and therefore usually answers to the Board of Regents of the College's governing body or the school President.

With the NCAA continually reevaluating its policies and regulations, the AD has become a politician in establishing a cooperative relationship between men's and women's athletic departments. This becomes even more evident when it comes to allocating limited available resources. Few universities still operate under segregated programs. However, this trend is changing and there is a shortage of female ADs who have both an athletic and administrative background.

Since balancing the books is the very reason this position exists, the AD of the future will be a successful financier and fund raiser. Depending on the needs of the program, many universities are now hiring public relations oriented ADs with associate or assistant directors taking on more of the administrative and operational duties.

The powers of the athletic director are not as absolute as the average fan may think. Though many schools' ADs are allowed to hire and fire coaching staffs, it is not unusual for departments with prominent football and basketball programs to have the department's power residing with these head coaches. If this is the case, the AD performs in nothing more than a coordinating capacity as opposed to actually performing directorship responsibilities.

This highly pressured and time consuming position can vary in salary from $30,000 annually in a Division III school, to over $100,000 per year at a nationally known institution. Assistant and associate athletic directors, who will perform specific administrative functions for ADs, will earn in the range of $25,000 to $50,000 per year.

Collegiate Business Manager

The Collegiate level business manager maintains a very low profile. This person may be required to coordinate all administrative functions, including travel. Little to no athletic knowledge is required in this position, but strong accounting and finance experience is a must.

Salary ranges from $30,000 to $45,000 annually. Only the larger institutions can afford the luxury of a business manager. For those schools that do not have a business manager, the AD will either assume or delegate responsibilities.

Director of Development / Fund-Raising

The concept of fund-raising — hence the position of development director — is crucial to the survival of intercollegiate athletic programs in these times of escalating costs. Contrary to public belief, athletic departments are self-sustaining — *not* subsidized by student tuition fees. Therefore, in order to meet the demands created by increased expenses, revenues must also increase. Entry level positions in development are one best avenues for breaking into collegiate sports administration. Positions in this area provide ideal opportunity to be involved in collegiate athletic program operation. Most Fund-raising directors work closely with the university's fund development office. Depending on the demands and needs of a particular school, typical responsibilities would include: donor prospecting and solicitation, alumni group organization, booster club coordination, distribution of donor benefits and responsibility for promotional trips. Fund-raising today is characterized by more than just outright cash donations. It now resembles an investment market. The sale of insurance policies, scholarship endowments, and bequests of wills are some of the methods now used to preserve collegiate athletics for the future. Another popular concept is for schools with successful basketball and football programs to require a donation for the rights to have season tickets at center court or the 50-yard line.

A good marketing background, along with a desire to work with the public are necessary attributes for someone wishing to pursue Fund-raising. Advanced degrees are not required as the salary range varies from a low of $17,000 for a non-experienced entry level assistant, to $80,000 annually for a seasoned director.

High School Athletic Directors

For coaches or teachers who enjoy working with young people, becoming a high school director can be very rewarding. A typical high school AD will put in long hours (usually after school) managing coaching staff, groundskeepers and secretaries, organizing sports schedules, ordering equipment and uniforms, attending booster club meetings and special interest group functions and overseeing home athletic events.

The scope of an AD's duties will depend largely on the district's needs and athletic priorities. The role can vary from that of a full-time position to a part-time spot with other teaching and coaching assignments. The AD's authority may be limited, since most policies on discipline and participation may be mandated from the district itself.

Vacancies are scarce and are usually filled by an in-house staff member. The many budgeting cuts in athletics has forced many schools to merge programs or utilize an area AD for several schools.

The salary range for a full-time director will usually fluctuate between $25,000 to $70,000 with part-time administrators receiving stipends in the neighborhood of $10,000.

Sports Marketplace Salary Survey

Title	Salary	Years of Experience
Primary Teams		
VP, Marketing	$88,245	9
Director of Broadcast/Ad Sales	$67,500	6
Director of Marketing	$65,660	9
Director of Sales	$61,490	7
Director of Promotions	$50,035	--
Secondary Teams		
VP, Marketing	$70,815	6
General Manager	$49,735	9
Director of Marketing	$38,295	6
Director of Marketing & Promotion	$35,000	3
Director of Sales	$30,000	4
College/University		
Associate AD	$46,000	>6
Assistant AD	$38,325	
Director of Marketing and Promotion	$33,340	3+
Director of Marketing	$32,860	4.5
Director of Promotions	$31,250	3.5
Sports Marketing Agency		
President	$70,625	10
VP, Marketing	$55,000	--
Director of Marketing	$35,000	8
Director of Public Relations	$25,000	--
PR/Advertising Agency		
Director of Marketing and Promotion	$35,000	--
Account Executive	$25,000	--
Corporation/Manufacturer		
Director of Marketing	$80,000	--
Brand Manager	$70,000	--
Director of Promotions	$63,750	3+
Director of Sports Marketing	$53,325	--
Arena/Venue		
VP, Marketing	$90,010	11
Assistant General Manager	70,000	8
Director of Facility	$55,000	--
Director of Marketing	$33,000	--
Horse/Race Track		
General Manager	$90,000	--
Director of Marketing	$55,000	--

Specializing Training Profile

The Sports Management Institute The Executive Program

As thousands attempt to enter and progress in today's world of sports administration, leaders are finding themselves in a business that is becoming more and more complex.

Whether in professional or intercollegiate sports, administrators are expected to do more than field winning teams. They are held equally responsible to run efficient operations in finance, ethics, personnel and public relations.

While other professions have kept their leading executives on the cutting edge by developing effective management programs, sports administrators have yet to realize the full range of similar programs. To address this need, the universities of Southern California, Notre Dame and North Carolina have formed **The Sports Management Institute**. The Executive Program includes a seven month course in which three weeks are in-residence, and is tailored to specifically for the needs of athletic administrators in mid- to upper-level management positions who either are or aspiring to be athletic directors in collegiate sports or general managers at the professional level.

The three major goals of the Executive Program :

- To encourage the participant to succeed in an instructional, participation-oriented environment.
- To form working teams at various levels of experience/competence and combine collective strengths for required exercises and simulations
- To complete the six month project while enhancing one's skills and the employer's effectiveness.

Enrollment is limited to sports administrators with significant professional experience. Each applicant must have the endorsement of his or her supervisor. For information contact:

Bill Shumard,
SMI Program Coordinator
Heritage Hall
University of Southern California
Los Angeles, CA 90089-0602

Telephone: (213) 743-2771

Resources for Collegiate Athletic Directors

NCAA
6201 College Blvd.
Overland Park, KS 66211

(913) 339-1906

NAIA
1221 Baltimore Avenue
Kansas City, MO 64105

(816) 842-5050

National Junior College Athletic Association (NJCAA)
1825 Austin Bluff Pkwy., Suite 100
Colorado Springs, CO 80907

(719) 590-9788

National Association of Collegiate Directors of Athletics (NACDA)
24651 Detroit Road
Westlake, OH 44145

(216) 892-4000

Collegiate Commissioner's Association
800 South Broadway, Suite 400
Walnut Creek, CA 94596

(415) 932-4411

Conferences and Meetings

NCAA Annual Convention
Early January: (913) 339-1906

NAIA Annual Meeting
Early October: (816) 8425050

NJCAA Annual Meeting
Early April: (719) 590-9788

NACDA Annual Convention
Early June: (216) 892-4000

Publications

Athletic Director
319 Barry Avenue S.
Wayzata, MN 55391

(612) 476-2200

Athletic Administration
1842 Hoffman Street, Suite 201
Madison, WI 53704

(800) 722-8764

National Directory of College Athletics
Specify for Men or Women
P.O. Box 7068
Amarillo, TX 79114

(806) 355-6417

NCAA News
Nall Avenue, 63rd St.
Mission, KS 66202

(913) 384-3220

Athletic Director & Coach
450 Lafayette Street
Salem, MA 01970

(617) 744-1793

Journal of Sport Management
Box 5076
Champaign, IL 61825-5076

(800) 747-4457

Resources and Publications for Business Managers

Collegiate Athletic Business Management Association
c/o Kenneth Buell
University of Minnesota
516 15th Avenue S.E.
Minneapolis, MN 55455

(612) 6243354

College Athletic Management
438 W. State Street
Ithaca, NY 14850

(607) 272-0265

Organizations

National Interscholastic Athletic Administrators Association (NIAAA)
P.O. Box 20626
11724 Plaza Circle
Kansas City, MO 64195

(816) 464-5400

Arena & Stadium Management

The Facility Executives

New arenas and stadiums continue to be built in every size, city and town all over the country, creating a need for specialists in facilities management. Opportunities are expanding in this area, but require promotional skills and the ability to coordinate many schedules of activity. Success in this phase of sports management will be based on one's ability to be flexible, foresighted, and efficient in planning details.

With the additional bookings of concerts, conventions and shows, multipurpose sports facilities seek individuals who possess a promotional background to schedule events on a year-round basis. This concept is expanding due to the fact that many arenas and stadiums are publicly financed and must show a profit to justify their existence.

Strong management skills with a business administration degree are prerequisites for someone wishing to be a facilities director. Experience and internships are attainable with existing stadiums and arenas. Long hours with considerable travel in order to book major shows and attractions are commonplace in this wide open field. Compensation for a managing director in a municipal arena or stadium could be as high as $40,000 to $60,000 a year. Smaller facilities managers, who may be required to take on additional administrative responsibilities, may earn in the upper $20,000s.

The Multi-Faceted Role of the Facilities Director

A facilities director's duties can include any or all of the following areas:

- **Building Engineer:** coordinating and controlling the physical condition of the facility.
- **Operations Director:** Plans and produces facility events. Coordinates concessions. Recruit, hire, train and evaluate personnel. Coordinates staffing for crowd control and facility safety.
- **Director of Marketing**: Coordinates all marketing activities, manages sales staff and contracted agencies. Handles all promotion, production and financial management of events. Act as liaison between facility management, corporate sponsors and the community. Handle all aspects of publicity, media relations, press releases. Solicit and close all advertising and group ticket transactions: corporate sponsorships, group sales, program advertising, signage, special promotions.

Resources

International Sport Show Produces Association
P.O. Box 1238
Wheat Ridge, CO 80034

(303) 422-3444

Publications

Amusement Business Magazine
49 Music Square West
Nashville, TN 37203

(615) 321-4250

Athletic Business Magazine
1842 Hoffman St., Suite 201
Madison, WI 53704

(800) 722-8764

Training Opportunities

Red Wing Technical College
Arena and Recreational Facility Management Program

Red Wing Technical College is one of the most unique programs in the country. Variety is what you'll experience in the this program The course of study includes topics such as: event scheduling, public relations, building an ice sheet, small engine repair, and much more.

The Arena and Recreational Facility Management is a 96-credit major that can be completed in two years.

To obtain an application for admission or to learn more about Red Wing Technical College, write or call:

Red Wing Technical College
215 Pioneer Road
Red Wing, MN 55066-3999

(612) 388-8271 or 1 (800) 657-4849

Sports radio talk shows have taken the mass media by storm.
Photo: Courtesy of **KSTP TV/Radio**, an ABC Affiliate.

10

Sports Communications & Mass Media

The many different specialities in sports communication are inter-related — whether it be generated from within an organization, through the public relations and marketing departments or outside and organization from the radio, television and print media. Similar resources — organizations and professional societies, publications — serve the needs of all these groups. For this reason, resources for all the different media areas are listed at the end of this chapter.

Public Relations

Public relations is one of the most exciting yet pressure-packed positions in any athletic or corporate setting. Strong communication and journalistic skills as well as the ability to represent the club to a variety of audiences are a must. Public relations specialists' responsibilities will vary by organization but will usually include coordination of all press activities, media campaigns, news releases, and developing and maintaining a positive team image. All publications, photographs, guides, and programs are developed by the PR office. Typically, promotional campaigns to fall under the public relations umbrella, if an organization does not have an advertising or marketing specialist. Depending upon the needs within the organization, the public relations director may have other titles and responsibilities as well including director of media events, director of community relations, communications specialist, or director of promotion. The sports public relations person deals primarily with print and electronic media. Ted Haraca, former PR man at both Purdue University and with the Chicago **Bears** notes, "…we are more accurately an information service than a public relations department."

A PR person can sometimes make or break a newly established franchise, especially when dealing with the media.

To enter the sports PR field directly, internships and prior background are absolutely necessary. It is a field that is learned from the ground floor up. Many PR directors perform similar positions for as long as 20 years before securing the role of PR director. Entry level public relations positions will have salaries in the mid-teens while PR directors are handsomely compensated in the range of $40,000 to $60,000 annually.

Sports Information Director

Sports Information Directors (SID) are the public relations specialists at colleges and universities. The SID staff serves as a communication line between the athletic department and the media. They coordinate and publish all statistics, programs, and informational news releases. The sports information department offers excellent opportunities for entry level individuals, but does not provide the environment or training needed for upward mobility within an athletic department. The sports information assistant is not likely to stay with any one SI department for more than a few years unless a promotion is forthcoming. This continuous turnover creates numerous entry level openings in the field. Strong journalistic skills, a nose for statistics, the dedication to work long hours under tight deadlines, and an ability to effectively deal with the media are prerequisites for anyone entering this line of work. The pay scale for this high energy position will start at $14,000 for an entry level assistant to possibly $35,000 annually for a director with considerable experience at a Division I institution.

A bachelor's degree is usually required to be an SID, although one fourth of SIDs today have a master's degree. Emphasis should be in journalism, English, communications and writing. You must develop the ability to organize information and have interest in a broad range of sports.

Marketing and Promotion

For all those who still believe that college athletics is dedicated to the ideals of humanity as well as to the old saying "it's not whether you win or lose, but how you play the game," please read on. The matter of winning or losing has been translated on the ledger sheet in the Athletic Director's office with an ultimatum for bottom line profits... or else.

With the pressures of fielding competitive teams, keeping alumni happy and having an athletic department operate with financial stability, university officials have turned to sophisticated marketing operations. The amateur ideals of college sports are fading away as TV rights, bowl payoffs, NCAA tournament appearance fees and season ticket sales are soaring.

Former University of Michigan athletic director Don Canham is the pioneer and all-time leader in college sports marketing. Canham was one of the first to apply classic marketing techniques to a big-time college sports program. He made enough money to provide state-of-the-art facilities at Michigan and approached each facet of his program as if he were a professional sports franchise marketing director. In a few short years, he took Michigan's season attendance from 40,000 to capacity at their 101,000-seat stadium and set the standards for all other university ADs. Even NCAA headquarters have recognized the necessity of establishing formal marketing procedures. With escalating television rights contracts, rigid licensing agreements and special event production, the organization has made the formidable task of meeting sports administration budgets a reality.

All university programs have some type of marketing and development team for five basic reasons:

- To update and build new athletic facilities
- To fund scholarship programs
- To meet budgetary needs for all athletic teams
- To develop relationships with alumni to raise money and sell season tickets
- To create community awareness for good will as well as attendance at revenue generating sporting events

Opportunities

Virtually every athletic program in the country at NCAA Division I, II or III level, NAIA, junior colleges in both men's and women's sports is in need of good marketing people.

Classical marketing plans incorporate: telemarketing, direct mail marketing, multimedia advertising in print, TV. and radio. Fund-raising plans that employ full-time development coordinators are being implemented at most schools.

Athletic programs need money to survive and realize the only way to make it long term is through first-class marketing efforts.

Every area of the marketing mix creates an opportunity in the athletic program: corporate sponsorship, advertising, promotions, ticket sales, event management, booster club and alumni relations, development and fund-raising campaigns.

"Every school is looking to gain visibility and gain revenue at the same time," says Jack Waters, Director of Licensing for the NCAA.

A degree in Business Administration or Marketing is essential for this area. Any type of sales background is almost as essential in today's environment. "You have to be able to sell: tickets, corporate sponsorship, souvenirs. You name it, we've got it for sale," says a marketing director for a PAC Ten university.

Job Search Strategies
- Create a bank of contacts and resources at target universities.
- Build up a background of sales and/or marketing that may be applied to athletic programs.
- Apply directly to the university athletic director, director of development or marketing director. For leagues, bowls or associations, apply directly to the commissioner or executive director.

Make sure your application package is includes applicable experience, classic marketing plans, references who are tied in directly to influential alumni, corporate sponsorship and administration officials.

Ticket Manager

A ticket sales director may also serve as a marketing director involved with group sales, similar to a promotion assistant. The people aspect of the job is important since ticket personnel are the only personal link between the public and the team.

Knowledge of computers, ability to keep accurate records, as well as a capacity to be organized are prerequisites to being a successful ticket manager. There is no travel and little contact with players and coaches. In fact, it is not unusual for ticket personnel to rarely see their team play, since their duties only begin once the patrons are seated.

The field is relatively easy to enter, but the average salary range is relatively low, ($15,000 to $30,000 annually), with little chance for job enhancement or promotion. Creativity and organization with an emphasis on presentation and sales appeal will not only develop excellent promotions, it will increase ticket sales and overall revenue.

The Mass Media

If you think playing baseball is competitive, broadcasting is worse. There are a lot fewer jobs and it's a vicious business. The woods are full of people who will say you're good, so many that you tend not to trust them

— Jim Kaat, former MLB pitcher, now TV baseball broadcaster

Without communications, sports undoubtedly would have never achieved the status it enjoys today. Take away the print and electronic media, which have provided the information and publicity on athletic events, and possibly the only ones interested in sports would be the participants themselves. If it weren't for the financial sponsorships provided by network broadcasting, many of today's sports franchises would not even exist, much less show a profit. The athletes themselves have the mass media to thank for indirectly allowing them to receive the high salaries of today that at one time would have been a far-fetched fantasy. Professional hockey teams illustrate the value of television sponsorship. Due to a lack of media sponsorship, many NHL clubs must charge in excess of $40 per ticket for their 41 home contests, only to discover that they still may not be able to break even financially. In contrast, an NFL franchise may not need to depend on ticket sales for revenue since each organization will eventually be awarded in upwards of $33 million for broadcasting rights before the season even begins. Imagine where professional soccer could have been if the sport were to have received such a lucrative television pact!

An in-depth look at the evolution of sport clearly documents the mass media's impact on popularizing sport. In the early 1900s, college football was strictly a regional sport played predominantly in the east. It wasn't until as late as the 1950s, that major league baseball news extended west of the Mississippi River.

Advancements in communications have changed both these scenarios making increasing football interest to epidemic proportions nationwide and allowing baseball to become America's number one pastime. Expanded wire services, increased radio broadcasting, and television programming have made sports more visible to the general public. The interest in sports generated by the media ultimately led to the development of new leagues and franchises.

Sports coverage in the 90s has blossomed to the point where many marketing experts believe that a certain degree of over-exposure exists within particular sports. An over-saturated product can lead to eventual disinterest if the supply exceeds the demand.

No one knows this better than the producers of NFL Monday Night Football and the organizers of the now defunct USFL. They believed the football fan could never see enough coverage on television, which led to expanded television coverage and a spring schedule. Both concepts failed.

Sports media personnel have become as familiar as the athletes themselves. And many enjoy a more lasting career than the sports performers. No longer is the reporter a behind the scenes person: Each journalist has developed a personal sphere of attention. It isn't uncommon for a sports enthusiast to watch a particular telecast, tune in a particular radio station, or read a selected column just to be entertained or amused by the coverage of the event from a favorite reporter or telecaster.

This lifestyle may appear glamourous but it is also fast-paced and demanding. The competition for sports media sports is fierce. Training and experience in sports media are definitely necessary.

Print Media

Sportswriting is the oldest and most basic component of athletic journalism. Most members of the sports media get their start by writing in one form or another. There is no substitute for sound writing skills with the ability to ferret out facts and separate them from fiction. Dedication and enthusiasm as well as a sense of humor are needed to attain a high level of proficiency. Without these attributes, it is doubtful that the aspiring reporter has much of a chance to make it to the big time.

There are several schools of thought about which route to pursue in becoming a newspaper sportswriter. The advantage of starting with a small newspaper provides the opportunity to be involved in every facet of the business writing, reporting, editing, laying out, and even taking pictures. In a sense, learning the nuts and bolts from the basic levels can be a proving ground to see if this is what you truly desire as a career endeavor.

Still, there are others who believe that once a position can be attained in a major metropolitan newspaper, the possibility for advancement will greatly increase. A majority of all applicants will take the latter approach. The downside is that opportunities on large metropolitan newspapers are scarce. The main advantage with this approach is that metropolitan area newspapers will provide more opportunity to cover highly visible events. In addition, reporters for larger newspapers enjoy greater readership, and this helps create media identification.

Try to acquire as much experience as possible, even if it is unpaid. Keep in mind that "if you are good enough, someone will discover you."

In Chapter 1, evaluation of lifestyle preferences was explained. Sportswriting careers definitely required some careful consideration to lifestyle preference — demands which can often be discouraging to the aspiring sportswriter. This field demands long hours. Usually, sportswriting means working nights and weekends while friends and family are at play. Even those who reach their lofty ambition of covering a team must realize that there are schedule drawbacks. Following a major league baseball team means spending a half the season on the road while the other half will be covering weekend and night games. Covering a professional football team means spending summer at a training camp, and covering exhibition games. This doesn't even take into consideration the weekends away from home. With the current play-off schedules, the Thanksgiving, Christmas and New Year holidays may also be spent away for family and friends! Pro basketball and hockey are just as demanding as are college and high school sports. Remember, sports are part of the entertainment business and working people are best entertained at night and on weekends.

Milton Richman, 40 year sportswriting veteran and renowned sports editor for United Press International, says that the first question he puts to any prospective sportswriter is: "Are you absolutely sure you want to do this more than anything else in the world? Or did you just happen to wake up this morning and say to yourself, 'Wouldn't it be wonderful to be a sportswriter?'

"If they're bone honest," Richman adds, "this question eliminates at least half of those so-called applicants."

There are three ingredients which are required when anyone is applying for a job: A feel for what has to be done, Judgment, Attitude. Of all three, attitude is the most important. "Give me a guy who is out hustling all the time for a solid, well-founded story, and I'll show you my future journalist," says Milton Richmond.

Training

Athletes are told that if they are to be proficient performers, they must talk, eat, and sleep every aspect of their chosen sport. The same holds true for sportswriters. They need to be sports historians, constantly reading publications and talking the language of sport. Specialized courses such as the geography of sport help prepare the trivia expert. So many of today's sports enthusiasts don't seem to understand that the history of sport did not begin with Pete Rose or Wayne Gretzky, but began in Greece. And somewhere along the way came the Cy Youngs and the Red Granges. The point is that a writer needs to put a singular event or an individual feat into a proper perspective within the total picture of the sport. How often do we hear sports media people proclaim a team, a game, or a play as being of an all-time or greatest moment magnitude. In actuality, if the competition, the conditions, or the technological advancements were taken into account, the feat may have not been so remarkable. If there was as much media exposure earlier in the century as there is now, we would be better equipped to make such comparisons.

In addition to acquiring street knowledge which is the prerequisite to any field in sports, without the necessary formal education required of the communications expert, there probably will be no future. An undergraduate degree in journalism is highly recommended, but majors in English and literature, coupled with an emphasis in a sports science could suffice. It can be said that, "you cannot really learn to write—*only to write better.*"

Experience

Don't think for a minute that all a sportswriter does is watch a game and report on it. Developing a style, transposing events into words, and making an article entertaining is the real art of writing. There's only one way to fine tune those already existing skills which cannot always be taught: By constantly refining them through experience.

Working for a high school or college daily paper, a local neighborhood publication, or even free-lancing can provide the necessary opportunities to develop your talents. Even by serving in the capacity as a non-compensated staff member, you possibly may be given a press pass to cover major events which could lead to contacts and other future assignments.

Educational Opportunities

United States Sports Academy Sport Management Education

The United State Sports Academy has introduced an exciting new program in Sport Journalism as an area of concentration in Sport Management. The graduate curriculum in Sport Journalism is designed to prepare students for the increasing number of career opportunities that are rising in the electronic and print media. Program electives will prepare students for a multiplicity of demands involved in professional and collegiate sport programs at all levels. Program objectives include:

- News writing and editing
- General assignment reporting
- Field trips to media outlets
- On air assignments
- Feature writing
- Sports reporting
- Photography
- Elements of sports publicity

For further information, contact:

United States Sports Academy
One Academy Drive
Daphne, AL 36526

(205) 626-3303

Wire Services

A sports journalist may choose to pursue working as a wire service reporter. This route serves as the best possible training ground for becoming a newspaper sportswriter since it will require the journalist to perform efficiently and accurately under tremendous pressure. Additionally, wire service reporters must also have a sound knowledge of all sports considering that the essence of time restraints will not allow them to be able to pick the story of their choice.

Working under the many deadlines will at times necessitate that reporters dictate their stories, forcing them to rely on keen thinking and fact finding. One of the drawbacks to wire service reporting is that wire reports can often be incorporated into locally-published accounts, thus diluting an individual wire reporter's style. In addition, wire service pressure to get the information out sometimes means that less than polished stories are sent to individual publications, where the staff reporters add the needed polish. For this reason, wire service reporters may be though less capable than their on-staff counterparts. The fact remains that wire service reporting is much more demanding. A newspaper staff writer may only write one story a day while a wire service reporter could have numerous assignments in one day. Needless to say, the workloads between the two journalism positions have quite a variance, but the training and experience gained as a wire service reporter will prove to be invaluable in the long run.

No matter what route you may choose, each day will present new challenges that will not allow you to live on past accomplishments. The advantage to such a work style is that there will always be a tomorrow to prove yourself all over regardless of the positives or negatives that occurred today. Writers do not always come across to the public as heroes. They can become very unpopular figures if they are unable to maintain a strong sense of objectivity. On occasion reporters may have no choice but to ask questions or report on incidents that the public may not want to know. Keep in mind that journalists are employed by the newspaper or wire service, not by a school, coach, or organization.

It is of utmost importance that personal biases do not cloud a reporter's objectivity. In other words, there is no room to be a fan much less having personal favorites. Good reporters strive not to break the cardinal rule against taking bribes or providing preferential coverage. There are too many other hungry writers willing to step in and report the facts "as is.". Once you have established a reputation as a *Homer*, it will stick with you wherever you go.

The future for print journalists remains good but due to the competitiveness of the field, many jobs will offer minimal pay scales. The writer's guild, to which most reporters belong, dictates the salary structure. For the most part, earnings are in the $16,000 to $45,000 range depending upon the size of the publication, experience, and the clout of the local writer's guild. Free-lancing for publications and magazines can be very profitable, but the financial rewards will not be attainable until you have been identified with your own writing style.

Television

In the minds of the public television represents the pinnacle of success in the sports mass media. Not only are the positions seen as prestigious and glamorous, but the salaries in this segment of the communications industry can rival those of highly paid athletes.

Even though the on-the-air personalities are the most recognizable members of any sports telecast, there are numerous behind the scenes personnel ranging from directors, producers, and camera operators, to stage managers, artists, and technicians.

Since the majority of aspiring journalists target television as their career endeavor, the competition to enter the market is extremely fierce with only a select few ever realizing their dreams. A misconception is that being an former athlete is a surefire way of attaining a broadcasting position. Though former athletes may get a foot i the door, how many do you see having their network contracts renewed or succeeding beyond the role of color commentator? A name cannot carry the audience's attention, but the dynamics of the presentation will. A sportscaster prototype must have a desirable on-camera image, excellent speaking skills, and an upbeat and energetic personality. Even though there is a definite need to amuse and stimulate the viewing public, sportscasters must be journalists first and entertainers second.

Besides projecting a positive image, sportscasters be artists in their use of language: speaking concisely yet colorfully. Becoming a trivia expert is not important since sports information or public relations department can provide any necessary statistics. The far more important task is to translate play-by-play action into an understandable and interesting format. The audience looks upon a sportscaster to interpret the game action.

Due to the instinctive nature of play-by-play telecasts, countless hours of preparation are needed before the event. This may include studying team profiles, interviewing players, or even memorizing numbers. A sportscaster becomes an instantaneous reporter without the luxury of editing words and sentences in order for the presentation to flow cohesively. This is the major difference between a play-by-play sportscaster and a color commentator, who will have the opportunity to rehearse a statement or summary momentarily before making an analysis. Many sportscasters begin in this capacity since it doesn't require them to be as reactive initially.

Getting Started

As with any other sports career, there is an element of luck in landing any broadcasting position. Theories differ on how to prepare for broadcasting and establish a successful track record, but no single strategy should be considered more noteworthy than any other.

A strong background in journalism and communications is necessary foundation for any aspiring sportscaster. A number of universities and colleges offer specialized training in broadcasting, and many have their own television stations, allowing for additional hands-on experience.

Some of today's most heralded media figures have begun their careers in a similar fashion.

Brent Musburger, the former CBS giant, is a graduate of Northwestern University. After majoring in journalism, he worked as a sportswriter shortly before turning to television. Vin Scully, who is especially known for his work as a football and baseball broadcaster, was one of Fordham University's first graduates in communication arts. He was hired as the voice of the Brooklyn **Dodgers** right off the college campus some 30 years ago. There are many other major network sportscasters who had their roots in an educational setting and were fortunate enough to be given internships or temporary positions on account of their formal training.

Upon completion of a formal education program, there are two basic directions to pursue in the sportscasting profession: as a play-by-play announcer or as a sportscaster on a television station news show. There are those sportscaster who have duo roles whereby they perform both at the station and have contracts enabling them to also work games at the college or professional level. But for the most part, the ideal situation would be to broadcast in only one aspect of the profession.

Despite the various paths and strategies that have proven to be successful for many of today's leading broadcasters, vast majority of the inexperienced media professionals will start their careers in a small market. Though this approach may appear to be somewhat unpromising and vague, it cannot be over emphasized that the competition to be a part of this field, especially in the larger markets, has few alternatives. No matter how desolate the location, the committed individual must seriously consider every offer in order to create an identity. Some impatient and ambitious entrepreneurs have taken matters into their own hands by starting or buying their own broadcasting stations. Though costly, this route does provide a considerable amount of flexibility to be creative.

The outlook for sports broadcasting remains fair at most. Salaries for top network play-by-play sports people can exceed $1,000,000 while color commentators can receive anywhere from $25,000 per telecast. As far as studio sports directors are concerned, a major metropolitan station may compensate its sportscaster to the tune of $100,000. But here again the size of the market will have the greatest bearing on the salary structure. For example, independent stations where may only pay their telecasters as little as $100 for a college basketball game.

Some of the universities that have established advanced curriculums in the television arts include Illinois, UCLA, Syracuse, and Missouri. For those with more focused goals, wishing to attend a more specialized and accelerated training program, there are also broadcasting schools. On such program is offered through Brown Institute in Minneapolis, Minnesota.

Brown Institute

> The Brown Institute is one of the most well-known radio and television broadcasting schools and was founded in 1946. Currently, Brown graduates are employed in radio and television from coast to coast.
> New classes begin quarterly. Entrance requirements include a special voice and reading analysis. Flexible scheduling allows students to attend evening sessions and many graduates complete their classes in as little time as 36 weeks.
> Brown has recently initiated an 18 month associate degree program which is geared toward individuals without a college background. The associate degree program includes college level general education courses in economics, sociology, and psychology, in addition to advanced broadcasting courses. The average Brown Institute graduate steps up regularly in salary and often moves to larger stations and more responsible positions. The school's placement service assists graduates nationwide, with many securing positions with the leading radio, television, and cable networks. Many graduates who prefer administrative work now own their own broadcasting stations. Radio and television broadcasting students who have completed at least 8 weeks may take the sports course at the same time. Play-by-play experience involves one or two major sports located in the Twin Cities area depending on the time of year the student wishes to attend. For more information on this exciting field, contact:
>
> Ralph Vieau, Chairman National Education Center of Broadcasting
> **Brown Institute Campus**
> 2225 East Lake Street
> Minneapolis, MN 55406
>
> (612) 721-2481

Television Support Personnel

On the air people compose only a small fraction of the total staff necessary to telecast a sporting event. There are positions available in television that will incorporate the talents and career interest of nearly every personality type. From the blue-collar worker who possesses sound electronic skills to the white-collar individual who has polished creative abilities, there will always be a demand for both people-oriented producers and sophisticated technical personnel at both the local and national network levels.

Producers and Directors

As the overseers of any televised sporting event, producers coordinate all aspects of coverage including preparation and coordination of announcers, production crew, and technical staff for every phase of a broadcast.

Even though the producer may have a set game plan going into any production, this person must be ready for any number of the unpredictable occurrences and be able to re-direct staff as needed. Events such as weather changes injuries call for a quick thinking on the part of producers.

Producers and directors work very closely. The major difference between a producer and a director is that, a producer pulls the total production together, and the director, on the other hand will execute the finer elements of the telecast. For example, a director will determine what cameras are handling different action and replays will appear on the screen and, if necessary, troubleshoot situations (i.e. mistakes made by the announcers or time lags that may affect the quality of the show).

Many skills that are necessary to perform either of these roles proficiently. Well-developed organizational and administrative abilities are crucial, but even more importantly, these roles demand keen attention to details. Putting together a sports program will involve precision down to fractions of a second. Consider that Super Bowl advertisements can run as high as $700,000 for each 30 seconds of air time. The slightest miscalculation can result in foregone coverage of the game or even worse, litigation by one of the sponsors for not meeting contractual time lengths. There is absolutely no substitute for extensive sports background along. The production crew must be thinking in the same terms as the coach or manager in order to anticipate plays or strategy. A producer's refined sense of objectivity and instantaneous judgment can be spare the network embarrassment from one of those unexpected occurrences in which the technicians are left flat footed. A first step in preparing for television production career is acquiring a thorough knowledge of communications and the mass media. It is never too early to gain exposure to all kinds of sporting contests and develop people handling skills. This can be attained while attending school or, like most major network producers, by becoming involved with a local television station. If possible, it may be even more beneficial to be associated with a cable station or independent network that specializes in local sports coverage since all your time then will be related strictly to athletics.

Television producers are handsomely compensated and it is not uncommon for a network producer to earn upward of $275,000 annually. In fact, production staff members have been known to equal the earnings of those on-the-air specialists.

Camera Operators

On-site camera operators are the folks in the trenches in the television industry. No matter what the conditions, heat, cold, or snow, they are required to perform at the same level of competence as if they were in the perfect confines of the studio.

Like the producer, the camera technician must be able to have a feel for the sport that is being telecast as well as be able to anticipate and often stay ahead of the commands from the control booth. Even with pre-planned camera coverage, situations will arise in which only the alert technician will be able to provide in-depth coverage to the viewing audience. It is in these instances that award-winning film clips and videos are made. Training for this line of work is available at area technical schools and usually can be completed in a relatively short period of time. Some programs even offer internship which can lead to full time jobs after graduation. But for the most part, camera operators begin their careers at a local station or cable company before being sought by a major sports market. Salaries vary depending upon past assignments and the size of the employing television station. A first time camera operator can expect a salary figure in the upper teens while a seasoned technician can usually demand a figure in the neighborhood of $25,000 per year.

Radio

Without a doubt, radio broadcasting presents the best overall opportunities in the sports mass media market for a quick entry with rapid advancement. In fact, many sportscasters who have become successful in the television sector have spent some time in the radio booth. Considering the number of stations that exist in even in the most desolate of areas, coupled with the fact that radio is primarily a local medium, the possibilities for employment are endless.

Radio can be a training grounds before moving into a larger market or to television. This is not to say that the competition is any less rugged, only that the initial upward movements are much more readily attainable in radio as compared to television sportscasting.

As in any other communications position, a fine command of the English language is vital since radio reports do not have the luxury of a television picture to describe the action. It will take patience, experience and practice to enable the listener to actually visualize the action from the announcer's description.

Many young radio reporters can be spotted by their inability to listen to athletes during interviews — leading to some very awkward blunders. Listening attentively is crucial to good sports casting and pertinent for maintaining rapport with players.

Many schools and vocational institutes offer short-term curricula. Brown Institute, described earlier, has one of the finest reputations in the country for this field. Radio broadcasting does not provide as lucrative of a compensation structure as its television counterpart, but it does offer a wider range of job availability.

There are some professional franchises and collegiate teams who hire their own voice to do telecasts. There is one added trade-off for radio: the radio voice for a team is often more popular than the sportscaster who is involved with the play-by-play on television.

A radio broadcaster's salary can vary immensely depending on the size of the station and the duties involved. Some reporters have their own shows as well as announce daily updates while others only broadcast a specific sport and may free-lance with other assignments. In any case, radio reporters can expect to receive as low as $10,000 to as high as $100,000 annually.

Sports Photography

Even in sports there is an appreciation for an artist — especially the photographer who can capture a single action of an athlete or play and raise it to dramatic proportions. Whether it be the intensity on the face of a tennis server or the exasperation expressed after a missed opportunity, how true it is that a single picture can speak a 1,000 words.

While the reporter may labor over phrases and words to describe a feeling or expression, the good photographer can put the whole story into perspective with just one click of the shutter.

Most sports photographers can have their beginnings traced back to their high school yearbook days or college newspaper experiences. It's never too early to start selling select action shots to local neighborhood newspapers or publications.

Like so many other artistic professions, there is little informal photography training, just fine tuning clinics and seminars. However, it will be necessary to put together a portfolio of your work to demonstrate your abilities. Again, there will be no substitute for experience or knowledge of the sport you are covering. The premier sports photographers need to know the personalities and the key players of each sport. Being at the right place at the right time is no accident. A fine example of this is the famed Dwight Clark catch in the end zone of the 1982 NFL playoff to allow the San Francisco **49ers** to beat the Dallas **Cowboys** in the waning moments. How often have you seen that one shot duplicated? Being in photography is much like public relations and marketing. Getting your work bought and published will require a certain element of hustling. ."The tough part in this line of work is that there's no routine in your life. You have to be able to have a flexible lifestyle," says Susan Camp, University of Texas photography supervisor. For the most part, photographers work independently on a free-lance basis. Primary sources of income are contracted photography sessions or sale of individual photos. Photographers can earn upwards of $30,000 annually, higher levels of success require not only superb photography skills, but excellent ability to market the work. Single photos may be sold for as little as $15.00 while unique shots can bring an unlimited fee. The outlook looks promising for the individual who has solid, disciplined work ethics.

Public Relations Resources

Public Relations Society of America
33 Irving Place
New York, NY 10003

(212) 995-2230

International Communication Association
P.O. Box 9589
Austin, TX 78766

(512) 454-8299

The Dream Job: Sports Publicity, Promotion and Public Relations
This thorough volume is often used as a course textbook. To order, contact:

Athletic Publishers
3036 Ontario Road
Little Canada, MN 55117

(612) 484-8299

College Sports Information Directors of America (COSIDA)
Texas A & I University
Box 114
Kingsville, TX 78363

(512) 595-3908

Annual Meeting: Early July

Athletic Fund-raisers of America
P.O. Box 1611
Clemson, SC 29633

(803) 656-2115

Annual Convention: Spring
College Sports Information Directors Association
Box 114
Texas A&I University
Kingsville, TX 78363

(512) 592-0389

National Association of Collegiate Marketing Administrators
c/o Roger Valdiserri, President
University of Notre Dame
Athletic Department
Notre Dame, IN 46556

(219) 239-7516

National Association of Athletic, Marketing and Development Directors
University of Michigan
Athletics Department
1000 S. State Street
Ann Arbor, MI 48109

(313) 747-2583

Association of Collegiate Licensing Administrators
Michigan State University
MSU Union Room 216
East Lansing, MI 48824

(517) 355-3434

Resources- Print Media

American Newspaper Publishers Association Foundation
The Newspaper Center
Box 17407
Dulles Airport
Washington, D.C. 20041

(703)648-1000

Associated Press Sports Editors Association
Jack Simms, Secretary
Department of Journalism
Auburn University
P.O. Box 1129
Auburn, IL 36831

(813)893-8111

Association of Women in Sports Media
c/o Kristin Huckshorn
1025 Schiele Ave.
San Jose, CA 95126

National Federal of Press Women
1006 Main Street
P.O. Box 99
Blue Springs, MO 64015

(816) 229-1666

American Council on Education for Journalism
563 Essex Court
Deerfield, IL 60015

(312) 948-5840

National Sportscasters and Sportswriter Association
P.O. Drawer 559
Salisburg, ND 28144

(704) 633-4275

The Newspaper Fund, Inc.
P.O. Box 300
Princeton, NJ 08540

(609) 452-2820

Professional Baseball Writers Association of America
36 Brookfield Road
Fort Salonga, NY 11768

(516) 757-0562

Professional Basketball Writers Association of America
c/o Bill Halls Sec/Treas
26 Woodside Park
Pleasant Ridge, MI 48069

(313) 222-2260

National Collegiate Baseball Writers Association
c/o Mark Brand, Secy/Treas.
Arizona State University Activity Center
Temple, AZ 85287

(602) 965-6592

Society of Professional Journalists/ Sigma Delta Chi
53 W. Jackson Blvd., Suite 731
Chicago, IL 60604

(312) 922-7424

Women in Communications, Inc.
P.O. Box 9561
Austin, TX 78766

(512) 346-9875

Resources – Television and Radio Broadcasting

National Association of Broadcasters
1771 North Street N.W.
Washington, D.C. 20036

(202) 293-3500

National Sportscasters and Sportswriters Association
P.O. Drawer 559
Salisbury, NC 28144

(704) 633-4275

Sportscaster Camps of America
P.O. Box 10205
Newport Beach, CA 92658

(800) 345-8730

American Sportscasters Association
5 Beekman Street
New York City, NY 10038

(212)571-0556

National Association of Broadcasters
1771 N Street NW
Washington, D.C. 20036

(202) 429-5300

National Association of Media Women
c/o Harlem Institute of Fashion
157 W. 126th Street
New York City, NY 10027

American Women in Radio and Television
1101 Connecticut Avenue, NW
Suite 700
Washington, D.C. 20036

(202) 429-5102

Sports & Media Publications

Professional Sports Publications
355 Lexington Avenue, 9th Floor
New York, NY 10017

(212) 6971460

The Sports Journal
Basement D
7 Glenbrook Place S.W.
Calgary, Alberta
Canada T3E 6W4

(403) 240-3258

Team Marketing Report
1147 W. Ohio, Suite 506
Chicago, IL 60622

(312) 829-7060

Photography Resources

Photographic Society of America
2005 Walnut Street
Philadelphia, PA 19103

(215) 563-1663

Professional Women Photographers
c/o Photographics Unlimited
17 W. 17th Street
New York City, NY 10011

(212) 255-9678

National Association of Women Artists
41 Union Square, W.
New York City, NY 10003

(212) 675-1616

192   Developing a Lifelong Contract in the Sports Marketplace

Though coaching represents one of the most desired non-playing careers in sports, it has been considered by many to be one of the most stressful occupations. Photo: courtesy of the **University of Minnesota.**

11
Coaching

There are two kinds of coaches - them who have been fired, and them who are gonna be fired.

—Bum Phillips, fired coach, Houston **Oilers**, New Orleans **Saints**

Coaching is said to be rewarding, challenging and fulfilling. It's also said to be exhausting, nerve-wracking and thankless. A wide variety of coaching opportunities exists for each aspiring teacher of sports from positions as a recreation volunteers, to the full-salaried professional mentor. Today there are not enough qualified coaches to meet the philosophical and athletic needs of sports enthusiasts. Coaches, especially at amateur and high school levels, are considered to be educators of life and sport. John Wooden, former coach of the UCLA basketball program, put it into perspective by stating, "I'm a teacher of life first and then a coach, whatever that is." Stop right now if you are pursuing coaching with ambitions of attaining legendary status, wealth and notoriety. Only a small percentage of coaches will ever reach such a level, the greatest rewards that a coach will receive will be the satisfaction of teaching and working with young people.

Coaching at any level is a "people-handling business," intended to bring the best out of every player. In addition to needing to be well-versed in the technical and strategic aspects of the prospective sport itself, coaches must also be proficient in directing a diverse group of individuals toward a common goal. Accomplishing this may at times seem complicated especially with the many interpersonal differences, social attitudes or lifestyle distractions that may exist within the team. With the recent public awareness of the prevalent use of alcohol and mind-altering drugs among athletes, the new function of chemical dependency counselor is also being added to the numerous multi-dimensional roles of a coach. Even though professional services are available to deal with such matters, many coaches handle these occurrences themselves in-house to minimize negative media exposure. Establishing a rapport with the media is a vital quality exhibited by successful coaches.

The Art of Mentorship

To coach either professionally or in a Division I collegiate program, it is almost a prerequisite to have been a collegiate performer of that sport. Individuals who have had illustrious careers as competitors are often highly sought after to fill coaching vacancies. However time and time again these such exceptional athletes have proven themselves unsuccessful coaches. This is due in part to the fact that coaching and performing are distinctly different careers. Personal interaction, communication and teaching ability are skills essential in coaching, but not necessarily in competing.

Usually those who aspire to be interscholastic coaches enroll in a physical education program and complete a coaching certification program. Physical education curriculums include the study of fitness, recreation and leisure time, but do not address issues related to competitive nature of sports, dynamics of individual and group behavior, or educational constructs. For most states, however, a physical education major is the only requirement for attaining coaching certification in the school systems. Physical education and coaching careers should be considered separate entities, not interdependent on one another.

Joe Paterno of Penn State epitomizes the non-PE coach. Coach Paterno received an undergraduate degree in English from Brown University intending to attend law school. Thirty years later he is still guiding the Nittany Lions. Paterno illustrates how coaches who stay with their teams for long periods of time experience the highest degree of success in motivating the players to perform at a maximum efficiency.

Even coaches such as Paterno who have established their reputations among the elite of their profession are finding that the awe and respect they once commanded is diminishing. Players who competed for the love of the game have been replaced by self-centered athletes who play for love of money. In this age of inflated salaries, product endorsements, post-career business opportunities and *me first* attitudes, the average playing career has been cut to only a few short years. Athletes, once hungry to make it to the top now have shifted their long-term career priorities to protect their future interests as opposed to putting it all on the line.

The Most Unique Position in Sports

There is no single formula for the ideal coach. A basic quality that every winning coach must learn to develop is working within the confines of his/her own personality. True leaders will not concern themselves with trends or what others are doing, but instead will dictate the style that will eventually be copied by others. Today's coach or manager is in the people business and must concern himself/herself with this aspect as much as his/her technical prowess in the Xs and Os.

Some of today's most prominent mentors realize that their success is as an objective leader. The most common mistake made by young coaches in an attempt to win the support of team members is by becoming one of the gang. This approach can only lead to a loss of respect and control.

For sports where a coach travels extensively with the team for months, maintaining the proper relationship conducive to winning may make for a somewhat lonely existence. Famed baseball manager Casey Stengel used to give his **Yankees** a list of saloons and watering holes saying, "These are my places. Now you find yours." Tom Landry, long-time coach for the Dallas **Cowboys**, was nicknamed the "plastic man" for his presumed insensitivity and aloofness. Landry later admitted that there were times he felt the tremendous warmth and good feelings that occurred within a dressing room, longing to be part of them. He contends there is no room for emotion in coaching since vital decisions need to be made objectively. He also believes that once you come down from the pedestal that players have put you on, you'll never be able to go back up in the eyes of your team.

Paul Brown was criticized for taking a similar approach in managing the Cleveland **Browns**. Though Brown never socialized with his players, some of whom he had coached since high school, he always looked after their needs. The distinctive coaching styles of Landry and Brown certainly not the only successful styles. Many times coaches are very involved with their players due to either the coach's personality or the emotional makeup of the team itself. With athletes of today requiring a more nurturing style from coaches, the parental image may be just the antidote needed to not only straighten out the athlete's personal life, but also to motivate individuals to higher levels of commitment and productivity.

Regardless of a coach's personal style, discipline is a necessary component for the team's success.

Do You Have the right Stuff?

Besides managing athletes, the keys to successful coaching are the capacity to recognize talent; and the ability to enable the that talent to develop it to its fullest potential.

Though high school coaches may never have the luxury of choosing players, collegiate coaches serve as recruiters who must be selective in distributing a limited number of scholarships. The evaluation of talent becomes even more critical to pro teams since the draft is the main mechanism in developing a sound franchise.

There is much more involved in the process of evaluating talent than physical measurements and statistics alone. Today, coaches are seeking personal attributes they believe are indicators of a winner. Often times, coaches select athletes with personality traits and playing styles similar to their own. A certain dynamic exists between coaches and players who function under frameworks that parallel one another.

With the emergence of sports psychologists and the development of sport personality inventories, personal attributes can be more readily pinpointed. **Cattell's 16 Personality Factors** and the **TAIS** (Test of Attentional and Interpersonal Style) are examples of such self-scoring profiles. These assessments will rank the following personality traits:

- Coachability
- Emotional Control
- Responsibility
- Pain Tolerance
- Commitment

- Self-confidence
- Leadership
- Mental Toughness
- Determination
- Aggressiveness

Talent selection and the evaluation of personnel has become such an important art in coaching that it now rivals one's knowledge of the technical aspects of sports. There is also an emerging philosophy that many of the behavioral problems now so prevalent off the field of play in both the collegiate and professional circles could be avoided or minimized if the athlete's character was given a more thorough psychological assessment at early stages in the player's development. The preferential treatment athletes receive at an early age has resulted in many of today's collegiate athletes being immature and not socially ready for the rigors of being student-athletes. Unfortunately, many scouts close their eyes to the off-field behavioral traits and choose to make decisions on talent alone. Today's problems in sports reflect the consequences of such decisions. For the majority of young athletes, their level of development will often be determined by the coach's approach to teaching. Coaches' who seek to move up the ranks will ultimately be gauged on their success as teachers and their track record in nurturing ability. At any level of coaching, there is no substitute for sound fundamentals that are reinforced by teaching the little things. The most successful head coaches have surrounded themselves with assistants who are good teachers. A coach who is too insecure to have a staff of the best possible assistants shouldn't be a head coach in any team sport and, in all likelihood, won't last long in that capacity.

Key Attributes of Coaching

Coaches become the overseers of all that happens with their assistants and players. Most coaches prefer to delegate responsibility among their staff and thus play an active role in only a few components of the *big picture*. They then become the decision makers concurring in position assignments, practice schedules, game plans, trades and other organizational moves. For some first time head coaches, the transition of taking on this new role which involves the total spectrum of duties as opposed to performing one speciality as an assistant, can become overwhelming. There are some coaches who even prefer to remain in an assistant's capacity since they do not feel comfortable with the added functions of a lead coach. The trademark of the great coaches is meticulous organization of time and energy. So often championship caliber teams will be characterized by spending the least amount of time in training camps while also having practice sessions that last no longer than 90 minutes. These same organized coaches are able to have time to themselves for outlet activities. Compare this to the workaholic type who has 23 hour practice sessions and who also spends nights sleeping in an office watching stacks of film, right up to game day.

A major drawback to this all-consuming approach is the high incidence of burnout among players and coaches alike. It is many times reflected in the on-the-field performance , especially late in the season. Knowing how to win is one thing, being able to get a team to peak is another.

Few coaches retire or quit coaching by choice. Success is short lived, and, for those who are unable to adapt and move on to another page in the journey of success, it can also lack fulfillment. Many coaches are forced to exit the mentor ranks due to their inability to move and roll with the times. The coach who is a pioneer of sorts in his approach to innovative techniques seems to always be ahead of his peers who are merely trying to maintain the status quo. Unfortunately, there appears to be one distinct advantage in becoming a trendsetter: job security.

Another major shortcoming many tunnel-visioned coaches encounter is not allowing the personnel makeup of the team dictate the type of play or strategy to be employed. Rigid or one-dimensional thinking here can only lead to under-utilization of talent.

Not only should a chemistry exist between the style of play and the team's personality makeup, but it should likewise be prevalent between the head coach and the organization's management. Too often in their desire to land a head coach's position, individuals will take a position without ever looking into the past history of why others left the team. A new coach should make sure that a *marriage* exists with the organization regarding philosophy and commitment to winning. Such a scenario is commonplace in the collegiate ranks, especially within struggling programs. The schools themselves play musical chairs when establishing their own institution's goals and priorities. More often than not, institutions may provide lip service to the theme that education is the focal point for their existence, only to come back later when ticket sales are down and bend NCAA regulations to preserve an entertainment commodity. If a coach is to function properly, then there can be no inconsistencies in the expectations to what is to be delivered.

Where the Jobs Are

The majority of all salaried coaches will be employed by secondary school districts. While professional game's mission is to *win at all costs* and secure a profit, the fundamental philosophy at the high school level is to educate and develop. So often coaches lose sight of this fact and subsequently get caught up in their own egotistical ideals. In developmental terms, the school coach is probably the most important member of all coaching ranks. The grass roots coach can encourage and motivate a student to further sports competition or on the other hand, possibly make the experience so negative that the child may begin to dislike sports and fitness in any form. There would be no college much less professional performers if the school coach does not seriously take on the responsibility of nurturing a healthy attitude and forming a serious foundation for the players. For a number of student-athletes, the coach can serve the role as a substitute parent or fill a void in the personal life of the child. Coaches finding themselves in these situations need to be sensitive of the power they bestow in a young person's life especially if the child has already placed them on a pedestal. Since coaches can easily get caught up in the mechanical side of sport will often times become blinded to adolescent needs and concerns. Few students will ever forget their coaches and the impact both on and off the field they had on their lives.

Secondary school coaches, however, do not have the luxury to relegate their involvement to the gym or playing field alone. They ultimately must work effectively with parents, booster groups, school principals and athletic directors. A secondary coach must have the moral courage to stand firm on issues involving character development and athletic sportsmanship. When establishing a system of priorities, a coach must understand that academics come first. Coaches need to recognize the impact their behavior or any statement they may have on students especially if it is not consistent with the student-athlete's family or school's philosophy toward discipline, education and athletic development.

A common concern expressed by many student-athletes and their parents is that coaches are not open to working with players with varying degrees of talent. It is easy to develop the highly skilled performer, but participation and enjoyment should be the main thrust at the school level. For the less talented young person, this may be the only opportunity he/she will have to achieve a sense of accomplishment in what probably will be a onetime involvement in athletic participation.

Not only does this teacher of sport need to be proficient at demonstrating physical skills, the Coach must also be adept at creating high sportsmanship ideals. Sports psychologists believe that athletic competition is becoming more conducive in building characters as opposed to character, as once perceived. Meshing standards of performance and sporting values coupled with teaching the physical components of sport, makes this sometimes thankless part-time position a near full-time preoccupation.

Those wishing to secure a coaching role will discover jobs are tougher to find due to declining enrollments and subsequent school closings. There also is a considerable turnover at this level with coaches moving on to college sports or other non-education careers due to the relatively low pay of the teaching and coaching profession. Though positions are more plentiful, coaching in the inner city has become even more challenging considering that the instructor must motivate to the point of soliciting students to become involved. Coaching salaries vary upon each community's or district's emphasis on extracurricular activities. However, the average scale would be $3,000 to $4,000 for a varsity position while assistants will receive a fee of approximately $1,500. Some school districts even have a sliding scale for longer season sports or for those which are non-revenue producers. You should be aware that each state has its own requirements for certifying physical education instructors, teachers and coaches. Keep your eye posted on job advertisements in the spring or call the local school district, or state coaches association regarding hiring procedures.

Coaching in the College Ranks

The collegiate coaching scene presents a completely different athletic environment then that experienced in the high school ranks. Considering that coaches will be involved with a much more highly skilled and talented athlete, the teaching process will therefore become more technical and specialized. The vantage point from which a collegiate coach will operate will be better equipped and considerably more prestigious. Even though this highly desired level of coaching has considerable benefits to be gained, they are not attained without a significant price to pay.

Coaches aspiring to become a part of a collegiate program should do so as soon as possible. The most direct route is to apply as an assistant at a Division II or III program or enter a Division I school as a graduate assistant. Most graduate assistantships do not offer a salary in compliance with NCAA regulations. However, the opportunity does provide room and board and more importantly a foot in the door at an early age.

Actually, a very small percentage of college coaching is spent on the practice field as the position can more or less be viewed as a three-fold role. For instance, a head coach will invariably spend one third of the time coaching, another third with administrative and organization duties and a final third recruiting. During the off-season months coaching segments are replaced by fund-raising.

Full-time assistants can expect to spend days and even weeks on the road recruiting potential athletes. This is the aspect that few coaches enjoy and many individuals leave the ranks for this reason alone. Recruiting is a difficult task that cannot be learned overnight and is an element of collegiate sports that is tough for any high school coach. Just ask Jerry Gaust, former coach of Notre Dame's football program, who only lost a handful of games in 17 years as a high school coach, but didn't even have a .500 record as a collegiate mentor.

The younger coaches or graduate assistants can expect to perform a myriad of tasks from splicing game films to recruiting athletes in unknown locations. Rarely will coaches serving in these capacities spend more than 23 years at any given institution since it is to maintain upward mobility. Salaries in the collegiate circles will depend upon the size of school and the conference. Assistants usually begin in the range of $20,000 to $30,000 at the Division I level. You can expect from 10% to 20% less at Division II and III. Head coaches can expect compensation for men's sports to go from a starting salary of $35,000 to as high as $75,000, while women's mentors will usually receive considerably less. Major conference head coaches in revenue-producing sports can earn as much as $100,000 in addition to outside income from radio and television shows, sports summer camps, endorsements and speaking engagements.

Professional Coaching

The professional arena provides the one true opportunity for the individual who wants to simply coach and nothing else. Pro coaches need not concern themselves with the unique problems experienced by school programs such as recruiting, counseling, determining academic eligibility, fund-raising and complying with NCAA Policies.

In order to secure a professional coaching position, one must first be successful at a lower level. It becomes obvious that the college football and basketball scenes are the proving grounds for both future professional players and coaches. But for the sports of baseball and hockey which adhere to a minor league system, a parent franchise may wish to keep a coach under a watchful eye for several years before any permanent decision is made. Amazingly enough, the win-loss records of a minor league coach are not the main criteria for being selected as a head coach. The ability to teach, develop and nurture raw talent are the key ingredients. Never be intimidated by the fact that you may not have played professionally as the most proficient players of the game rarely become hall of fame mentors.

Salaries for professional coaches are often twice as high as they are for collegiate assistants and head coaches. However, the emphasis will be placed on winning over anything else. This allows individuals to establish a reputation quicker than is possible within collegiate sports. There is no job security in the professional ranks. It is rare to see a professional coach or assistant remain with one club for more than 5 years. Most assistants make continuous moves to enhance their possibilities of becoming a head coach in the future.

Other Coaching Opportunities

Amateur club sports

Tennis clubs, golf courses and driving ranges, swimming clubs, gymnastics clubs, and ski areas all offer career opportunities for teaching and coaching amateur athletes. Many of these jobs are primarily instructional in nature. Some combine instruction with the development of competitive club teams. The pay tends to be low, the hours are long, and some of the jobs will include peripheral duties, as maintaining facilities, stocking and selling merchandise at the pro shop and sales.

Sports camps and summer camps.

There has been recently significant growth in the form of sports camps which focus on team sports for school-age youth. This field expands a job market that already includes summer sports camps for youth. Most of these jobs are seasonal with low pay, unless an individual can get involved in the management or client-recruitment side of the business. The U.S. Olympic committee recognizes nearly three dozen national sports organizations which are all in need of dedicated instructors. By obtaining a copy of the USOC's directory, you will be able to obtain contacts in your local area.

Never rule out YMCA's or the nearest recreation center. These organizations are always in dire need of additional help.

Making It Happen

No state certification is required for amateur club teaching/coaching, although several sport associations either require or recommend their own certification. Whether certification is required or not, a person with certification is a more attractive job candidate. A call to a club will provide information as to the need for certification and what it entails. Experience as a college athlete is often enough for an entry level job as a club sport teacher/coach.

Resources

Black Coaches Association
P.O. Box J
Des Moines, IA 50311

(904) 644-1408

American Baseball Coaches Association
P.O. Box 3545
Omaha, NE 68103

(402) 733-0374

Annual Meeting: Early January

American Football Coaches Association
7758 Wallace Road
Orlando, FL 32819

(407) 351-6113

Golf Coaches Association of America
P.O. Box 8082
Statesboro, GA 30460

(912) 681-9100

National Association of Basketball Coaches of the U.S.
P.O. Box 307
Branford, CT 06405

(203) 488-1232

Annual Meeting: Early April

National High School Athletic Coaches Association
P.O. Box 941329
Maitland, FL 32751

(407) 628-8555

National Federation Interscholastic Coaches Association
11724 Plaza Circle
Kansas City, MO 64195

(816) 464-5400

National Youth Sports Coaches Association
2611 Old Okeechobee Road
West Palm Beach, FL 33409

(407) 684-1141

U.S. Professional Tennis Association
One USPTA Centre
3535 Briarpark Drive
Houston, TX 77042

National Wrestling Coaches Association
University of Utah
c/o Athletic Department

(801) 581-3836

U.S. Olympic Committee
1750 E. Boulder Street
Colorado Springs, CO 80909

(719) 632-5551

Publications

The Coaching Clinic
P.O. Box
Princeton, NJ 08536

(516) 466-9300

National Coach Magazine
341 N. Maitland Avenue, Suite 150
Maitland, FL 32751

(904) 622-3660

Scholastic Coach
730 Broadway
New York, NY 10003

(212) 505-3000

Today's Coach
2236 Blue Mound Road
Waukesha, WI 53186

(800) 633-2823

Professional Scouts

Just before Jocko Collins retired in 1982, in his 43rd year as a scout, he said a scout is a "guy who played the game as far as his talent took him, even if that was just to the low minors, and kept hanging around." All coaches, most general managers, a few owners and all scouts constitute a species all their own, distinguished by willfulness and independence. They dislike supervision, hate bureaucracy, but do their work for the love of the game.

They better do it for the love of something. Does this sound like a thankless job:

- For every hundred players signed to a professional contract, only seven will ever appear in a major league game (Basketball and Football most likely go direct to the Big Leagues).
- Yearly turnover rate ranges from 30% to 40%.
- Normal development takes 3 to 4 years but competitive pressures are calling for results in 12 months.

"No matter how much we try to do to improve the minor league's life, we still lose more talented ball players to bad girlfriends, bad managers, bad attitudes, alcohol and drug abuse than we do to ballplayers who just don't have enough ability to make the majors," says Paul Snyder, Jr., Scouting VP for the Atlanta **Braves**. Scouting has been the basic backbone of Major League Baseball and Pro Football since the organizations have been in existence. Even though this ancient art form had been practiced well over 100 years, the reality is that business of scouting really hasn't changed that much. In 1974, after a couple of test programs, seventeen clubs put up about $120,000 each to establish the Major League Scouting Bureau, a centralized scouting system that tracks down prospects and makes scouting reports available to clubs. Football has developed the Scouting Combine and likes to think of itself as more sophisticated and scientific in its thinking. Baseball, by nature of its system, is geared more toward the grassroots mentality. Most professional sports teams staff their development system with speciality coaches, roving instructors, nutrition experts, strength and conditioning coaches, psychologists and even financial advisors to handle a wide range of problems a young pro player might encounter away from home.

Most Major League Baseball franchises each have at least six minor league clubs operating and developing talent. The NBA uses the Continental Basketball Association and Europe as its minor leagues, while Football is now developing a system through the WLAF. Typically, each team will have 1530 full-time scouts and 1030 part-timers, and a salary range of $15,000 to $60,000 with a median in the low $20,000s. Part-timers usually receive a small stipend and expenses. Clubs spend about $4 million annually developing their talent. "We look upon our minor league operation in the way that many companies would look upon their research and development operations," says Joe McIlvaine, baseball operations VP for the New York **Mets**. All clubs are dedicated to hiring good scouts. "No question about it," says McIlvaine, "I look for certain characteristics in a potential scout, including people skills, business savvy, intelligence, an ability to empathize and an intuitive sense of what scouting involves. After that, it's a matter of hustling, learning from one's mistakes and simply staying with it."

In the hiring process, scouting directors might spend entire days with candidates. They range from coaches, former players, officials and people who simply can't stay away from the game. "They have to know, love and be a student of the game," says one scouting director.

Each year the typical major league ballclub drafts and signs from 40 to 60 new players. Thus, an equal number of players who are under contract from the year before are released. Since an average organization has no more than 120 to 140 players in its entire system, a yearly turnover rate of 35% is common. With the other major sports leagues facing similar challenges, Scouting is here to stay.

Resources

Major League Scouting Bureau
23712 Birtcher Drive, Suite A
El Toro, CA 92630

(714)458-7600

National Football Scouting
5350 East 46th St., Suite 125
Tulsa, OK 74135
(918)66-33750

Recommended Reading

Dollar Sign on the Muscle: The World of Baseball Scouting
by Kevin Kerrane

208 *Developing a Lifelong Contract in the Sports Marketplace*

Sports agents are involved with much more than just negotiating player contracts as it is commonplace for them to represent clients in all areas of sports such as announcers. Photo: courtesy of the **Seattle Mariners.**

12

Sports Agents & Legal Representation

As an athletic director, I learned to appreciate the pressure connected with the job. It was a difficult procedure to reconcile six irreconcilable parties coaches, student athletes, senior administrators, committees, alumni, faculty. They all have different agendas and that creates different kinds of pressures.

–Mike Slive, sports attorney

Sports law was practically non-existent 15 years ago, but now it touches every area of sports. It is no exaggeration to say that today's athlete or club executive is often as familiar with a court of law as the sports court. Athletes, coaches, administrators, officials, spectators, physicians, equipment manufacturers, and sports facilities operators share a common bond: the risk of sports litigation.

In the last decade, professional leagues and colleges alike have spent millions of dollars in legal fees defending against damage and liability action of every conceivable kind. Many professional teams have now taken even greater care when acquiring players who have been previously injured. The skepticism that exists in such a situation is the result brought about that once the player's career is ended, he will sue the team and try to recover for physical injury. Some teams will even go to the extreme of moving or waiving a player once he is healed. There is room on both sides of the legal bench for lawyers to become involved in sports law. Nearly 100 law schools in this country now have courses in sports or entertainment law. Due to the unexpected growth of the sports businesses, an ethics committee has been formed comprised mainly of sports lawyers.

An allied profession to that of sports lawyers is the sports agents. Many agents are also sports lawyers. Agents know each sport's nuances and possess an inside perspective not so much in the technical aspects of the game, but more so in the personal demands the sport places on its players. Many of these agents invariably become close confidants and care-takers of sorts for their clients due to the fact that athletes have been taught from their early years on to achieve and excel without also being schooled on how to deal with the inbred securities of competitive sports.

The sports agent prototype has often times not been very clear-cut: anyone, it seems, can become an agent. All you have to do is convince an athlete to allow you to represent him, agree on financial terms, notify everyone that you are the agent, and simply go at it. What this process represents is a lack of standards, a lack of recognized ethics and disciplinary procedures, and no clear guidelines for expected performance. The results have been a litany of horror stories about agents who are interested only in getting their percentage, not contacting the player or doing anything on his behalf.

Anyone contemplating this career should bear in mind that each sport has a different personality and while a contract may be a contract, the terms and stipulations can be influenced by the sport itself. Many top flight agents deal with only one sport in which their expertise is comprehensive and their knowledge of the management principles is complete. There are some agents who have reputations for extracting big bucks across all sports, but management sources will secretly claim they are not as effective. A legal background is a good base from which to work even though it is not necessary to be a lawyer to serve as a sports agent. The monetary aspects of sports will become so mind-boggling in the next few years that an athlete-entertainer will be foolish not to have a financial planner to invest that money with only the client's best interest at heart. As this more thorough mindset becomes the standard, self-interested sports agents will become a thing of the past, thus allowing a level of credibility for the profession.

On Becoming a Sports Lawyer

Note: The following article was written by Gary R. Roberts, law professor and editor of **The Sports Lawyer** *in response to the many requests he and other sports lawyers have received on the question of how to become a sports lawyer. It is reprinted with his permission.*

The first and perhaps most important thing to note is that there is no formulated body of doctrinal substantive sports law. Rather, sports law is the body of all substantive areas as it relates to a factually and structurally very unique industry. A sports lawyer is someone who practices or is involved in some way in the legal problems of the sports industry. A sports lawyer might represent a league, a team, a player union, a player in a team or individual sport, an equipment manufacturer, a coach, a stadium or arena authority, a college or high school district, a conference, a city or county, a trainer or physician, a referee/umpire, a television syndicator, a corporate sponsor of an event or program, etc. And in this representation a sports lawyer might become involved with contract, tort, antitrust, labor, workmen's compensation, broadcast, regulation, copyright and trademark, property, immigration, tax, pension, procedural, constitutional, or even international or foreign law issues. Unfortunately, even criminal law and procedure is becoming ever more involved in sports.

Because sports law is so diverse, the best advice to an aspiring sports lawyer just entering law school is not to worry about sports law —or more specifically, the legal problems of the sports industry— until you are a lawyer. A good sports lawyer must first be a good lawyer. Thus, pick the best law school you can and once there, take the full range of courses covering as many of the areas mentioned above as possible. It is crucial that a sports lawyer have a great depth and breadth of legal knowledge. This multifaceted dimension makes being a sports lawyer more challenging and difficult than the average counselor who must primarily master only one substantive speciality.

If you are at a school where there is a sports law expert on the faculty, it would be useful to take whatever course(s) he or she offers, but it is not important as simply taking a wide variety of relevant courses. There are several law schools at which there is a sports law teacher, but only a few have a faculty member who makes sports law a major part of his/her professional career.

The schools at which there is a primary sports law faculty person (in alphabetical order) include: Boston College, California Western, Duke, Illinois, Loyola of Los Angeles, Tulane, Tulsa, and Widener.

Several other schools have part-time or regular faculty who spend a fair amount of time and energy on sports law included in this group is Denver, Detroit College, Kansas, Southern Illinois, Vanderbilt, Indiana at Bloomington, and Marquette.

Do not choose a law school primarily because it has a sports law person on the faculty. While that might be one small relevant factor, you should choose the school that is right for your ability, your personality, and your interests. Because sports law is really the application of substantive law to a unique industry, it is also important in your preparation to become a sports lawyer that you become as informed and familiar as possible with that industry. You can't convince a team general manager or an arbitrator that your client deserves more money unless you thoroughly understand the game he plays, how he has performed, and how the other players on the team as well as in the league have performed relative to him/her. You can't negotiate a stadium contract or worry about liability for injuries if you do not understand the nature of the business and the activity it involves. Thus, the good sports lawyer is not only a good lawyer, you should be someone who knows a lot about sports: the game(s), the business, the economics, and the personalities who are important both on the field and in the background. It is highly recommended that you read the sports pages, not only in your local newspaper, but in more national publications as well; *USA Today*'s sports section is an excellent source of a lot of general information. Magazines and other periodicals are also good. Nobody in the world can read all of the sports magazines published, but reading a few covering a variety of team and individual sports is invaluable. A favorite is *The Sporting News* which comes out weekly and covers all major team sports in depth, and most of the individual sports to a lesser degree. I should also add that the discontinued publication of *Sports, Inc.* magazine earlier this year was a tragic loss for the industry; I only hope something similar comes along soon to replace it.

Once out of law school, getting a job as a sports lawyer can be problematic. Probably the single largest group of sports lawyers is that composed of player agents. This is so simply because players constitute by far the largest single group of sports clients. The first problem is getting a client. The highly publicized dog-eat-dog tactics that go on in soliciting clients are truly sobering. But if you are not willing to hustle, you better either be very lucky, be the sibling, neighbor, or college roommate of some star player, or be able to land a job with an established agent or organization. It is not impossible to find clients, but it is not easy, either.

A second sobering factor involves money. A few years ago it was jokingly said that to be an agent all you needed was a briefcase and a client. That is no longer true. Today, not only do you need a client, but you also must be certified with the athlete's player union (except in hockey), which involves an initial one-time processing charge and an annual fee running in the hundreds of dollars. Then there are a plethora of states that have registration and surety bond requirements that, if complied with in every state, can be quite onerous both financially and administratively. On top of all this, union certification guidelines limit the fees an agent can collect from each player client to a small percentage of the players' earned income above the union negotiated minimum. Thus, unless your client is a high salaried star with other endorsement income, or you have a large number of clients, it is unlikely your income will justify the expenses involved in soliciting clients, getting and staying union certified, and complying with the state laws.

The upshot of this is that except for the very lucky, there are realistically only two avenues open for getting into the business. The first is by finding a job with an established agent or organization that already has clients and in which you can work your way up. The three largest organizations of this type that come to are: Advantage International, Pro Serve (both in Washington, D.C.), and International Management Group headquartered in Cleveland. However, there are many smaller groups or firms that might consider hiring a young associate. The major problem with this approach is that there are precious few of these jobs to be had and many very highly credentialed people looking for them. The second approach is simply by practicing law generally to pay the bills while gradually building up a sports clientele. Those who are not committed to this profession and not willing to work hard and sacrifice in the beginning might want to consider some other type of law. Many prospective sports attorneys have gotten jobs or landed significant clients simply by beating the bushes. Writing letters to firms or businesses of all types involved in sports, and if possible, following up with telephone calls or personal visits can sometimes pay off. Every league, every team, every tournament, every union, every stadium/arena, every equipment manufacturer, every college and high school district, in fact, every person or entity involved in the industry needs in-house counsel and/ or a firm to represent it. You simply have to identify all of these prospective employers/clients and go after them. It will probably be discouraging after you get two hundred rejections, but persistence pays off. And it should be said again, in any type of law practice, getting good clients requires a lot of hard work and creativity and the ability to withstand a lot of initial rejection. Another good device for getting clients over the long run is to do things to increase your name exposure.

Become involved in the Sports Lawyers Association and attend its annual seminar in May. You will be astounded at how many important figures in the sports world will be there, and you can make their acquaintance easily. Join and become involved in the ABA and its Forum Committee on Sports and Entertainment Law and the Antitrust Section's Subcommittee on Sports and Entertainment. To gain credibility and exposure, write articles for publication in various journals. Thee are two young lawyers who have had dramatic gains in their sports related careers because of articles they have sent to me and I have published in this Journal. Getting your name known and being respected is critical to your success, and writing good articles for journals like *The Sports Lawyer* is one easy way to accomplish that goal.

The primary message to be remembered that while there is a significant demand for sports lawyers, but there is equally a considerable number of lawyers who would like to fill the available need. Being one of the few who land jobs or clients in the sports industry will rarely involve only luck. You need first to build a solid background by doing as well as you can at as good a school as you can. You also need to be as familiar as you can with the industry, its structure, and its participants. Then you need to find clients or a job, which will entail a lot of hard work and probably some financial sacrifice for a time.

Agents and Sports Representatives

Agents, sometimes called representatives, act as the players' intermediaries with the team's owner and general manager, to secure the best financial and playing arrangement for the athlete. The use of agents occurs in several professions. For example, writers use literary agents and those in show business use booking agents. Agents are usually lawyers or accountants. They obtain their salary as a percentage of the income the player will receive from the team (or athletic event, as in boxing).

In addition, to negotiating contracts, many serve as financial agents for players, making suggestions for investments, product endorsements, and handling income taxes. Some act as representatives for organizations such as the football players or for baseball umpires. In doing so, they work to obtain better salaries, retirement benefits, and improved working conditions. Richie Phillips, well-known attorney and representative for several players, coaches, as well as the Major League Baseball Umpires Association and National Basketball Associations Official, believes he plays an important role in negotiating contracts. Phillip feels that the representative lends objectivity to a situation, since the player or management may not be able to evaluate the athlete's contribution to the team, that is, the player's bargaining position. He believes he additionally serves his clients through careful examination of the language of a contract for example, the wording of no-cut clauses. Following the signing, as the contract goes into effect, Phillips keeps his clients informed on legal developments, such as the free agent rule; he may become involved if a contract breach occurs. If you're interested in the career, attend law school and do a good job for your clients, suggests Phillips.

For many years, players made their own arrangements with team owners. With the introduction of television, rivalries between leagues, and the expansion of players' legal rights, salaries increased greatly. Many athletes in past years were underpaid for the performance; today some players are grossly overpaid. Hopefully a leveling of salaries will occur before sports are seriously damaged in terms of public support.

Opportunities for agents in the future will remain small and the salaries will continue to be excellent. If you're seriously interested, the best background is law or accounting. For law, this means four years of college in which you must do well academically followed by three years of law school. Accounting will require undergraduate school coursework. While in school, association with sports as a player, writer, or broadcaster will provide excellent experience.

Educational Profile:

Marquette University National Sports Law Institute

Marquette University Law School established the National Sports Law Institute in February of 1989. As the first of its kind in the nation, the institute aims to educate law students, lawyers and other participants in the sports industry in the legal and ethical practices in all phases of amateur and professional sports. To ensure that students are properly trained and well prepared for this speciality practice, Marquette University Law School will integrate sports law instruction into its traditional law curriculum.

The Law School will incorporate speciality courses, including sports and the law, current issues affecting the sports industry, sports Industry contracts and negotiations and regulation of amateur athletics.

In addition, the Institute serves as a repository of sports-related resource material; publishes a national sports law journal; sponsors continuing education programs for educators, lawyers and sports industry professionals; assists in procuring funding for an endowed chair in sports law at the Law School; and its directors are author of a sports law book to be utilized by both law students, practitioners and sports management personnel.

For information about the program, contact:

Martin J. Greenberg
National Sports Law Institute
1103 W. Wisconsin Avenue
Milwaukee, WI 53233

(414) 288-5815

Associations

Sports Lawyers Association, Inc.

Sports Lawyers Association, Inc. is an international professional organization of Lawyers. The Association was founded in 1976 with three basic objectives and purposes:

- To establish a society for those with specialized interests in the areas of sports law for the purposes of providing educational opportunities and disseminating information regarding those specific areas of the law.
- To provide a forum for lawyers representing athletes, teams, leagues, and those otherwise involved in sports for the purpose of permitting the discussion of legal problems affecting their sport law practices by providing a variety of perspectives and positions.
- To promote and, where necessary, establish rules of ethics for lawyers involved in this specific area of practice.

The Sports Lawyers Association's bylaws stipulate that regular members be qualified or licensed to practice law in, or admitted before the highest court of any jurisdiction. Associate members include accountants, other professionals, and entities that may be affiliated with or have a legitimate interest in the affairs of professional athletes, teams and sports games. For more information contact:

Sports Lawyers Association, Inc.
c/o Barry Mano
2017 Lathrop Ave.
Racine, WI 53405

(414) 632-4040

The Society for the Study of Legal Aspects of Sport & Physical Activity

Current membership includes individuals and institutions from the United States, Canada, Australia, and Japan. Each of the Last 6 years a spring conference is held at a revolving site.

Program Coord.
Dr. Lori Miller
Department of HPER
University of Louisville
Louisville, KY 40292 U.S.A

(502) 588-6642

Publications

A Complete Guide to Sports Agents, Robert O'Connor, Pierce CollegeThis book clarifies the role of agents and guides athletes toward proper selection of a representative. It features a nationwide survey of agents, athletes (college seniors and professionals), athletic directors, coaches, the NCAA, and representatives of professional athletes' associations, including: Joe Paterno, Larry Smith, Bob Woolf, Steve Arnold, Tony Attamasio, and F. Harrison "Buzz" Green.

1990 / 155 pages / ISBN 10774 / $29.95

Minding Other People's Business is a fast-paced user's guide to the art of dealing with clients from all walks of business life and prospering along with them. Donald Dell is the founder and chairman of ProServ, the multi-million dollar international sports management firm that includes the likes of Jimmy Connors, Arthur Ashe, Michael Jordan, Stan Smith, Yannick Noah, Patrick Ewing, James Worthy, Dave Winfield, Pam Shriver and Gabriela Sabatini among its elite clientele. Dell is a master at getting and keeping first rate clients. Now he has organized the principles that have made him among the best client managers anywhere in a cohesive plan of action for winning big in any client-oriented business. The result is *Minding Other People's*

Business, a street-savvy handbook for coping with the most complex, mysterious and challenging people in business: clients. ***Minding Other People's Business*** covers all aspects of client relations, from getting the kind of clients you want to implementing strategies for keeping them satisfied; from winning them over to your side of dealing with the most difficult client types; from being effective with clients to being effective on their behalf.

The book is available for $18.95 from:

Villard Books
New York, NY 10022

Periodicals

The following periodicals are considered to be foremost trade journals utilized by the most prominent sports agents and lawyers.

Agent & Manager: The Bible for Entertainment, Literary & Sports Agents & Managers.

This monthly publication provides insights into the issues and developments in sports and entertainment representation. Unlike many periodicals, *Agent & Manager's* focus is to educate and inform, not advertise. For subscription information, contact:

Bedrock Communications, Inc.
650 1st Avenue
New York, NY 10016

(212) 5324150

Entertainment: Law & Finance

A comprehensive publication that encompasses a broad base approach to servicing the *total* needs of the client. For subscription information, contact:

Leader Publications
111 Eighth Avenue
New York, NY 10011

(800) 888-8300

Amusement Business

The International Newsweekly for Sports and Mass Entertainment. In addition to addressing the trends of the sports market, Amusement Business interfaces with every aspect that confronts the entertainment field as a whole with weekly issues. For information, contact:

BPI Communications, Inc.
1515 Broadway
New York City, NY 10036

(800) 648-1436

Financial Services

The crest of the pro sports big money wave is attracting the attention of many financial service advisors who have a knack for trapping and nurturing those big dollars of today's sports stars. They are attempting to provide products or services to anyone even remotely related to the sports industry. The quickest avenue to the dollar is in providing financial services for the athletes themselves.

What Services are Needed? Where Does the Money Go?
- Agents command 3% - 10% of the athlete's gross income to negotiate contracts.
- Fees of about 20% of gross income are paid by the athlete to acquire endorsements and appearances.
- Commissions paid for insurance premiums for career income protection policies are between 5% - 10% of the annual premium.
- Commissions paid for life insurance protection vary widely based on the exact type of insurance and the company.
- Investment commissions vary according to the investment product. Acceptable levels are in the 3% - 7% range depending on the dollar volume and type of investment made. The larger the investment, the smaller the per dollar fee.
- Accounting fees should be paid on an hourly basis. They usually range from $65/hr. to $125/hr. depending on the complexity of the task. In the past, sports agents attempted only to get the highest paying performance contract and keep the athlete out of trouble. Ten to fifteen years ago, the agents began to realize the additional income they were missing by not controlling the athlete's income after it was made.

We have all heard tragic stories about yesterday's heroes ending their careers penniless and embarrassed. Checks and balances need to be added to the system now. Here are some guidelines for those who are entering the business for the right reasons and are willing to take the responsibility of fair and prudent judgment with a high level of integrity:

Traps to Avoid

- ***I'm Your Man* System.** This system exists when the *I can do everything for you* agent says "all you have to do is perform, I will take of your money for you." Any agent who accepts the responsibility of negotiating the contract and doing the tax returns and making the investment and insurance choices for the performer (sometimes going as far as paying the bills and giving the performer an allowance) should check his ethical credentials at the door. There are just too many conflicts of interest and opportunities for financial abuse of the client in the One House System.

- ***Trust Me* Theory.** This exists when the performer won't take the time to find one competent investment and insurance advisor, or firm he or she can trust. The weakness is spreading the investments around. When the athlete is continually able to be persuaded by an ever increasing number of new geniuses to change prior financial plans, the investment and insurance planning will: lack direction, not be cohesive, cost the athlete much more, and not be effective. Many athletes acquire their investments and insurance haphazardly based on friendships and the desire to be liked. Some, for no reason, feel obligated to buy from those with no extensive background, no credentials and little experience in their chosen field. These include family, friends, the family attorney, their minister, etc. These well intended "advisors" generally fail miserably and squander small (and large) fortunes that our heroes won't have a chance to recapture. An athlete will make more money with consistently average investment returns using one well-informed advisor than in finding a "new genius" every six months. The process of staring over at square one, each time, loses both time and money.

An advisor who gets selected by athletes should have:
- **Applicable experience**.
- **Credentials**: CLU (Chartered Life Underwriter); CHFC (Chartered Financial Consultant); CFP (Certified Financial Planner).
- **Clients**: Currently working with ten or more, professional athletes.
- **Solutions**: Will know what to expect in athlete's financial life before critical situations arise. A seasoned advisor can plan well and deal with the inevitable surprises.

Game Plan

- There must be a separate CPA firm who reviews the cash flow and approves of the financial plan and products proposed by the investment and insurance advisor.
- CPA's should never share in fees or commissions from investment and insurance purchases.
- The agent should never be personally involved in receiving commissions or fees from an investment or insurance purchase.
- Create a proposal that makes economic sense and does not exceed the athlete's ability to easily complete the program and still pay everyday living expenses.

Opportunities

- Accounting in the areas of cash flows, financial statements, tax returns, tax planning, investment suit ability and general planning reviews.
- Trust officers in handling the assets and banking needs of the successful athlete.
- Investment and insurance advisors in providing prudent financial products to meet the needs and cash flow limitations of a professional athlete.
- Financial planners in providing a blue print for success in budget needs and appropriate investment analysis.
- Attorneys in reviewing all contracts entered into. Preparing the appropriate wills, trusts, pre-nuptial agreements and any other legal documents protecting the athlete from unreasonable liability.

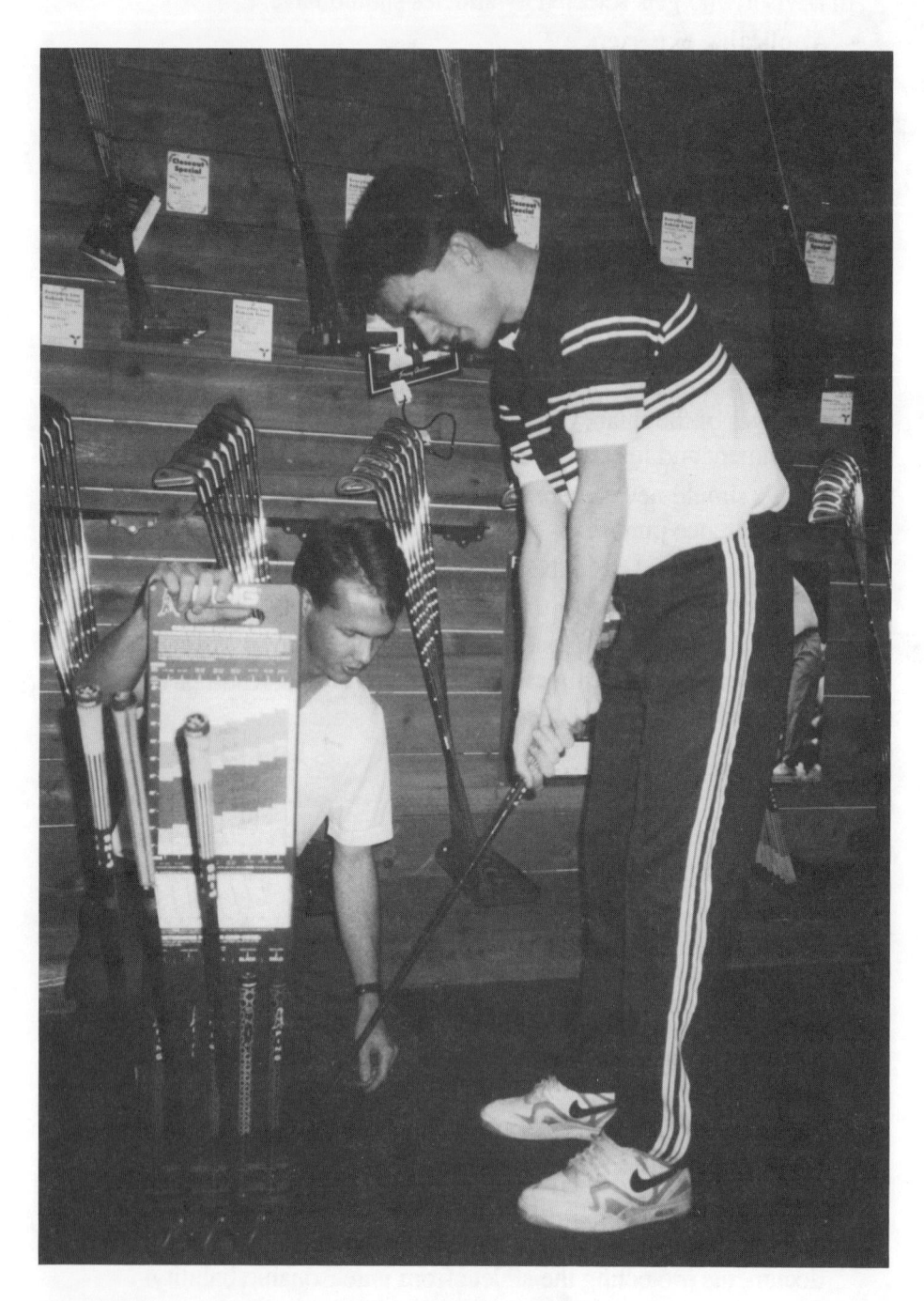

222 Developing a Lifelong Contract in the Sports Marketplace

Sports retailers need to be well-versed in a variety of sports activities and product lines in order to best serve the sophisticated sports consumer. Photo: **Athletic Achievements.**

13

The Business of Sport

Until the mid 60s, business and sports only flirted with the idea of becoming big time. Now it is a rare occasion when a major corporation does not involve itself in some way with sports. The central theme in advertising, marketing, sales, or purchasing will attempt to involve a sports-related concept whether it be food, apparel, automobiles, or a predominating lifestyle,

With the arrival of sports on the business scene, the demand has increased for those who can speak and conceptualize the ramifications of how sports applies to other walks of life. Take for instance the insurance industry which has expanded its special risk coverage to include athletics. It now is commonplace for a football quarterback to have an arm insured or a runner to set a premium on his/her legs. Or how about the lawyer who handles contract negotiations and investment procedures for his/her professional athletic clients who regularly have their salaries deferred for tax purposes sometimes as along as a 20 year period of time.

As a new sport gains public acceptance, there will also be a need for advertising and promotion of the activity that along with a whole new line of sporting equipment that will evolve to meet the newly created interest. Each new sports entry will ultimately increase the demand for sports related business personnel.

You don't have to be an athlete, much less an avid fitness participant, to be successful in a sports-related business career. Success in any sports business field requires the same disciplines and skills that are the foundation of successful retail sales people, corporate lawyers, public accountants, and middle managers. There is no substitute for knowledge, dedication, ability, foresight, experience, and hard work.

The Sporting Goods Industry

The sporting goods industry exemplifies the need for sound business principles in a sports environment. The segment of sports is composed of people with expertise in personnel, production, finance, marketing, sales and research.

Individuals working in this industry need not be sports experts. Quite frankly, those competing athletes who have utilized the sport specific products and equipment are often times less qualified to sell or much less even market the equipment. The disadvantage of hiring successful athletes may be that they already have a prejudice about equipment that may not even be within the realm of the company's product line. How often do you see high profile athletes employ the competition's product line as opposed to the company they supposedly endorse? Therefore, the only real demand for the athlete-specialist is in the phase of product development and design. Employment opportunities in sporting goods sales are increasing, but not without a high turnover rate which can be attributed to the exorbitant amount of traveling that may be required of the marketing representative. The two prerequisites that all companies seek in prospective employees are: college degrees with emphasis in business and marketing, and hands-on experience. Neither of these elements may take precedence over the other unless the applicant has already established a successful sales track record with another firm.

Marketing and sales staff people will usually receive a base salary plus a commission. An entry level earnings range of $13,000 through $20,000 can be expected in the early stages of sales with increases and bonuses occurring rapidly as sales volume and contracts increase.

Retail Sporting Goods

Due to America's preoccupation with physical fitness, sporting goods retail businesses have experienced tremendous growth. The store that stocks everything from uniforms to baseball gloves along with fitness equipment to tennis apparel still dominates the market. A growing trend is speciality outlets or sport-specific stores featuring a particular line of recreation or sports merchandise such as camping equipment, bicycles, or fitness machines.

No longer is the trend for retail businesses to be owned by sole proprietorship. Specialization has also increased the need for regional chains which keep costs competitive. This conglomerate effect has created a whole new market for management staffs including those with expertise in promotions and sales. Knowledge and firsthand usage of the many product lines can only enhance the success and future advancement of the retail salesperson. Since new product lines are flooding the market on almost a daily basis, the retailer's education and experience with each product will better enable the purchaser to make a correct choice and become a repeat buyer. Entrance into the retail market is not difficult considering sales staff personnel often start with rather conservative hourly salaries. For those with management aspirations, salaries will begin the area of $14,000 with quick advancements. The retail industry is noted for its low salary structure and long hours, but with the right attitude and some capital backing, ownership of a sporting goods dealership is attainable within 5 to 10 years. Very few sporting good retailers actually receive formal training and preparation to enter this industry. However, those individuals who are successful will have a strong background in sales, marketing, and business administration.

The institution that does offer a structured program designed for career work in the sporting goods industry is the University of Massachusetts in Amherst. This school has already been outlined in an earlier section for providing flexible coursework in sport facility management, recreation, and athletic administration.

Sporting Goods: The Retail Business

According to John Ruskin, a 19th century English author, there are three things needed for people to be happy in their work; they must be qualified for it, they must not do too much of it, and they must have a sense of success in it. It has been suggested by people in the retail sporting goods industry that a fourth factor be added; they must be paid well for it.

Resources

National Sporting Goods Association
1699 Wall Street
Mount Prospect, IL 60056

(312) 439-4000

Benefits retailers in the sporting goods industry. Services for members: Directory of members' 800 numbers, information center; sports retailer magazine.

Sporting Goods Agents Association
P.O. Box 998
Morton Grove, IL 60053

(312) 296-3670

Membership: Individuals who are independent agents for sporting goods manufacturers.

Services: Annual meeting, educational seminars, job placement assistance; *SGAA Bulletin,* monthly newsletter.

Tackle Shooting Sports Agents
1250 Grove Avenue, Suite 300
Barrington, IL 60010

(708) 381-3032

Sporting Goods Manufacturers Association
200 Castlewood Drive
North Palm Beach, FL 33408

(305) 842-4100

Serves as a forum for exchanging ideas and information as a means of building a better industry.

Membership: Professional manufacturers of sporting goods.

Services: Conventions, seminars; information (on trends, marketing studies) available; newsletter.

Trade Journal & Publications

The Sporting Goods Dealer
P.O. Box 56
St. Louis, MO 63166-1056

Sports Trend
Shore Communications
P.O. Box 1505
Riverton, NJ 08077

Sporting Goods Business
Reader Service Management
P.O. Box 5278
Pittsfield, MA 012035278

SportStyle
Semi-monthly source book on the sporting goods industry.

Fairchild Publications
7 East 12th Street
New York, NY 10003

(212) 741-4054

Showtime: The Means of the Sporting Goods Industry

Thousands of retailers, manufacturers, dealers, sellers and leaders in the sporting goods and active wear market meet to discuss, share and explore a myriad of new styles and innovative products at the continent's largest sporting goods shows.

The National Sporting Goods Association World Sports Expo.

Nicknamed *The Show That Works*, this 5 day event will admit 85,000 attendees who will parade one million square feet of space occupied by 1,700 exhibitors and 4,100 booths. During the course of the three-day program, over a quarter of a million products are exhibited at the Chicago McCormick Place Convention Complex.

The Expo is organized in a way that allows attendees to efficiently discover the products that interest them most. The Show is divided into 17 separate pavilions. Those attending have no difficulty finding new products or suppliers in a particular product segment, from The Activewear Pavilion to the Team Licensed Products Pavilion.

"The General Licensed Products Pavilion and the Team Licensed Products Pavilion is the largest exhibit of licensed products ever in the world," says a public relations manager for NSGA.

To attend, contact:

N.S.G.A.
1699 Wall Street
Mount Prospect, IL 60056

(708) 439-4000

The Super Show

The Super Show is the largest and perceived to be the most valuable sporting goods trade show in the world.

More than 2,000 manufacturers of sports products exhibit their merchandise to buyers from all over the world. Over 85,000 attendees view over 6,000 booths occupying more than 1.6 million square feet of floor space. More than 180 sports celebrities, business seminars, fashion shows and demonstrations are featured. Exhibitors are grouped into 16 complete and distinct shows: The Activewear Show, The Outdoor Sports Show, The Bowling and Billiards Show, The Cycle Show, The Fitness Show, The Footwear Show, The Golf Show, The Imprint and Apparel Show, The

International Show, The Licensed Sports Show, The Marine and Water Sports Show, The New Products Show, The Team Sports Show, The Tennis Show, The Trophies and Awards Show, and The WinterWear Show.

Owned and operated by The Sporting Goods Manufacturers Association (SGMA), it is held each February in Atlanta and produced in cooperation with The National Sporting Goods Association.

This equipment extravaganza generates over $4 million annually which is redistributed to various industry related associations and special interest groups. If you are even remotely related with the sporting goods industry, this is a must attend event.

To learn more about the Super Show, contact:

The Super Show
1450 N.E. 23rd St.
N. Miami, FL 33161

(800) 327-3736

The Quest for Excellence Seminar Series

The most comprehensive continuing education program of the industry. The QFE Seminar Series has an expanded format which will include every element of professional development necessary to enhance industry related skills for the 1990s.

The QFE Seminar Series is on the leading edge of the industry because of its hard-hitting practical approach.

The seminars cover key areas of managing a sporting goods business from financial management to customer retention: effective buying to managing employees; self-improvement to effective sales and marketing techniques, and from managing an individual speciality shop to managing a multi-unit national chain. The diversity of the sessions provide attendees with solid revenue increasing ideas and profit making techniques. The QFE Seminar Series has established a faculty of industry leaders, experts and innovators from across the country.

Forms of Sports Marketing

There are five basic areas of sports market involvement; sponsorship, use of athletes and sports celebrities, advertising, public relations, and sales promotion.

Sponsorship

There are eight basic areas of subgroups for sponsorship: Title sponsorship - where a company attaches its name or the name of a product to the title name of an event or promotion; Co-sponsorship - where two companies share equal billing in the name of an event; Presenting sponsorship - where a company receives less prominent billing than the title sponsor; Team sponsorship ; Vehicle sponsorship - where a company sponsors a vehicle that travels on ground, air or water; Associate or supporting sponsorships - sponsors who pay less for their involvement than title and presenting sponsors; Broadcast sponsorship - which involves a company purchasing commercial air time on a television or radio broadcast of a sports event, and; Official supplier relationships, which involves a company providing its goods or services to a sports event or organization for their use and endorsement.

Use of Athletes and Sports Celebrities

A sports celebrity is any individual who has achieved a level of local or national prominence and exposure who may or may not be athlete, but who is in some way connected to sports. Examples of a sports celebrity include: sports commissioners or presidents, managers and coaches, retired athletes, umpires and officials, TV broadcasters and commentators, team owners, agents and anyone connected to sport who receives any significant media attention.

Advertising

The use of sports in advertising is everywhere. Sports programs are the most watched television shows of any kind in the world. Commercials and print ads use sports as a background theme to send subliminal messages to target audiences who have active lifestyles. Many companies place significant portions of their advertising in television sports programming due to the high concentration of adult male viewers.

Other uses of advertising include printed local team schedules, billboards and signage at sports stadiums, ads in sports event programs and displays at sports events.

Public Relations

Public relations includes handling the publicity needs of sports events and companies involved in sports. Publicity programs utilize sports designed to generate awareness and recognition of a company and its products or services.

Some forms of public relations include the development of sports, achievement awards, sports clinics, corporate entertainment and hospitality using sports related activities and athletes.

Sales Promotion

Trips to the Super Bowl, Olympics, World Series and other sports events of international stature which are commonplace as prizes in contests and sweepstakes. Whether used to influence consumer purchases or to reward employees and dealers, sports holds terrific potential for a company that wishes to increase the response of its sales promotion efforts.

Studies have shown that after money and family, there is no greater motivational factor than sports!

Sports Event Marketing

Companies spent $1.7 billion on domestic sports event sponsorships in 1990. The total spent for sponsorship of all events, including music, festivals and the arts, was $2.5 billion. Thus, sports represented a whopping 67% of all corporate sponsorships (see accompanying charts). That's big business.

With numbers like that being thrown around, it takes a large and diversified agency in the middle of the mix to keep the corporations, events executives, other sponsors and the athletes content and to make it profitable for all of the above.

Why are corporations so willing to part with substantial dollar amounts to have their name associated with a sporting event? Studies show that corporations get more than a decent return on their investment, which makes the event profitable for all participating entities. Michael Trager, Chairman and founder of Sports Marketing and Television International, Inc. (SMTI), a Greenwich, Connecticut consulting firm, says it's a judgment call for corporations on which types of sports events they wish to have their name identified with.

Trager, says corporations have to go outside their organization for marketing help for their sponsorship to be most effective, and not to advertising agencies. "Some of the worst decisions are made in corporations that think they know what's going on (in the sports event field)," comments Trager. "They (corporations) rarely have that expertise in-house. Many of them have the tendency to turn to advertising agencies. "It is a very difficult market in which to compete, and ad agencies just don't have the necessary focus to make the event as financial lucrative. They are almost solely concerned with the media."

Even though many individuals begin their own sports event and sponsorship agencies, the three major companies which dominate the industry are International Management Group (IMG), Proserve, Inc., and Advantage International. To illustrate the 'bigness' of IMG's impact in the industry, its 1990 revenues exceeded $700 million from its 43 offices in 20 countries! Events, management and sponsorship solicitation is a more lucrative and less risky field than individual client representation. Look at it this way. Ivan Lendel can break a leg; the U.S. open cannot.

However, if you are aspiring to make an impact in the industry, you must first establish yourself with either a branch of the "big 3" or by learning the business with a firm in the marketplace that serves clients in high media demographics. The only tried-and-proved training will occur in the field itself as no formal training curriculum could ever substitute for practical experience. Most successful event management executives will earn salaries in the six figures, but keep in mind the attrition rate of those who pursue any sports related field in the marketplace.

Economic, political and societal concerns also play a role in corporate sponsorship of athletic events. When economic conditions are unfavorable, sports event sponsorships can be one of the first things to be trimmed from a company's budget.

For example, the PGA Tour will reportedly lose several corporate sponsors within the next two years. A recent trend also has corporations turning to other modes of sponsorship representation, most notably music. According to a survey by *Special Events Report of Chicago* corporate sponsorship of music, concerts and tours has grown to 16% of total sponsorship dollars in 1990 from 5% in 1986. Sports sponsorship has fallen from 88% of the total in 1986 to 67% today.

Sports Entrepreneurship: Franchising

Franchising is the single most successful marketing concept ever

- John Naisbitt, *Megatrends* author

Over 525,000 franchise businesses generate more than $716 billion in sales. With a new franchise opening somewhere in the U.S. every 17 minutes, it is indeed the success story of the 1980s and 1990s. If you want to own your own business and be your own boss, there's a place in franchising for you. Investors at all levels are finding that few financial investments can compete with the potential of a sports related franchise.

Franchising it especially attractive because it offers an opportunity for people with various levels of capital and experience. Small business people are attracted, not only for the chance to be on their own, but also for the chance to do so within an established system.

Franchise owners like franchising because they can be in business for themselves but they're never left by themselves. Franchisors like franchising because it is the best growth system ever devised. The public likes franchising because franchised stores offer known names and dependable standards of quality. And that's the real reason for franchising success - the customers give it their wholehearted support at the cash register.

What is Franchising

When you hear the word *franchise* you probably think of fast food restaurants like McDonald's, Burger King and Wendy's. But there are many more types of franchise businesses. One out of every three dollars spent by Americans for goods and services is spent in a franchised business. Franchising is a method of doing business. It is a method of marketing a product and/or service which has been adopted and used in a wide variety of industries and businesses. The word *franchise* literally means to be free. There are two different types of franchise arrangements; product distribution arrangements, in which the dealer is identified with the manufacturer/supplier, and; business format franchises in which there is complete identification of the dealer with the buyer. Franchises offer the owner (franchisee) not only a trademark and logo but a complete system of doing business. A franchise receives assistance with site selection, personnel training, business setup, advertising, and product supply. For these services, the franchise pays an up front fee and an ongoing royalty which enables the franchisor to provide training, research and development, and support for the entire business. In a nutshell, the franchisee purchases someone else's expertise, experience and method of doing business.

Is Franchising For You?

Before buying a franchise, the carefully consider the following self-assessment questions:

- Are you willing and able to take on the responsibilities of managing your own business?
- Will you enjoy the franchise?
- Are you willing to completely follow the franchise system?
- Do you have a history of success in dealing with people?
- Can you afford the franchise?
- Have you carefully studied the legal documents?
- Does the franchise you are considering have a track record of success?
- Are the franchisees generally happy and successful?
- Do you like the franchisor's staff?
- Do you have the family support?

Key Issues to Clear up:

- Personal liability and obligations of franchisee and family members.
- Location and marketing area.
- Trademark issues.
- Omissions from the franchise agreement.
- Renewal rights.
- Termination and its consequences.
- Sources of essential products.
- Transfer restrictions of the franchise or ownership interests.
Advantages and Disadvantages:

The Advantages

The Experience of the Franchisor

A proven franchise may eliminate many start-up problems. This permits one to open a franchise business with little or no previous experience in the sports industry.

Training
This is usually done at the home office and at the franchisee's place or business, and should prepare the new owner in all facets of the business.

Buying and Advertising
Most small business people cannot afford to inventory products in bulk or do extensive advertising.

Ongoing Advice, Research and Development
Franchisees need assistance throughout their business endeavors. The franchisor's staff of experts is available to give help in all aspects of the business and the franchisor is also in a position to provide ongoing research and development.

Business Synergy
Often, some of the most effective ideas come from franchisees who in turn share their ideas with the corporate office and with other franchisees.

The Challenge: Working within the System
Conformity to the franchisor's system is critical if consistency among franchises is to be maintained.

The Risk
The franchisor may have a great program and a respected name, but in the final analysis much of the risk in your hands.

Working With the Franchisor
Your relationship with the franchisor/staff is extremely important. Get to know the franchisor through the following methods:
- Visit the corporate headquarters to get a feel for the staff.
- Talk to other franchisees.
- Read as much about the franchise as possible.

False Expectations
Some people expect instant success. Obtain from the franchisor a realistic

picture as to what is required in operating the franchise.

Managing the Business

Honestly assess your preparation to run a business. If you find that you have little or no experience, you may want to seek special assistance from the franchisor in business management.

Entrepreneurship

Where is sports heading in the 90s? Many writers are picturing average athletes with $5 million salaries and Joe Fan as having four season tickets to different sports teams across the country, courtesy of pay-per-view TV Will our signage become saturated by corporate logos to the point of overload? College athletics have jumped into the marketing mania big time, with Georgia Tech selling each of its seven football home games this season to sponsors for $75,000 to $175,000 each. With competition becoming fierce at every level of the sports game board, one skill necessary to survive is becoming very high in demand - entrepreneurship. With the advent of formal university sports management programs at over 100 colleges, a high degree of sophistication is brought to entry level positions. The next level of specialized college education is growing rapidly with entrepreneurial instruction.

More than 250 colleges and universities across the United States have initiated entrepreneurial courses, at both graduate and undergraduate levels. Sports is among the many industries that are causing the institutions of higher learning to take notice of America's burgeoning small business climate. No where is it more apparent as thousands of niche markets are becoming available with the addition of a professional sports franchise or all-purpose athletic facility.

"No matter what industry, if America is to continue as a world leader, we have to become more entrepreneurial," says Fran Jabara, director of Wichita State's program, a noted leader. "The future of our country is in the hands of our youth. We provide a learning atmosphere for the students and improve their probability of success in new ventures," he adds. Classes explore every avenue of starting a business from scratch, buying existing businesses as well as how to develop and manage a growing enterprise. All programs are designed to be interchangeable, with the ability to apply certain principles taught to particular industries.

That's where sports can be fed into the entrepreneurial computer and *success* is printed out. One basic formula in all entrepreneurial courses is the exposure to business leaders who have made their mark in the industry. Wouldn't you like to go one-on-one with Ted Turner or Donald Trump? "These sessions provide invaluable information and insight to students, and show them that prosperity isn't out of their reach," adds a noted professor. The advent of these classes and special programs has created a nonprofit organization designed to aid in the development of young entrepreneurs by serving as a support and networking resource the Association of Collegiate Entrepreneurs (ACE). More than 300 universities from 35 countries throughout the world boast active chapters of ACE, comprised of students, faculty, and recently graduated young entrepreneurs.

The Top Ten Entrepreneurial Schools

Harvard University
Soldier's Field Rd.
Morgan Hall
Boston, MA 02163

(617) 495-6000

University of Illinois
P.O. Box 802451
Chicago, IL 60680

(312) 220-2670

University of Calgary
123 Scurfield Hall
2500 University Dr. N.W.
Calgary, Alberta,
CANADA T2N 1N4

(403) 220-6117

University of Arizona
Karl Eller Center
Tucson, AZ 85721

(602) 621-2576

University of Southern California
University Park
Los Angeles, CA

(213) 743-2098

Ball State Small Business Management University Program
Muncie, IN 47306

(317) 285-5300

Wichita State Center for Entrepreneurship
008 Clinton Hall
Wichita, KS 67208

(316) 689-3000

Babson College
The Center for Entrepreneurship
Wellesley, MA 02157

(617) 239-4420

York University
4700 Keele Street
Toronto, Ontario
Canada M3J 1P3

(416) 786-5060

Wharton Snider
Vance Hall, 4th Floor
Philadelphia, PA 19104-6374

(215) 898-4856

Marketing Consultants

If the age of an industry can be discerned by the amount that has been written about it, then the event marketing industry is in the throes of adolescence. Few books are available on the how and why of the subject, which some observers are already calling the fourth marketing medium, behind television, radio and print. As a result, many of those responsible for marketing events don't know much about the industry outside of their own events, even though it reached the $1.8 billion mark by 1988 and $2.1 billion in 1989.

"In its $2.1 billion adolescence, the special events industry is still often unsteady on its feet and some strengthening is needed," according to Robert Jackson and Steven Wood Schmader, authors of a totally practical how-to approach on event marketing called *Special Events: Inside and Out*. Overall, over 3500 firms participate in one form or another of sports marketing. As this area continues to gain popularity, it becomes harder and more expensive to gain recognition through sponsorships. With increasing costs and rising salaries causing fewer sports organizations to show a profit, many administrators are now contracting specialists in advertising, promotions, and fund raising to assist them in generating additional sources of revenue. Universities and professional franchises are finding this approach of rendering the services of a consultant more cost effective than employing additional staff members since specialists can spend more time and perform a more thorough evaluation for a particular need. Marketing specialists have been especially effective in the acquisition of television and radio sponsors, ticket sales, and promotion events to targeted groups.

Before franchises can be awarded or stadiums erected, marketing and feasibility studies must be completed. Marketing studies are utilized to measure a designated market for interest, potential growth, such as a television market, and income diversity. A feasibility study will ensure predictions of meeting environmental standards, stadium accessibility for crowd control, and the demographics of a particular populated area. This type of sports involvement has been attractive to the non-athletic individual who can serve as a corporate executive and still be a part of the sports world. Degrees in business administration with graduate studies in finance, advertising, and marketing are necessary components for developing a sound background. Most professional consultants have as many as 20-30 years of practical experience before they enter private practice, but once an associate has created an established reputation, fees for consulting services can range as high as $5,000 per day.

Advertising Agents

Sports has become a dominant theme in advertising with some of the most popular television ads dealing with past and present sports figures. Unfortunately very few agencies concentrate exclusively on sports marketing concepts as sports advertising is not all-consuming to the buying public as a whole.

For those entering this highly competitive field, a thorough understanding in marketing, sales, and advertising, along with creative instincts and a knowledge of sports and athletics will provide the perfect blend of working attributes. The key to success in this business is being able to tie in the athlete or sports related message with a client's product and attract attention to it. This can only be accomplished if the agency understands the sports market and knows the strengths and weaknesses of the sports figures in relation to the product.

Tenacity, perseverance, and imagination are essentials to entering the world of advertising. It will take several years to become established within a firm, but for those who can weather the dues paying process, a handsome compensation structure will begin in the $30,000s. Becoming a junior partner or assisting in volunteer campaigns are the only proving grounds for an advertising hopeful who possesses little experience. To learn more about sports marketing networking opportunities, contact: National Association of Collegiate Marketing Administrators (NACMA). NACMA is a nonprofit organization targeted at those working in collegiate marketing, promotions and related fields at NCAA member institutions, as well as administrators at members of the National Association of Intercollegiate Athletics (NAIA) and the National Junior College Athletic Association (NJCAA). The proliferation, thrust and impact of marketing and promotional effects and programs on the collegiate level in recent years have served to accelerate interest in an organization where practitioners can exchange ideas, formulate concepts and practices, and establish operating and ethical standards.

For information on NACMA , call

(219) 239-7516 or (205) 284-2400

Sports Marketing Agencies vs. Sports Marketing Firms

Until recently, the term *sports marketing agency* didn't exist. The term was recently developed by the American Sports Marketing Association to distinguish competent and independent sports marketing consultants from their counterparts at sports marketing firms. The reason for this new distinction was the fact that many corporate managers became disgruntled with the proliferation of sports marketing firms. Today, over 2000 companies in the United States alone classify themselves as sports marketing firms. In reality, these firms do not provide marketing advice and counseling. Instead, they own or represent various sports events, athletes, television programming or sports that they are charged with selling for corporate sponsorship.

The new sports marketing firms founds an incredible amount of opportunity and wealth in representing corporations. They now could obtain larger sponsorship dollars for their events and athletes and then charge the companies it sold its product for showing them how to use the product. Sports marketing firms have grown at a record pace. The sports marketing firms now own and sell sports event sponsorships. They represent athletes and sell them to corporations. They also represent entire sports through their governing bodies, while at the same time selling sports they represent to the networks and advertisers.

This trend has continued until recently, when spiraling costs and increased competition made corporate managers realize that it was necessary for them to justify their decisions and budgets. As more and more money was shifted from traditional mass media budgets to various areas of promotion, including sports marketing, corporate managers were faced with the challenge of measuring the return on their sports marketing investment.

Distinctions
- Agencies solely represent corporations and their wholly-owned properties, products and/or events.
- Agencies charge only for time and expense in the same manner of a public relations firm or professionals (accountants, attorneys, etc.)
- Firms charge whatever the market will bear.

- Agencies use integrated marketing plans that utilize sophisticated elements of public relations, sales promotion and advertising support, as well as corporate sponsorship.
- Agencies sell the corporate client and its products via sports.
- Firms sell sports marketing events, promotions and activities.
- Agencies fit into a sports marketing special interest group using classical corporate marketing techniques.
- Firms fit into the sports entrepreneurship special interest group under the areas of sports promoters. They certainly utilize many key elements of the marketing mix while growing their business ventures.

Functions Performed by Agencies

- Analyze a corporate client's past, current and prospective sports marketing endeavors.
- Conduct audits of client's sports marketing program and activities.
- Conduct evaluations and feasibility studies.
- Make specific recommendations on the selection of opportunities which meet specific client marketing needs and objectives.
- Develop sports marketing plans where recommended programs, opportunities, budgets and schedules are outlined.
- Negotiate and contract for client purchasers of sports sponsorships and opportunities.
- Evaluate and measure the return on client's sports marketing investment.
- Conduct both primary and secondary sports marketing research.
- Coordinate, supervise or implement the execution of client's activities.
- Establish corporate policies, objectives and strategies for client's use of sports marketing.

Functions Performed by Firms

- Management and representation of professional athletes.
- Financial planning for athletes and corporate executives.
- Development and promotion of sports events for sale to corporations.
- Development, production and sale of sports television programming.
- Representation of sports federations and sporting events for the sale of sponsorship to corporations.

- Sports marketing counseling of corporations.
- Licensing and merchandising of specific sports properties.
- Contract negotiations and procurement of corporate endorsements for athletes and other sports celebrities.

Benefits Provided by Agencies
- Assistance in making successful sports marketing decisions.
- Strategic placement of the sports marketing budget.
- Sports marketing campaigns which complement existing marketing plans geared toward realizing sales and marketing goals.
- Classical integrated marketing plans which take into account overall corporate business strategy and philosophy.

Benefits Provided by Firms
- Convenience and one-stop shopping for the client's sports marketing opportunities.
- Experience in promoting and organizing sports events.
- Broad based knowledge and background in several different elements of corporate packaging with the savvy to execute the program.

Corporate Client Needs
Knowing exactly what the client needs and how to execute will spell the difference between any successful sports marketing agency or firm.

Client Questions:
- What does the client want sports marketing to do for the company?
- What specific marketing, communications and business needs does the client want sports marketing to address?
- How large a budget will the client apply toward sports marketing?
- What type of sports marketing services will the client require?
- Does the firm or agency have the resources and capability to handle all services required by the client?
- Which tasks can be handled by the client internally?

New York University Summer Institute in Sports and Special Event Marketing

The NYU Summer Institute is an intensive, two week program whereby students will learn how the sports business is structured as well as master many of the key skills used in sports marketing and communications. Participants will hear presentations from leading sports practitioners in and use the city of New York as a lab for the study of reporting events from a marketing point of view.

The full program is built on the following assumptions:

- Marketing orientation: the program teaches how to focus as a business person on practical marketing techniques that help build multiple revenue sources for sport and cultural entities.

- Sports as a model: students learn how sports marketing is effectively accomplished by major teams and leagues as a model of what can be done not only in other athletic environments, but in other areas of event marketing altogether (i.e., cultural and community events).

- Local to international scale: cases and examples are used that help students develop an understanding of sports marketing at all levels. Included will be NCAA athletics, minor and major leagues, non-team sports, and global events such as the Olympics and the World Cup.

- The role of the media: students will learn how broadcast and print media are essential partners in every aspect of the sports marketing process and how to work effectively with them.

- Career applications: students will learn the many different environments where upon sports marketing expertise is in demand and just how to approach prospective employers. The goal of NYU is to assist students make the transition from the perspective of fan to that of marketer by providing experiences and tools which are necessary to effectively function in the field.

For more information contact:

Jonathan Pollack, Director Sports Sciences
New York University
48 Cooper Square
New York, NY 10003

(212) 998-7217

Specialized Training Programs

Sports Marketing Institute
This annual spring conference is held in Orlando, Florida for the purpose of educating and creating awareness to the latest techniques and issues in the sports marketing field. In addition to the conference, the institute offers sports marketing enhancement tools which include videos, directories of who's who in sports marketing, and a monthly newsletter. For more information, contact:

Sports Marketing Institute
109 58th Avenue
St. Petersburg Beach, FL 33706

(813) 367-6545

Sport Summit
For the past 15 years, the Sport Summit provides the most established executive platform on the business of sport events and sport facilities. This international trade show and conference is a high profile event designed to meet the needs of corporate executives in the media, player management and sports marketing.

To receive additional information, contact:

Monica de Hellerman
International Sport Summit Headquarters
372 5th Avenue
New York, NY 10018

(212) 239-1061

Career and Job Placement Services

Sport It
Sport It's mission is simple, "to provide entrepreneur types with the opportunity of fulfilling the dream of owning a sporting goods business. Sport It employs a team approach in securing dealers and franchises as well as supplying in-depth strategies and techniques in making sporting goods a successful career endeavor.

For more information, contact:

Sport It
429 Production Blvd.
Naples, FL 33942-4724

(800) 328-3820

Sherco
Dan Sheridan, is a recognized leader in sports sales training who recruits quality sales agents for national manufacturers seeking quality distribution. A unique feature of Sherco's services is that Dan Sheridan travels extensively across the United States seeking viable candidates as well as staying abreast with the industry's happenings.
For more details call (919) 722-9183.

Teamwork Consulting, Inc.
Teamwork has established the reputation as the leading executive search firm to the sports and event management industry. Led by its president, Buffy A. Filippell, Teamwork retains clients from major league professional team owners to small business owners and from sport trade associations to professional player associations. Due to the high profile clientele that Teamwork services, it recruits middle management and executive types only. Therefore, entry level applicants should seek an agency that recruits with broad base sports industries.
To learn more about Teamwork's services, contact:

Buffy G. Filippell, President
Teamwork Consulting, Inc.
Shaker Heights, OH 44122

(216) 751-3306

Insurance Reps

The insurance policy designated for athletes is appropriately termed special risk. So risky is this field that very few independent agencies in the country even attempt to write such policies. There is one distinct advantage that comes along with writing these extremely high premiums - high income. Only sound insurance entrepreneurs with a background in the risk areas will be able to develop policies for athletes and teams or for advertisers that use athletes for endorsements. Knowledge of sports or athletics is not essential, but a sound knowledge of sports law will be invaluable.

The type of insurance policy to be dealt with is not unlike those written on the late Jimmy Durante's famous nose or Betty Grable's legs. These physical features were essential to these individuals' popularity and the revenue that they brought to themselves, their studios, and the many who promoted their careers.

Before writing such a policy, a special risk insurer must develop a special sense for determining an athlete's market value by projecting proposed salaries and establishing the true existing physical condition of his/her athlete. The insurer should also have a feel for the nature of the sport and the risks involved that might bring a rise for such a claim. Since the insurance industry has its own method of certifying agents, it is better to contact the industry directly to acquire proper procedures and information.

Due to the enormous number of athletic contests played on any given day, the role of the athletic trainer becomes crucial.
Photo: courtesy of **Colpin Physical Therapy.**

14

Sports Medicine

The typical sports enthusiast's involvement, once relegated to that of a passive spectator, has now transcended to the role of an active participant. Today's get involved attitude is clearly evident upon examination of a recent study which indicates that 44% of the American population is participating in some form of athletic activity or fitness program. There is, however, one overriding side effect that has transpired through this fitness boom - an outgrowth of activity related injuries. The drastic rise in the numerous physical disablements can usually be attributed to one of the following conditions; improper training techniques, poor levels of physical conditioning, ignorance about the physical complexities of the activity. Beginning fitness and recreational buffs are not the only ones experiencing an increase in injuries. The number of non-traditional sports is cropping up daily. Along with the increase in athletes starting to compete in the more established activities, the figure for individuals seeking sports medicine assistance is growing exponentially.

Sports Injuries

The table below shows estimates of injuries, deaths and participants associated with various sports as reported by the National Safety Council during a 12 month period of time in 1990. This list is not complete, as the number of participants varies greatly. Therefore, no inference should be made concerning the relative hazard of these sports or rank with respect to risk of injury.

Sport	Participants	Injuries	Fatalities
Archery	5,100,000	3,366	—
Baseball	13,900,000	348,539	0
Basketball	21,200,000	467,160	4
Bicycle Riding	49,700,000	561,764	—
Boating	38,200,000	3,501	—
Bowling	34,200,000	17,152	—
Boxing	500,000	5,671	—
Fishing	47,500,000	65,021	—
Football	12,000,000	329,987	4
Golf	20,000,000	22,648	—
Gymnastics	1,800,000	34,217	—
Handball	1,700,000	4,113	—
Hang gliding	7,000	—	8
Hockey	1,900,000	23,679	0
Ice Skating	4,400,000	12,270	—
Lacrosse	400,000	—	0
Parachuting	115,000	—	28
Racquetball	7,800,000	19,761	0
Rugby	300,000	6,943	—
Scuba Diving	2,600,000	—	76
Soccer	8,000,000	86,409	3
Softball	20,900,000	—	0
Snow skiing	14,400,000	49,483	1
Snowmobiling	3,600,000	10,289	—
Swimming	72,600,000	94,053	2,000
Tennis	18,000,000	19,627	0
Volleyball	20,700,000	91,639	—
Water skiing	11,900,000	22,583	36
Wrestling	1,300,000	35,585	1

The onset of uncommon injuries is often out of the ordinary everyday practices for most family physicians. The emergence of athletic injuries has thus opened the door and created an imminent need for specially trained physicians and therapists.

The impact sports medicine research has provided in the rehabilitative is apparent. However, of equal importance and not yet receiving much attention, is the field's contributions to the prevention and diagnosing of potential injuries before they occur. Yet still another positive breakthrough that has evolved from sports medicine's advanced technology is in its physiological testing of new approaches to training techniques, which can assist athletes in optimizing their levels of performance.

It should be noted that sports medicine's rehabilitative process does not include medical personnel alone. It also utilizes the expertise in a host of other interrelated specialities such as nutrition, kinesiology, exercise physiology, psychology, physical therapy and podiatry. In the next decade, no other sports associated field will offer a wider range of opportunities, advancement, job security or compensation positions in the sports medicine field.

The training involved in these highly specialized disciplines is both rigorous and very competitive. However, due to a shortage of qualified practitioners in several areas, there should be an abundance of possible options for the patient and dedicated person. With an evoking interest in sports and a fitness conscious society, the need for sports medicine related services will continue to grow. The field will employ and attract all types of individuals, from the research minded to the application oriented.

Sports Physicians

Before the term sports medicine really had any legitimate meaning, a team doctor treated everything from broken bones to head colds. Sports specialization has now become a need in the ranks of medical doctors as well. The three distinct groups that comprise the physician specialist are as follows: Doctors of Medicine, MD; Doctors of Osteopathy DO, and Doctors of Chiropractic, DC.

Several MDs offering services in sports medicine will be general practitioners, GPs, serving as team physicians. The majority of sports physicians involved in clinics and rehab centers will ultimately have their training as orthopedists. The orthopedist will be the primary caretaker of injured individuals authorized to make delicate decisions and, when necessary, supervise the follow-up treatment administered by other support personnel. Osteopaths and chiropractors on the other hand have only begun to gain respect within the medical community and general public. Their roles as consultants to schools, teams, and health centers has now diversified into private practices. One key reason is the acceptability of health insurance coverage for their services.

To be proficient and credible as a sports physician, doctors must be trained in all procedures for the prevention, recognition and treatment of soft tissue and skeletal injuries. Physicians should have a clear understanding of the sport in which they are involved. This includes the mechanism of the injuries occurring, the protective gear and equipment utilized and the emotional well-being of its performers.

The physician who undertakes the responsibility of being a team doctor must remain objective and firm with coaches and parents. The ethical considerations in these situations represent the one aspect that so many sports medicine doctors find most difficult to handle. There are many instances in which a physician will be forced to take action contrary to both the coach's or injured athlete's beliefs.

Orthopedists

As has already been indicated, a greater percentage of all sports physicians will have an orthopedic background. Orthopedists, who are also surgeons, will treat injuries and abnormalities of the skeletal system and musculature by implementing a wide range of techniques to restore the athlete to his/her playing capacities.

Few orthopedists will restrict their practice to sports injuries alone and therefore will usually be a staff member at a hospital or a rehabilitative clinic. Long work days are the norm, but these specialists enjoy fine working conditions and a position of prestige in the medical community. Orthopedists earn excellent salaries with starting yearly incomes in the area of $100,000. The outlook for these physicians is excellent for both men and women, but the competition for entrance into medical school will always remain fierce.

Education

Despite a growing interest in careers within the sports medicine field, there are no formal sports educational program that results in a recognized AMA degree. The only route at this time is to attend one of the 126 accredited medical schools in the United States. Upon completion of a 4-year undergraduate degree and acceptance into a medical school, those interested in sports medicine will most likely pursue an orthopedic residency lasting from 2 - 5 years.

However, numerous institutions that offer speciality course offerings in selected areas of sport medicine. Also, a group of physicians have now organized the Sports Medicine Curriculum Study Group in order to identify which subjects need to be taught to cultivate competencies in this area.

Resources

Medicine & Science in Sports & Exercise
Box 1446
Indianapolis, IN 46206

(317) 637-9200

The Physician in Sports Medicine
McGraw Hill Book Company
4530 West 77th Street
Minneapolis, MN 55435

(612) 835-3222

American Health: Fitness of Body and Mind
American Health Partners
80 Fifth Avenue, Suite 302
New York, NY 10011

The National Strength and Conditioning Association Journal
P.O. Box 81410
Lincoln, NE 68501

American Medical Association
535 N. Dearborn Street
Chicago, IL 60610

(312) 645-5000

Journal of Physical Education and Recreation
American Alliance for Health, Physical Education, Recreation & Dance
1900 Association Dr.
Reston, VA 22091

Association of American Medical Colleges
The DuPont Circle N.S., Suite 200
Washington, D.C. 20036

(202) 828-0400

American Orthopedic Society for Sports Medicine
70 West Hubbard Street, Suite 202
Chicago, IL 60610

(312) 644-2623

American College Health Association
15879 Crabbs Branch Way
Rockville, MD 20855

(301) 963-1100

Certification in the American College of Sports Medicine

Sports medicine, a rapidly growing sub-specialty in the field of medicine, has evolved from the special needs of persons engaged in sports, exercise and fitness activities. The American College of Sports Medicine, headquartered in Indianapolis, Indiana, is the largest sports medicine organization in the world with nearly 12,000 members involved in science, medicine, education and sports. Its primary mission is to generate and disseminate research and information on the benefits and effects of exercise, as well as the treatment and prevention of injuries incurred in sports, exercise and fitness activities. The ACSM professional certification program, established in 1975, emerged in response to the need for establishing competency standards for exercise personnel. The Preventive and Rehabilitative Exercise Programs Committee of the ACSM is charged with the responsibility for the development of competency standards, examination design and supervision of the certification program. The committee has grown from a handful of leading professionals in the field to a standing committee of over 50 ACSM experts in science, medicine, education and professional practice.

The ACSM now provides two tracts for certification - preventive and rehabilitative. Each tract has three levels of certification representing progressive levels of knowledge, skills and competencies. Preventive

The preventive tract is designed primarily for personnel who function in programs serving adult clients who do not require significant medical oversight during their exercise. Health clubs, corporate fitness programs and wellness programs are the example settings.

Preventive Certifications

Exercise Leader

Individuals certified at this level are considered to have demonstrated competence for entry level service and would normally be expected to serve under the supervision of a health/fitness instructor and/or a health/fitness director. They serve as the exercise floor leaders either for group sessions or individual exercise participants. The exercise leader (EL) is required to document 250 hours of experience and/or training as a prerequisite.

Health/Fitness Instructor

Certification at the level of Health/Fitness Instructor (H/FI) requires a greater depth and breadth of knowledge from the EL in each of the areas encompassed by a multi-disciplinary approach to prevention. The Health/Fitness Instructor has the responsibility of training and/or supervising Exercise Leaders during an exercise program but may also serve as an exercise leader. In addition, the Health/Fitness Instructor has demonstrated a knowledge base which enables him/her to serve very basic health counseling functions encountered in the exercise program setting (e.g., diet, smoking cessation, coping strategies for stress). The minimum educational prerequisite is a baccalaureate degree in an allied health field or the equivalent.

Health/Fitness Director

The individual certified at this highest preventive level is required to have a command of the behavioral objectives for the EL and H/FI levels and, additionally, incorporates the administrative knowledge and skills as the director of a preventive program. The Health/Fitness (H/FD) has background and experience with the administrative aspects of preventive programs and also has leadership qualities which ensure competence in the training and supervision of personnel. The minimum educational prerequisite is a postgraduate degree in an allied health field or the equivalent. In addition, in order to qualify as a Health/Fitness Director, an internship or period of practical experience in program administration of at least one (1) year is required. Rehabilitative

The rehabilitative tract is designed for professionals who are primarily responsible for working with diseased individuals enrolled in medical treatment programs of which exercise is a part. Example settings are medical clinics, cardiovascular and pulmonary rehabilitative programs. Rehabilitative certifications are offered for exercise test technologists, exercise specialists and program directors.

Rehabilitative Certifications

Exercise Test Technologist

The primary responsibility of the exercise test technologist (ETT) is to administer exercise tests safely in order to obtain reliable and valid data on functional abilities and limitations. Significant knowledge and skill in administering graded exercise tests and the essentials of stress electrocardiography are required. While there are no explicit field experiences or educational prerequisites for the exercise test technologist, study in the fields of the biological sciences, physical education and health related professions are examples of appropriate foundations.

Exercise Specialist

The unique competence of the exercise specialist (ES) is the ability to supervise and/or lead exercise programs for persons with medical limitations, as well as healthy asymptomatic populations (competencies of the H/FI). The exercise specialist, in conjunction with the program director and the attending physician, is able to:

- Design an exercise prescription based on the results of an exercise test.
- Evaluate participants' responses to exercise and conditioning.
- Assist in the education of patients.
- Interact and communicate effectively with the referring physician, program director, and other related professionals.

The exercise specialist demonstrates the competence required of the exercise test technologist and health/fitness instructor. The minimum educational prerequisite is a postgraduate degree in an allied field or the equivalent. In addition, in order to qualify as an exercise specialist, an internship or period of practical experience in a cardiac rehabilitation program of at least four months/600 hours is required.

Program Director

In addition to the knowledge and competence of all other certification levels, the program director is capable of organizing and administering all types of programs in any situation. The program director must possess the ability to plan and initiate new programs, as well as to reorganize and upgrade existing ones. Prerequisite include studies for an advanced degree in fields such as exercise physiology, physiology, medicine, or physical education. The minimum educational prerequisite is a postgraduate degree in an allied health field or the equivalent. In addition, in order to qualify as a program director, an internship or period of practical experience in a cardiac rehabilitation program of at least one year is required.

Exam and ACSM Information

ACSM membership is not mandatory to either attend the workshops or take a certification exam. However, the test fees are $50.00 less if you are a member. The exams have a written and practical portion. Written exam fees are between $125-$150. The health/fitness, exercise program and exercise specialist exams carry an extra fee for the practicum of between $100-$200. The written exam takes about three hours and the practical exam from half to a whole day. For additional career information contact: Paula Elliott, Public Information Assistant for ACSM.

To obtain a 1992 calendar of workshops and certification dates and locations, contact :

>American College of Sports Medicine
>Certification department
>P.O. Box 1440
>Indianapolis, IN 46206-1440
>
>(317) 637-9200.

Doctor of Osteopathy

Like the orthopedists, DOs concern themselves with the musculo-skeletal systems: bones, muscles, ligaments and nerves. Osteopaths also offer an additional health care service: manipulation. The use manipulative therapy is the basic treatment of osteopathy. Osteopathy places its emphasis on treating the whole person. Those specializing in osteopathy take into consideration the total health of a person when treating an injury.

Osteopaths, like chiropractors, have fought a long battle to gain the respect of the medical profession. The average salary is typically lower than an MD, approximately $75,000-$95,000 annually.

Their educational training is similar to that of a medical doctor with the addition of osteopathic manipulation. Osteopaths must also undertake residencies upon graduation, which will eventually lead to licensing necessary to practice.

Resources

American Association of
Osteopath Medicine
4720 Montgomery Lane
Washington, D.C. 20014

American Osteopathic Association
212 East Ohio Street
Chicago, IL 60611

(312) 280-5800

Doctor of Chiropractic

Chiropractic doctors implement manipulation as their primary treatment. It is their belief that a person's health is directly related to the nervous system. It is theorized that any interference with the nervous system will impair the body's normal functions, which will in return lower resistance to disease. Therefore, DCs will take the emphasis of their treatment with the spinal column to restore proper functioning.

Chiropractors do not believe in prescription drugs or surgery. To supplement manipulation techniques, they utilize water, acupuncture, massage, ultrasound and various temperature controlled therapy modalities. Special diets, nutritional supplements and exercise are commonly prescribed during rehabilitation by DCs.

The cold war that once existed between the American Medical Association and chiropractic medicine has dramatically rescinded in recent years. In fact, both disciplines have learned to understand the importance of each practice, to the point where each will refer patients to their counterparts, if it is in the best interest of the injured athlete.

With the recent approval of chiropractic services as a part of health insurance coverage, the popularity of chiropractic continues to grow and receive acceptance. Holistic medicine's emphasis on prevention represents the philosophical trend in the health care of the future.

Education

Though few people realize it, the educational training of chiropractors is as intense as that of physicians. Upon completion of their educational requirements and clinical experience, DCs must pass the licensing requirements in the state in which they wish to practice. For those wishing to perform as a sports medicine practitioner, there is a certification program which requires additional coursework and the completion of an application examination.

As the field has developed, so have earnings. Chiropractors currently average from $45,000 to $85,000 annually in an established clinic. One of the most well known institutions for formalized chiropractic training is the Northwestern College of Chiropractic Medicine located in Minneapolis, Minnesota. A unique feature of the school is its sport medicine certification curriculum.

Resources

Dr. Donald M. Cassata
Northwestern College of
Chiropractic
2501 West 84th Street
Bloomington, MN 55431

(612) 888-4777

Council on Chiropractic
Education
3209 Ingersoll Avenue
Des Moines, IA 50312

(515) 255-2184

International Chiropractors
Association
1901 L Street
M.S. Suite 800
Washington, D.C. 20036

Council on Sports Injuries
American Chiropractic
Association
220 Uroom Avenue
Spring Lake, NJ 07762

(201) 449-8530

Physical Therapy

Physical therapists are involved with patients who have become disabled from an accident, a birth defect, an illness or possibly an injury during sports participation. A good share of a sports therapist's time will be spent with athletes referred by a physician following surgery or recovery from a disabling sports injury. At this point, the main function of a physical therapist is to administer therapy in order to restore function, relieve pain, prevent re-injury and return the athlete to action as soon as possible. Rehabilitation treatments include exercise for increasing strength, endurance and range of motion, application of temperature controlled modalities, ultrasound, acupuncture to relieve pain and massage techniques.

In addition to healing skills, physical therapists need to have good interpersonal communication abilities. Besides working closely with patients, these professionals are required to communicate effectively with all types of health care personnel, from radiologists to orthopedists. Most sports physical therapists become certified as athletic trainers. They must first meet the requirements for certification and be recommended by an acting team physician or a NATA certified trainer.

In looking at experience factors, the sports therapist should be concerned with the training and care of injured athletes, the alteration of protective padding, nutrition and body maintenance skills, the development of conditioning programs, the administering of pre-season screening examinations and the selection and fitting of equipment. The outlook for physical therapists is excellent considering there are far more job opportunities than applicants. Sports medicine, though, is only one of the many segments in which PTs perform. The highest percentage of therapists will be employed by hospitals, clinics and research centers. The current shortage of rehabilitation specialists allow for a continued increase in salary scale, which is in the range of $15,000 to $40,000 annually.

Education

There are more than 90 colleges and universities in the United States which offer accredited undergraduate programs in the general field of physical therapy. However, the American Physical Therapy Association has mandated that each certified member must have a master's in physical therapy. One of the more prominent sports medicine programs is offered at Ball State University in Muncie, Indiana. The focus of Ball State's curriculum is on turning out well-rounded practitioners who are able to step into any sports medicine environment.

Resources

American Physical Therapy Association
1111 N. Fairfax Street
Alexandria, VA 22314

(703) 684-2782

Promotes the professional practice, research, and education of its Established physical therapists.

Services: Career Kit (available free of charge), which includes employment facts and information, publications list, educational requirements and career opportunities available.

Athletic Trainers

Athletic trainers represent the core of all sports medicine practitioners. Their basic duties consist of the implementation of injury prevention programs, initiation of immediate treatment for an injured athlete, and the supervision of injury rehabilitation procedures set forth by the team physician. Undoubtedly a trainer's expertise must be varied considering that he/she will be required to attend to everything from the simple treatment of cuts and abrasions to the imaginative custom tailoring of protective equipment. Since athletic trainers work within the traditions of numerous sports, their roles could very well expand into the unique needs of each. Speciality functions may include establishing conditioning programs, planning menus, supervising diets, and even serving as a counselor of sports to the players themselves. Though it may appear that the main function of athletic training is aimed to deal with injuries "after the fact," Otho Davis, NFL trainer of the Philadelphia **Eagles** and Executive Director of the National Athletic Trainers Association, believes, "The most important role of the trainer is to prevent an injury from occurring. At the professional level, a player cannot afford to even miss practice." Otho also feels his greatest satisfaction "...comes from seeing an individual return to maximum potential by performing well following an injury." A proficient trainer will be sensitive to the personalities of everyone with whom he or she must be associated. The trainer must identify who truly needs assistance and who is making much ado about nothing. On the other hand, it is necessary to know those individuals who will do anything or say anything to be able to play full time once again. A common dilemma exists with college freshman especially in football. Many are not accustomed to playing with everyday injury nuances and therefore must be made to understand the different types of pain.

Trainers must be careful not to be influenced by coaches or management who may want an athlete to return to playing status sooner than rehabilitation will allow. Only by being in the middle of such situations can a trainer begin to realize the commitment he/she has to adhere to the ethical practices of the profession.

Before you contemplate entrance into this field, be absolutely certain that you have a sincere interest in athletics and the well-being of those involved in sport. Trainers are for the most part healers and must therefore be sensitive to the needs and concerns of each individual athlete. In addition to being people oriented, other necessary attributes include an ability to work well with one's hands, a sense of ingenuity, meticulously clean health habits and an understanding that the dedication to serve others will involve long and unusual hours.

Professional Athletic Team Trainers

There exists much diversity among the working environments for athletic trainers from sport to sport and within each organization. A professional football franchise may employ as many as 4 full-time trainers in addition to part-time trainers for game days. On the other hand, while a professional soccer team may only contract the training services of a sports clinic, should an injury arise. Unmistakably, though, professional football is the ultimate goal and hotbed for most aspiring trainers.

Employment with a professional team is glamorous, exciting and provides numerous additional benefits. However, securing such positions will continue to be a difficult task.

Collegiate Teams

The greatest number of potential opportunities exists for athletic trainers at major universities, four year colleges and junior colleges. Though the working conditions may resemble any typical professional organization, the major difference is that the trainer will work with numerous teams and sports through the course of a season. A major university will usually employ only one head athletic trainer with several assistants and student trainers. For students, the pay will be minimal but the experience will prove to be invaluable in both securing a position and in treating clients.

Certification in the National Athletic Trainer's Association

The National Athletic Trainer's Association Board of Certification was established in 1970 to implement a program of certification for entry level athletic trainers. The purpose of the certification program is to establish standards for entry into the profession of athletic training.

Certification Requirements

In order to attain Certification as an Athletic Trainer, the following core requirements and one of the section requirements must be fulfilled. If one or more of the core requirements are not fulfilled at the time of application, the application will be returned.

Core Requirements

- Proof of graduation (official transcript) at the baccalaureate level from an accredited college or university located in the United States. Students who have begun their last semester or quarter of college are eligible to take the certification examination prior to graduation provided the other core and section requirements have been fulfilled at the time of application.

- Proof of current American National Red Cross Standard First Aid Certification and current basic CPR. (EMT equivalent instead of First Aid or CPR will be accepted.)
- At the time of application, all candidates for certification (curriculum and internship) must verify that at least 25 percent of their athletic training experience hours credited in fulfilling the certification requirements were attained in actual (on location) practice and/or game coverage with one or more of the following sports: football, soccer, hockey, wrestling, basketball, gymnastics, lacrosse, volleyball, or rugby
- Endorsement of certification application by an NATA certified athletic trainer.
- Subsequent passing of the certification examination (written, oral practical, and written stimulation sections).

Section Requirements

Section One: Graduate of an NATA approved curriculum. Successful completion of an NATA approved athletic training education program from a college or university sponsoring a NATA approved graduate or undergraduate program.

For more information, contact:

NATA
Board of Certification
P.O. Box 1726
Greenville, NC 27835

(919) 355-6300.

Employment Opportunities

With an emergence of specialized sports centers across the country, the demand for certified trainers has increased drastically. The salary and working hours at such clinics and hospitals are surpassed only by those trainers employed in the professional ranks.

The one possible drawback that may exist here is that a majority of a trainer's time spent in this type of setting will be involved only in areas of treatment and rehabilitation of injured athletes and recreational enthusiasts. It is not uncommon for the dedicated therapist to become frustrated with the recreational athlete, who may not be as disciplined in the rehabilitative process as the competitive athlete. When choosing a prospective clinic for employment, find out what kind of people will be seeking assistance and the role in which you will be required to perform beyond normal conditions. This may, in the long run, prevent any future job dissatisfaction. The National Institutes of Health have estimated that as many as 18 million Americans sustain sports related injuries each year. According to *Forbes* magazine, over $10 billion dollars is spent annually on rehabilitation treatment from sports injuries. Estimates on the number of formal sports medicine clinics run by professionals in the United States are close to 1500. There are many kinds of facilities included in that number, ranging from rehabilitation centers to full service sports medicine wings of hospitals. A typical full service sports medicine clinic can expect to generate over $30,000 monthly revenue against operating expenses of $20,000 per monthly for a typical pre-tax profit margin of 35%. That type of return is fueling the sports medicine fire.

The Future

The need for certified trainers will only continue to increase as it is estimated that high schools alone offer the possibility of 10,000-20,000 jobs! Currently, women athletic trainers are in short supply, as are trainers needed to cover the astronomical numbers of youth contests. While salaries remain only moderate to good, $14,000-$30,000, potential salaries will increase in the years ahead.

Resources

National Athletic Trainer's Association
2952 Stemmons, Suite 200
Dallas, Texas 75247

(214) 637-6282

American Athletic Trainer's Association & Certification Board
660 West Duarte Road
Arcadia, CA 91006

(818) 445-1978

National Athletic Health Institute
6666 Greer Valley Circle
Culver City, CA 90230-7068

(213) 649-6244

Sports Nutrition

In the athlete's quest to gain the competitive edge; the relationship between nutrition and performance has recently been recognized as a key factor. The advances in sports nutrition and the acceptance of its importance in attaining total health and wellness will allow sports nutritionists to perform a major role in enhancing performances in the years ahead. Most nutritionists involved in sports serve in a consulting capacity, usually self-employed in a private practice. Their function is mainly concerned with the analysis and development of the athlete's diet for teams, sports medicine clinics and camps. They offer expertise in weight control, pre-game meals and vitamin/mineral supplementation.

Many practicing sports nutritionists have acquired their education and background in medicine or nutrition with their experience usually in nursing, or as a dietician. Those wishing to pursue this growing field will need to complete at least a master's in nutrition with a doctorate desirable for added credibility.

Nutritionists are receiving excellent fees for their services, as earnings from $20,000 to $80,000 annually can be expected depending upon whether the practice is private or within a health care clinic.

Resources

Sports and Cardiovascular Nutrition
American Dietetic Association
430 North Michigan Avenue
Chicago, IL 60611

(312) 280-5000

International Center for Sports Nutrition
502 S. 44th Street
Omaha, NE 68105

Podiatry

It is estimated that 80% of all people have foot problems, in one form or another. Since nearly every sport puts a great strain on its participants' feet, the need for podiatric care has grown in importance. These Doctors of Podiatric Medicine, DPM are concerned with the diagnosis, treatment, and prevention of foot and lower extremity injuries. DPMs utilize a variety of methods, including medical, surgical and physical techniques. Podiatrists may practice privately, be a part of a hospital staff or sports clinic. DPMs enjoy excellent working conditions and usually don't work the many long hours of other sports medicine practitioners. Aspiring podiatrists must complete an intensive educational curriculum involving premed undergraduate degree, a four year professional program, an internship, residency emphasizing foot surgery, biomechanics, and sports medicine.

DPMs must pass state and national licensing exams, which are monitored by the American Academy of Podiatric Sports Medicine (AAPSM). The academy also is active in promoting and presenting research on podiatric sports medicine. The future of podiatry will continue to be bright as earnings for DPMs should range from $40,000 to $80,000 annually depending on the size and location of the practice or clinic.

Resources

American Academy of Podiatric Sports Medicine
1729 Glastonberry Road
Potomac, MD 20854

(301) 424-7440

Schools With Recognized Curriculums in Podiatric Medicine

California College of Podiatric Medicine
Box 7855
San Francisco, CA 94120

(415) 563-3444

University of Osteopathic Medicine & Health Sciences
3200 Grand Avenue
Des Moines, IA 50312

(515) 271-1400

Other Sports Medicine Related Careers

There are various sports opportunities in fields which assist sports medicine practitioners, but are not able to sustain a full time business with sports clients. Technicians in sports prosthetics and orthotics are frequently being called upon to develop and design knee and elbow braces, foot supports, body jackets, and on occasion, tailor protective equipment for injury rehabilitation.

These design experts work closely with sports medicine personnel for the purpose of providing injury prevention mechanisms which will not alter performance. Few technicians will exclusively work with athletics.

Resources

The American Orthotic & Prosthetic Association
717 Pendleton Street
Alexandria, VA 22314

Sports Vision

Sports vision consultants believe that the vision system directs the muscular system, thus allowing the successful athlete to have a greater reaction system. It is this innate reaction system that some feel determines an athlete's ability. Optometrists estimate that almost every athlete can improve his/her game if they practice visualizing their goal in their minds, while using their eyes to concentrate on the ball.

Visual concentration does not necessarily mean concentrating on what the eyes are seeing. In basketball, a player can keep an eye directed to the opposing guard while visually concentrating on a teammate. Optometrists specializing in sports vision have found that the shorter the period of time a person visually concentrates on something, the more intense the concentration is. When an outfielder or football receiver misses an easy catch or a basketball player misses an easy shot, it may be that there was too much time to concentrate and the athlete was not concentrating intently enough at the right moment.

As with other medical personnel, the education and training of ophthalmologists, MDs and optometrists, DOs requires a serious commitment and long study. An interest in science and academics generally exists as an important criterion for success.

Resources

American Optometric Association
243 North Lindbergh Boulevard
St. Louis, MO 63141

Sports Medicine Paraprofessionals

For each professional practitioner there is at least one support staff member who will assist in a variety of capacities. These paraprofessionals are trained health aids who are permitted to perform numerous functions once undertaken by the doctor or physical therapist.

A career as an assistant will usually involve a short, yet intense, formal training program in the related sports medicine field. All sports medicine professionals utilize paraprofessionals in their practices. Many of these paraprofessionals will later choose to further themselves as professional practitioners.

Entrance into any one of the sports medicine paraprofessionals fields is not difficult and fulfilling the education requirements can take as little as 6 months to two years. Hourly wages paid to assistants will range with an income in the neighborhood of $12,000 to $16,000 per year.

The job outlook for paraprofessionals remains good, as it should experience a steady increase in the future.

Sports Dentistry

> *When I've tried pitching without the mouth guard I get tired quicker and feel more pain in my arm afterwards. Some might say its psychological, but I don't think so.*
>
> –Hank Iervolino, Former baseball pitcher
> New York Technological University

One of the areas of sports medicine that has created excitement in recent years has been the use of special mouthpieces. Interest in these devices skyrocketed following a 1980 Sports Illustrated report. Technically called a mandibular orthopedic repositioning application (MORA), this dental apparatus fits over the lower teeth and readjusts the mal-alignment from which many athletes suffer. Some players reported increased overall performance and particularly improved strength.

Few, if any, dentists involve themselves with sports on a full time basis. In addition to their regular practice, some dentists serve athletic teams as consultants. They are paid a yearly fee for their duties relating to the team. Others volunteer their services to school and community teams. The input of dentists into the design of mouthpieces and face guards has seen a reduction in the number of injuries to the mouth area by nearly 60%.

The American Dental Association (ADA) has outlined the primary functions of the team dentist:

- The dentist is responsible for making sure that players have good oral health at the start of the season.
- The team dentist helps set up and implement the school mouth protector program. Each year, the dentist and school officials should discuss when the program should take place, by whom and how it will be run, what kind of protectors should be used, and what the costs will be.
- The team dentist can treat emergency dental problems if the player's own dentist is not available, or can administer first aid if the team physician is not present.

Resources

American Dental Association
211 East Chicago Avenue
Chicago, IL 60611

Academy Sports Dentistry
12200 Preston Road
Dallas, TX 75230

(214) 239-7223

Sports Massage

The newest and fastest developing concept in the sports medicine field is the art of massage. Body massage treatments are considered to be therapeutic and have been clinically proven to be successful; in relieving mental and physical strain, in assisting as a complementary procedure during injury rehabilitation and in preventing possible injury through stretching and flexibility principles. Sports masseurs and masseuses have been extensively called upon by both individual athletes and race organizers to perform their services at triathlons, marathons, and track events. Athletes are not the only ones who have experienced the benefits of body massage as mental health centers and hospital clinics are more often adding these specialists to their therapy staffs. However, the majority of massage artists are in private practice with their own exclusive clientele. Once a reputation has been established, a good masseur or masseuse can earn anywhere from $25 to $75 per hourly session.

Education and Training

Requirements on education and training vary among the states. Many states require tests for licensing, and some do not.

Most therapists learn their skills in schools that teach massage. A number of vocational schools throughout the United States offer programs in massage. The American Massage Therapy Association (AMTA) has approved 55 massage programs in North America. They vary in length from six months for full time enrollees to 24 months for part time students. Some schools teach only one form of massage. Others teach different kinds of massage. Workshops and short courses are also available. Students take anatomy, physiology, and the theory and practice of massage. Persons of any age may study for this work, but most programs require students to have a high school diploma. Helpful high school courses include those in sciences, especially biology. Business courses will prove helpful to those who plan to set up their own practice.

Eight massage schools in the United States are federally accredited. Students attending these schools may be eligible for federally sponsored student loans. Some schools offer scholarship assistance or workstudy programs.

Licenses, Certification, Professional Societies

Thirteen states require licensing for massage therapists. Texas offers a registration program, and Connecticut has state certification for massage therapists. In most states that require a license, therapists must take a state licensing examination after they complete their training. The AMTA sets nationwide standards for training and practice. This organization has helped give massage therapy a good name and has made it a respect occupation. Membership in AMTA indicates that the therapist has met its standards for practice.

Schools approved by AMTA operate in more than half the states. Some of these states do not require massage therapists to be licensed. To have the approval of the AMTA, a program must offer at least 500 hours of classroom instruction lasting at least six months. Some last a year or longer.

To become members of AMTA, therapists must complete a program at an AMTA approved school or pass an AMTA approved examination. In a few states, the AMTA will admit therapists who hold a state license.

Employment Outlook

The demand for massage therapists is growing. The interest in fitness has made people more aware of the value of massage. Even when money is tight and people are spending less, they still like to receive a massage. Massage fits in with the new approach in health care treating the whole person and stopping trouble before it starts.

The American Massage Therapy Association now has more than 6,500 members, four times as many as in 1984. The number of schools with AMTA approved programs has doubled since 1983. There are now 55 of these schools. Most states are considering licensing legislation.

For all these reasons, the employment outlook for massage therapists is excellent. The trend toward health and wellness will continue, and massage is an important part of that trend.

Two institutions noted for their specialized training are The Sports Massage Training Institute and the Minneapolis School of Massage.

The Sports Massage Training Institute

The SMTI program includes pre, post and preventive massage, injury care, trigger point, P.N.F. stretches, clinical internship and more. The 500 hour/ 15 week program is concise and comprehensive, giving the student a thorough background in sports massage, injury care, sports pathology, anatomy and physiology. Graduate students have gone from their training into jobs with sport oriented chiropractors, orthopedic surgeons, fitness clubs, sports medicine clinics and massage therapists for sports teams. SMTI publishes the *Sports Massage Journal* and is recognized worldwide as a leader in sports massage training.

For information, contact:

The Sports Massage Training Institute of Encinitas
121 West "E" Street
Encinitas, CA 92024

(619) 942-6128

Minneapolis School of Massage, Inc.

The philosophy of this sports massage program is that the human body needs to be in balance to prevent injury and optimize performance. A student who wishes to be certified in this 12 week sports massage program must first complete training in the basic two week massage course. A unique concept of this program is that students may proceed at their own pace of study before completing an internship with the local Division I college athletic training department.

For information, contact:

Minneapolis School of Massage, Inc.
Jim Traver, Director
220 Lowry Avenue
Mpls, MN 55418

(612) 788-8907

Publications

Massage Journal Quarterly
American Massage Therapy Association
P.O. Box 1270
Kingsport, TN 37662

The Book of Massage
by Lucy Lidell
192 pages, $9.95 softbound
Simon & Schuster, Inc.
1230 Avenue of the Americas
New York, NY 10020

Healing Massage Techniques:
A Study of Eastern and Western Methods.
by Frances Tappan
$14.95 softbound
Appleton & Lange
25 Van Zant Street
East Norwalk, CT 06855

Physical education represents the backbone of athletic competition and healthy living. Photo: courtesy of the **Catholic Athletic Association.**

15

Sports Education & Performance Consultants

Within sports education, there are two distinct career routes individuals may choose to pursue. One is in a teaching capacity working within the educational system. The other is that of a practitioner of sports sciences principles. Each branch of sports education interrelates with the other. Skill training serves as a practical laboratory for academic studies while academic studies become a source of new ideas and techniques for coaches and instructors.

To be proficient at the sports sciences, a marriage must exist between the intellectual and experimental components of athletics. If an individual enters sports from an exact discipline (i.e. sociology or psychology), then there will be a need to increase expertise in physical education applications and sports knowledge. At the same time, those already experienced as athletes and coaches may need to take a step back to understand the intellectual and theoretical aspects of their training.

However, this interrelationship between theory and research with the practical application approach has not transpired well in the United States. This lack of awareness, coupled with the public's apprehension to utilize the many sports sciences advancements, has created little demand for the practicing sports consultant. The underlying result of this curfew state is that a majority of those employed in these fields will remain in an educational environment performing research. Any private consultation will be relegated to that of a part time avocation.

Physical Education

Physical educators are involved in both teaching about and developing the science of human movement. Despite the schools' emphasis on fitness over the last decade, test scores show that today's youth are actually decreasing their state of physical conditioning. The physical state of young students presents the biggest challenge for physical educators in the 90s.

Most physical education careers are within the public school system. However, with budget cuts and diminishing student populations, the trend will be to seek career opportunities in the private sector in the realm of resorts, health clubs, and social agencies. There are other sidelines that PE personnel with their flexible schedules are able to pursue. As mentioned earlier, some will take on coaching duties, sports officiating, aerobics instruction, or in fitness personal consulting. Even though a physical education career may appear ever changing, there is little room for upward mobility unless an advanced degree is attained. Many choose to take additional coursework in administration or use their graduate work to secure a collegiate teaching position. Although most of these instructors have a graduate degree, many of their tasks are the same as those of physical education instructors in high schools. They help students acquire sports skills. Some direct athletic programs that range from local to sectional tournaments. Other physical education instructors are researchers in exercise physiology. These workers may serve in industry, health spas, or community centers where they guide workers or members in physical fitness programs. Physical education can be divided into several areas, elementary education, secondary instruction or college teaching. The age group preference is strictly a personal one, but keep in mind that in grade school and possibly secondary schools, many students will be in your class as a requirement, not as an elective. Being able to motivate young people to commit themselves to self-improvement may take precedence over other aspects of teaching physical education.

The main responsibility for a physical education instructor at any level is to develop a wide variety of skills in students such as agility, balance, coordination, endurance, flexibility, power, rhythm, strength and timing.

When choosing a college for educational training, it is important to make sure it is accredited for the purposes of acquiring a teaching license. Check with your state requirements when developing your curriculum. For certification in most states, candidates must have a bachelor's degree with a major in physical education and ten to fifteen semester hours of education theory and practice. Requirements vary with states and schools. Physical education courses may include biology, anatomy, psychology, sociology, physiology, chemistry or physics. Others are growth and development, biomechanics, physiology of exercise, principles of play, tests and measurement, and physical education activities.

Those who plan to teach in college or become principals in high schools should have a graduate degree. They should also be qualified to teach a subject besides physical education.

The outlook for teaching physical education remains only fair. Therefore, it becomes imperative to diversify your education and experience in order to take advantage of opportunities that may arise in a non-PE environment.

Physical education instructors work a nine-month or ten-month school year. In the summer they may head local recreation programs or serve as camp counselors. Some go back to college to take graduate courses. They also prepare curriculums and sports programs for the coming school year. College instructors or professors teach their subjects during the school year, and they may teach summers as well. Many work part time in research laboratories, direct teachers in public schools, and work on school or college committees.

The pay of physical education instructors is comparable with that of other teachers with the same amount of education and experience. Starting pay ranges from $11,000 to more than $15,000 a year. Public school teachers with years of seniority earn from $17,600 to $30,000 or more a year. Exact wages depend on the qualifications of the instructor and the size, wealth and location of the town or city school system.

Instructors receive extra pay for the after school hours when they coach, supervise sports, and organize cheerleaders. Extra pay may range from a few hundred dollars to $4,000 or more in a school year.

College salaries range from $24,000 to $50,000 or more. Education, academic rank, duties, and the instructor's competence affect earnings. Pay increases more rapidly in public schools. In the long run, however, income may be higher for those with a doctoral degree who are college teachers.

Weight Training Instructor

At one time, weight equipment was usually found primarily in body builders' gyms and Ys. Today, the concept of weight training has become so popular that you will find some form of equipment in almost any fitness facility or gymnasium you visit. Until the mid-50s, training to enhance muscular strength and endurance was done almost exclusively by lifting barbells and dumbbells. Specialized exercise machines have now appeared and produce far more thorough training effects than traditional weight lifting. These high-tech exercise machines have become the most widely used form of weight training by professional athletes and fitness enthusiasts. The weight training instructor may be one of the most important positions in the facility due to the great risk of injury of an individual who is unfamiliar with the equipment.

Job Description

An instructor in the use of free weights, standard resistance machines or variable resistance equipment, should have an understanding of two things; the human body and the facility's weight equipment. An instructor should be able to answer questions and help club members work out. They are responsible for establishing a program for individuals interested in body building.

Education

A bachelor's degree in physical education with an emphasis in exercise physiology is a good start. Training provided by an equipment manufacturer is also a plus. However, most practical hands on knowledge will invariably come from attending certified clinics, national conferences and by subscribing to relevant journals.

Income

A weight trainer whose background includes only on-the-job training may be working at minimum wage. However, if the trainer has formal educational background and extensive experience, you can expect to make up to $30 per hour depending upon the place of employment.

Sports Psychology

An emerging field that has recently created considerable interest is the mental side of athletic performance. Whether the issue is enhancing mental toughness, coping with pressure or maintaining concentration, athletes are constantly seeking techniques that may provide the competitive edge.

Though still a relatively new concept in the training regimens of American athletes, sports psychology has now made its inroads in the amateur circles and is gaining acceptance in the professional ranks. Without an established market, sports psychologists who aspire to become practitioners continue to struggle for recognition. Sports psychologists are most prominent as teaching professors at the collegiate level or are involved in a clinical practice. Sports consultants as a whole have recently begun to take active roles working with athletes who suffer from alcohol and drug abuse in addition to serving as instructors for youth coaching effectiveness programs. There is much concern with the direction that youth sports is taking, especially in its character formation processes. It is the hope that sports psychology as a field can address such issues and provide education to coaches on the how and why in motor learning and child development.

Other conditions that may require the expertise of a sports psychologist are mental and/or physical burnout, anorexia and bulimia, aggressive behavior, injury rehabilitation and/or post-career life transitions for professional and amateur athletes.

A current controversy exists with the future legal status of sports psychology. Since a majority of these specialized consultants have completed their educational training in either a physical education or motor learning program, licensed clinical psychologists on the other hand who have acquired their academic training in the school of psychology, question the validity of their psychological counseling background. It will be some time before this issue will be resolved.

Sport Psychology Resources

Association for the Advancement of Applied Sport Psychology
Dr. Charles J. Hardy
Dept. of Physical Education
CB #8600, 315 Woollen
University of North Carolina
Chapel Hill, NC 27599-8600

(919) 962-2021

Promote the development of psychological theory, research, and intervention strategies in sport psychology. The organizers of the AAASP believed there was a strong need to insure that sport psychology is recognized as an orderly body of professional researchers and practitioners applying scientific principles in a systematic manner.

North American Society for Psychology of Sport & Physical Activity
Deborah Feltz, MD
Youth Sport Institute
Room 210, IM Sport Circle
Michigan State University
East Lansing, MI 48824

(503) 686-4106

The NASPSPA encourages the study of human behavior in sport and physical activity and to improve the quality of teaching and research in sport psychology, motor development, and motor learning. The society's members include scholars from a variety of behavioral sciences and professions.

Sports Psychology Education

There is an increasing number of graduate programs in sports psychology now being offered. Research a number of institutions to determine if their curriculum meets both your educational and career goals. Some will be more research based while others will be more application oriented.

To receive a comprehensive list of all institutions currently offering sports psychology degree programs, please send $12.95 to:

Athletic Achievements
3036 Ontario Road
Little Canada, MN 55117

(612) 484-8299

Resources

Journal of Applied Sports Psychology
University of North Carolina
C.B. No. 8700 Fetzer
Chapel Hill, NC 27599

Philosophical Society for the Study of Sport
Professor Joy DeSensi
University of Tennessee
Department of Health & Physical Education
Knoxville, TN 37996-2700

Conferences

Sports Psychology Conference University of Virginia

For the past 15 years, the University of Virginia has been the site for one of the most hands-on conference of its kind in the field of sports psychology. This educational opportunity is held annually for one week (Monday through Friday) during the last week of June. Its 1991 theme *Real Issues in the Real World of Sport Psychology* typifies its practical application focus. The presenting faculty represents the field's leading consultants and professors from around the county. Participants have the option to seek academic credit if desired. The format is designed to meet the needs of those interested in the psychology of sport performance from an athletic, coach's or sport psychologist's point of view.

University of Virginia Curry Memorial School of Education
405 Emmet Street
Charlottesville, VA 22903

(804) 295-7390

Conference on Counseling Athletes

Springfield College has been the sponsoring institution (for this progressive conference) for the past nine years. The three day, annual program held during the last week of May, features sessions or practical strategies to concerns in athletic academic advising, performance enhancement, and counseling strategies in addressing racism, substance abuse, and career planning. Roundtable forums are designed to create in-depth understanding regarding future trends and issues in meeting the ever changing needs of the student athlete. To learn more about this educational offering, contact:

Department of Continuing Education
Springfield College
Springfield, MA 01109-3797

(413) 788-3111

Exercise Physiology

The movement toward maximizing athletic performance has expanded to the application of exercise physiology principles. The study of exercise physiology involves the analysis and improvement of cardiopulmonary endurance and capacity, muscle power and joint flexibility.

Like other emerging sports sciences, exercise physiology practitioners have yet to gain the respect they deserve in the private sector of health. Therefore, the greater proportion of exercise physiologists involved with research at human performance laboratories are usually at university fitness centers. But for those who are able to be employed in a consulting capacity, they will more than likely serve in; evaluating the potential of athletes, developing conditioning and injury prevention programs for teams in conjunction with coaches and other sports medicine personnel and/or assisting elite and weekend athletes to achieve fitness.

Exercise physiologists utilize state of the art technology in evaluating performance and implementing training techniques. The combination of slow motion films, videotapes, and computer analysis provide direction in perfecting performance.

At the present time, the field remains wide open for the research oriented individual, but somewhat restricted for those seeking employment in the private sector. Exercise physiologists who are able to secure a corporate fitness directorship can earn upward of $35,000 to $90,000 at a national health center. Their teaching and research counterparts can expect a beginning salary in the low $20,000s.

Exercise physiologists are one of the few sports sciences that require graduates to pass a national certification exam. There are some practitioners who have acquired only a master's degree, but the trend is to complete the doctoral program. Over half of the states in the union have at least one institution which offers an exercise physiology curriculum. When contacting the school of your choice for inquiry, address all materials to the department of physical education.

To learn more about this field, contact:

American Physiological Society
9650 Rockville Pike
Bethesda, MD 20814

(301) 530-7171

Biomechanics

This science is the sister field to exercise physiology. Biomechanics however involves the analysis and correction of athletic movement in relation to the body's musculoskeletal system. Those who may best use these services include: Manufacturers of athletic equipment; Research health centers, or; Fitness clubs. Since biomechanical testing is not in demand for individual consultation, job opportunities are limited. In addition to teaching and performing research at human performance laboratories, the best possibility for career advancement will be in corporate fitness applications. Much like exercise physiology, a master's degree leading to a doctorate will be required of aspiring biomechanics students, but one drawback is the salary structure which will range from $17,000 to $35,000 annually.

Sports Sociology

Though a relatively unknown segment of the sports sciences, sports sociology involves the research and instruction of sport as a social institution, a social process, and structural social activity. The present applications of this science are minimal at beast as most sports sociologists will be committed to research, writing and lecturing on the subject.

Since there has been little demand for the practical usage of sports sociology, few institutions offer a structural program. A master's degree or a doctorate in physical education with emphasis in sociology, or a sociology degree with a concentration in physical education are necessary educational requirements. As in all academic careers, advancement comes through completing and publishing research coupled with teaching expertise. The job market outlook is not encouraging and for those sports sociologists who can be innovative and aggressive, earnings would be in the range of $18,000 to $35,000 annually.

Publications

Journal of the Philosophy of Sport
P.O. Box 5076
Champaign, IL 61825

(217) 351-5076

Journal of Sport Behavior
University of South Alabama
Dept. of HPERS
Mobile, AL 36688

(205) 460-7131

Sociology of Sport Journal
P.O. Box 5076
Champaign, IL 61825

(800) 747-4457

North American Society for the Sociology of Sport
c/o Jim Frey
Dept. of Sociology
University of Nevada Las Vegas
Las Vegas, Nevada 89154

(702) 739-3322

With an ongoing emphasis now being placed on the need for physical exercise and activity, personal trainers, most notably aerobic instructors, provide great part- and full-time opportunities. Photo: **The Aerobic Center.**

16
Health & Fitness

The health fitness movement is an outgrowth of the American obsession with youth and beauty. It is also an indictment on a high-tech medical system whose climbing costs sometimes seem to outweigh its benefits. Across the country, health fitness programs are keeping people healthy, active and productive. Over 500 major companies and many smaller ones are offering some sort of fitness program for their employees and the number is rising rapidly. These corporate programs consist of varying combinations of employee access to; jogging paths, exercise machines, aerobic dance instruction, classes in stress reduction techniques, smoking cessation seminars, counseling for alcoholics, nutritional advice. There are sports medicine clinics, health spas, Ys, gyms, hospitals, schools, church basements and many other creative sites where Americans are reshaping their bodies inside and out.

The health fitness boom is sticking and the improvement it has made in many people's lives has given hundreds of thousands more people the inspiration they needed to join the movement. According to recent statistics, men and women experience more job satisfaction in the health fitness career field than in any other field.

Dance Exercise Instructors

Dance exercise is a term that encompasses all the forms of exercise that are set to music. Dance exercise instructors lead group classes or give individual instruction. They demonstrate an exercise, explain its purpose, supervise clients to ensure that the exercise is done correctly and determine the entire program. The dance exercise instructor can choose to work full time or part time. Formats vary from beginning to advanced aerobics, Jazzercise, aquacize, stretch hand tone and prenatal/postpartum. No matter which phase of dance exercise you enter, you will need adequate training with a basic course in anatomy/physiology and CPR. You will need the knowledge of health appraisal techniques and submaximal exercise testing results to properly recommend an exercise program. In addition, you should be able to demonstrate appropriate techniques in motivation, counseling, teaching and behavior modification to promote lifestyle changes. If you plan to become an independent contractor, you should also have experience teaching and choreographing dance exercise.

Getting Started

Usually in the smaller organization, it costs nothing to get started. You may be required to purchase a uniform and pay for your training or certification. You also might have to provide your own cassette player. Training and certification costs vary greatly. In a large organization you may have to pay a franchise fee as high as $2,000, which may include your uniform, cassettes, music and training.

As an independent instructor the minimum amount you will need to get started is $2,000. This amount covers promotional fliers, clothing, shoes, music, accounting, telephone bills, business cards and other teaching accessories such as mats, hand weights and exercise bars. In addition, you may need to pay monthly rent on your studio. You should also be covered with liability insurance for protection if someone in your class is injured.
Income

A dance exercise instructor working in a small organization may make an hourly wage from $7.00 to as much as $35.00. Large organization employees can make an hourly wage of $20.00 to $50.00. You may also have opportunities to receive a percentage of the gross amount collected from each class. In a franchise position, the average part time income could be as high as $20,000 per year.

Resources

AFAA's American Fitness
15250 Ventura Blvd., Suite 310
Sherman Oaks, CA 91403

(818) 905-0040

American Fitness Quarterly
6065 Frantz Road
Suite 205
Dublin, OH 43017

(614) 766-7736

Aerobics & Fitness Association of America
15250 Ventura Blvd., Suite 802
Sherman Oaks, CA 91403

(818) 905-0040

International Dance Exercise Association
6190 Cornerstone Court, Suite 204
San Diego, CA 92121

(619) 535-8979

Jazzercise
2808 Roosevelt Street
Carlsbad, CA 92008

(619) 434-2101

Dance Therapist

The dance therapist uses movement in the treatment and rehabilitation of neurologically impaired, physically handicapped and emotionally disturbed adults and children. This work is distinguished from other types of dance by its focus on the nonverbal aspects of behavior and its use of movement. A dance therapist, sometimes referred to as a dance movement therapist, works with people who require special psycho-therapeutic services because of behavioral, learning, perceptual, and/or physical disorders. The therapist uses knowledge of how the body moves in relation to space and rhythm, which helps a person to develop coordination, improve gait and correct problems in mobility. The emotionally disturbed are rehabilitated by the dance therapist's observations, which aid in the development of a behavior modification program utilizing dance and music.

Job Description

Skilled dance/movement therapists must be well-trained in the art of dance and versed in psycho-therapy. Dance/movement therapists work with individuals who have social, emotional, cognitive and/or physical problems. Places of employment include psychiatric hospitals, clinics, day care, community mental health centers, developmental centers, correctional facilities and special schools, and rehabilitation facilities. Therapists work with people of all ages in groups, as well as individually. They also act as consultants and engage in research. Job opportunities for trained professionals vary in different locations. Many dance/movement therapists are pioneering job development in their region and the American Dance Therapy Association (ADTA) is actively engaged in a program to enhance jobs for dance/movement therapists.

Education

A bachelor's or master's degree in special education, dance, psychology or a related field may be sufficient if the person's dance background is very strong. Additional dance therapy training and a supervised clinical internship are considered pluses. The following is recommended: a broad liberal arts background with an emphasis in psychology; extensive training in a variety of dance forms with courses in theory; improvisation, choreography and kinesiology, and; experience in teaching dance to normal children and adults. Introductory or survey courses in dance/movement therapy can help students evaluate their interests and aptitudes before entering a graduate program. Professional training is concentrated at a graduate level. Studies include courses such as dance/movement therapy and practice, psycho-pathology, human development, observation and research skills and a supervised internship in a clinical setting.

Income

A beginning salary ranges from $15,000 to $20,000, depending on the these facts: training and experience of the practitioner; the region of the country, and; the type of facility employing the dance/movement therapist.

Resources

Dance Educators of America, Inc.
Box 470
Caldwell, NJ 07006

American Dance Therapy Association
Suite 108, 2000 Century Plaza
Columbia, MD 21044

(301) 997-4040

Corporate Fitness Director

The concept of fitness is changing, and so is corporate America. From the corporate viewpoint, these programs help reduce the incidence of cardiovascular disease with its astronomical costs to the company.

Job Description

A corporate fitness instructor may work in a large or small business, government organization or hospital, providing individual and/or group programs for employees, based on specific needs. Your work environment may be in a company's meeting room or gym, or teach the company's employees at a local fitness club. The instructor works with the company's medical staff in preparing and planning programs. Employees are provided with a comprehensive fitness and lifestyle assessment, education in lifestyle change and exercise classes. Many employers are looking for people with an exercise physiology background with knowledge in fitness testing, nutrition, stress management, business management and human relations.

Education

A master's degree in exercise physiology, physical education or a related field is usually required of the applicant. Corporate fitness is a rapidly growing field and the number of Universities offering degrees specializing in corporate fitness is expanding rapidly.

Income

As a corporate fitness instructor you can expect to make $15,000 to $30,000 per year depending on education, experience, and the size of the company. The company must be experiencing profitable business conditions before a fitness director will be hired. Most fitness director positions will be available with well established Fortune 1000 companies.

Resources

Health and Fitness Career Resources
P.O. Box 151
Bloomfield, MI 48303

(313) 737-0779

American Association of Fitness Directors in Business and Industry
400 6th Avenue, S.W.
Suite 3030
Washington, D.C. 20201

Association for Fitness in Business
310 N. Alabama, Suite A
Indianapolis, IN 46204

(317) 636-6621

The National Institute for
Fitness and Sport
250 N. University Blvd.
Indianapolis, IN 46202

(317) 274-3432

YMCA National Health and
Physical Education Department
101 North Wacker Drive
Chicago, IL 60606

(312) 977-0031

Health Club Administrative Personnel

The administrative members of the club include managers, salespeople, administrative assistants and operations assistants. Salaries in these areas are dependent upon club size, your education and experience.

Club Manager

A manager's responsibility is to coordinate the efforts of all administrative, fitness and auxiliary personnel. The manager sets the tone for the entire club. The quality of the facility is a reflection of the manager's concern and expertise. This is probably the most stressful position in a health club since the manager/assistant manager constantly deals with the people problems.

Exercise Program Director

The exercise program director heads the fitness staff. This key person must have a number of attributes in addition to a personal commitment to physical fitness. These skills include: managing, testing and communicating. The ability to plan, implement and evaluate programs is critical. Exercise program directors design, implement and administer safe, effective and enjoyable rehabilitative exercise programs. They are responsible for seeing that class instructors and supervisors deliver a consistent level of service. Staff training is essential, instilling the required knowledge and skills necessary for administration of these activities. A qualified director usually has a background oriented more toward exercise than business. The director may have a degree in physical education, exercise physiology, certification in sports medicine or training in another related area.

Resources

IRSA Jobline
132 Brookline Avenue
Boston, MA 02115

(617) 236-1500

IDEA Today
6190 Cornerstone Court East
Suite 204
San Diego, CA 92121

(619) 535-8979

CLUB Industry
1415 Beacon Street
P.O. Box C9122
Boston, MA 02146

(617) 277-3823

Club Managers Association of America
1733 King Street
Alexandria, VA 22314

(703) 739-9500

Aerobics Center
12200 Preston Road
Dallas, TX 75230

(214) 239-7223

Dance for Heart
American Heart Association
P.O. Box CH
7320 Greenville Avenue
Dallas, TX 75231

The National Association for Human Development
1620 Eye Street N.W.
Washington, D.C. 20006

(202) 331-1737

Wellness Bulletin Board Systems
I-20 at Alpine Road
Blue Cross and Blue Shield of South Carolina
Columbia, South Carolina 29219

(803) 788-3860 ext. 2604 or 2121

National Fitness Foundation
2250 E. Imperial Hwy
Suite 412
El Segundo, CA 90245

(213) 640-0145

Job Placement Services

IRSA Jobline

This monthly publication lists job opportunities in the racquet and fitness club industry. For information, contact:

Mary Albert
132 Brookline Avenue
Boston, MA 02115

(617) 236-1500 or (800) 232-4772 (USA)
(800) 228-4772 (Canada)

The need for recreation specialists for young and old alike continues to grow. Photo: courtesy of **YMCA**.

17

Recreation & Leisure

Opportunities

Economic indicator forecasts show increasing significance for recreation services over the next ten years. The potential of leisure career ladders will provide creative, satisfying jobs which help people attain true self-realization. The umbrella of leisure services covers three broad areas; natural resources, leisure education programs and commercial recreation.

Natural Resources
- public park systems (local, state, regional and national),
- programs utilized for outdoor recreation.

Leisure Education Programs
- indoor, outdoor (cities, schools, colleges, institutions, private, voluntary agencies).

Commercial Recreation Services
- tourism
- amusement parks
- attractions
- transportation.

Swimming heads the list of 40 participant sports surveyed in 1990 by the National Sports Goods Association.

More than 66 million Americans took the plunge last year, and swimming was followed in the poll by exercise walking (58.1 million). A participant is defined as someone 7 or older who plays a sport more than once a year. In swimming, exercise walking, bicycling, exercising with equipment, running/jogging and aerobics the participant must have engaged in the activity six times or more during the year. The top 20 are

Sport	Million Participants	Sport	Million Participants
1. Swimming	66.1	11. Running/Jogging	24.8
2. Exercise walking	58.1	12. Volleyball	23.6
3. Bicycle riding	53.2	13. Aerobic exercising	23.1
4. Fishing	45.8	14. Softball	--
5. Camping	44.2	15. Hunting/Shooting	20.7
6. Bowling	40.1	16. Golf	20.3
7. Exercising/Equipment	34.8	17. Roller-skating	19.8
8. Boating (motor)	30.9	18. Hiking	17.4
9. Billiards	29.3	19. Calisthenics	17.1
10. Basketball	25.1	20. Tennis	16.9

You can easily picture the benefits of being outdoors all day, taking part in the sports you enjoy most while enjoying a healthy atmosphere. However, finding the right career path in today's managed recreation and leisure field takes a considerable amount of determination, hard work, and an effective strategy implemented through highly specialized training and experience. It is clear that the future of the recreation and leisure industry promises an increasing rate of expansion. The industry is growing not only in size, but in the demand for greater variety and quality of services. Americans today have more free hours and discretionary money to spend than any generation in the past.

The tightening of governmental funding for recreational facilities in the public sector is a great challenge to recreational financial management. Many private sector managers, on the other hand, are riding on a boom of expansion, which is based largely upon the new emphasis of wellness and fitness. Today's professional recreation and leisure specialist can choose from a widening field of specialization. Career potentials begin with work at the public recreation sites such as zoos and parks at national, state and local levels. They continue at elementary and secondary universities, municipal recreation programs and special grant programs. Private sector facilities range from tennis and health clubs to athletic clubs and industrial recreation facilities.

The available career choices touch nearly every aspect of human activity and condition. There are many other choices in allied fields such as programs for the handicapped, leisure counseling, education or communications.

Taking advantage of the available opportunities is entirely up to you and the choices you make at the entry level. You can specialize or become a generalist, concentrating on any of these areas; people, nature, technology.

How we Americans spend leisure time might seem to have little bearing on the strength of our nation or the worth and prestige of our free society. Yet we certainly cannot continue to thrive as a strong and vigorous free people unless we understand and use creatively one of our greatest resources - our leisure

–John F. Kennedy

Leisure Related Occupations

Leisure time occupations refer to the various jobs which provide opportunities for other people during leisure hours. Since leisure time activities are numerous and diverse, the occupational specialities associated with them are as well.

The list of titles or positions on the next page represents the top 50 of today's recreation and leisure service careers. The future relies on the retention of public funding and private entrepreneurship.

Many of these occupations are naturals for people who are highly skilled athletes or entertainers. Such persons might become golf pros, tennis or ski instructors. However, for most recreation leadership positions, the best avenue is through a college program in some aspect of recreation and park management.

Divisions of Recreation

The recreation field has been logically divided into four groups; recreation services, recreation resources, tourism, amusement and entertainment.

Top 50 Recreation and Leisure Careers

1. Aquatics Specialist
2. Armed Forces Recreation Leader
3. Camp Counselor
4. Campground Attendant
5. Camping Director
6. Carnival Game Operator
7. Church Recreation Director
8. College Teacher (Recreation)
9. Commercial Game Center Director
10. Community Center Director
11. Community Development Specialist
12. Community Education Worker
13. Concert Promoter
14. Concessionaire
15. Condominium Social Director
16. Cruise Ship Activity Director
17. Dance Instructor
18. Environmental Interpreter
19. Fisheries Conservationist
20. Forester (Recreation Emphasis)
21. Golf Pro
22. Handicapped Program Planner
23. High-Rise Recreation Facilitator
24. Industrial Recreation Leader
25. Leisure Counselor
26. Leisure Education Specialist
27. Municipal Recreation Leader
28. Museum Guide
29. Naturalist
30. Outdoor and Waterway Guide
31. Outdoor Recreation Manager
32. Park Ranger
33. Park Superintendent
34. Playground Leader
35. Prison Recreation Specialist
36. Recreation Facility Manager
37. Recreation Therapist
38. Resort Manager
39. River Guide
40. Senior Citizen Programmer
41. Ski Instructor
42. Tennis Pro
43. Tour Guide
44. Travel Planner
45. Volunteer Agency Supervisor
46. Wildlife Agency Supervisor
47. Youth Agency Recreation Leader
48. Youth Sports Coach
49. Zoological Director
50. Botanical Director

Recreation Services

The recreation services group involves leadership in organized recreational activities. This includes: creating and supervising programs, planning activities, and providing leadership and instruction.

These leisure time experiences take place in a variety of settings: parks, playgrounds, camps, and community centers

Recreation Resources

The recreation resources group includes jobs relating to: planning, development, maintenance, and protection of resources. These jobs deal with recreational areas and facilities form a support system for recreational experiences.

Tourism

The tourism group includes jobs related to travel for pleasure and activities for tourists. Within this group are five major components attracting a market for tourism: providing transportation to places of interest, providing attractions for tourist participation, providing housing, food and service, providing information about attractions, services, facilities, and transportation, and providing specific arrangements.

Amusement and Entertainment

Occupations in amusement and entertainment include: entertaining clientele, commercial amusements, live or filmed performances, presentation of shows and professional athletic contests, and personal services in entertainment establishments.

The first two groups of occupations (recreation services and recreation resources) constitute the more professional portion of this occupational field. These two groups would employ those who pursue a college education in preparation for leisure time occupations.

In addition to the people working in the four categories described above, the leisure oriented fields support a number of other occupations. These include construction of facilities, commercial establishments, and industries involved in the production of a great variety of recreation equipment. If leisure time were suddenly eliminated, a major portion of the economy would suffer significant damage and a very large number of people in a variety of occupations would become unemployed.

New developments in technology affect the demand for recreational services. For example, modern mechanical lifts have revolutionized skiing. Dam building and reservoir developments, coupled with mass production of boats and marine equipment, have contributed toward a dramatic increase in water sports. Golf may be significantly affected by new computerized equipment utilizing limited space.

While highly specialized jobs require their own particular individual characteristics, there are some personal traits which are essential for any leadership position in the recreational field.

Park and recreation professionals must continue their progress toward overcoming a longtime public image of playground baby-sitters. Their responsibilities are too great for this image to continue. They must enhance their image by improving their qualifications as executives, innovators, planners, teachers, supervisors, and leaders of complex leisure oriented programs.

Park and recreation professionals must be competent in working with various kinds of natural and man-made areas supervised by government and nongovernment agencies. More importantly, the professionals must always be aware that the resources are for the optimum use of people.

Professional Preparation

The professionals in the field of recreation and parks are those serving in administrative, supervisory, and other leadership capacities, They are employed primarily by public and voluntary agencies providing recreational services. However, some of those who are professionally prepared choose to pursue private or commercial recreation careers. The professionals equip themselves for leadership through professional education and professional experience. Generally speaking, the professional in this field must be a promoter, a planner, an organizer, a teacher and a motivator. In the past there has been a serious lack of public knowledge about the scope and opportunities in leisure time occupations. However, because of the increased importance of leisure time occupations in recent years and this lack of understanding is being overcome rapidly. There is an increased awareness in communities across the nation of the need for competent recreational leaders who are well prepared. Recreation and park curricula currently exist in more than 165 two year colleges and almost 200 four year colleges. It is important to recognize that the college and university recreation departments are not the only programs involved in supplying this professional field. A portion of the leaders in the leisure industries have degrees in liberal arts, physical education, forestry, sociology, business and landscape architecture.

Resource oriented recreation curricula generally are housed in schools of forestry or natural resources. Recreational education and administration curricula are included in schools of health, physical education, and recreation. Field work is another important part of a student's formal training in parks and recreation. The majority of programs offer field work opportunities in municipal recreation programs. Others provide opportunities with hospitals, therapeutic agencies and resource management agencies and school camps.

Graduate Preparation

Often the administrators of the large and more complex recreation and park programs are required to hold master's degrees. College teachers and research specialists almost always must have earned at least a master's degree and, preferably, a doctorate.

For a master's degree, a minimum of 30 semester hours is required beyond the bachelor's. For a doctorate, a minimum of 90 graduate semester hours is required. The graduate program includes extensive field experience.

Scholarships and Internships

A national internship program is provided through the National Recreation and Park Association (NRPA). It provides special advanced training for a number of college graduates showing outstanding potential for administrative careers in the field. Stipends vary from $8,000 to $10,000 per year. The host agency provides a broad based and diversified experience designed to move the intern quickly into a responsible administrative position.

The scholarship office of every college or university will furnish information upon request about the scholarships offered by the particular institution. In some cases the specific department where the recreation curriculum is administered has limited financial aid available for selected students.

Specialized Educational Training

North Carolina State University

The Department of Parks, Recreation and Tourism Management has been in existence since 1947, was nationally accredited in 1977, and is considered one of the premier programs of its type in the United States. There are three primary goals of the Department: to provide professional education to individuals seeking careers in recreation, parks and tourism management; to conduct research relative to the planning and management of recreation and leisure service areas and programs, and; to provide consultation services to recreation and leisure service agencies and organizations.

Minor in Parks, Recreation and Tourism Management

The academic minor in parks, recreation and tourism management is offered to students interested in gaining a basic knowledge of the parks, recreation and tourism fields and an understanding of the importance of leisure and recreation in American society. It is not intended to prepare students for a professional career in parks, recreation and tourism. Seven hours of required courses and nine hours of electives are necessary to complete the minor.

Recreation Resources Administration

The Department of Recreation Resources Administration offers two master degree programs. The Master of Science degree is offered for students desiring a comprehensive understanding of research techniques and their application to applied recreation resource management. The Master of Recreation Resources is a professional degree emphasizing advanced applications of theory and administrative principles of the specialized areas of recreation resources management. Illustrative specializations include the following:

- recreation and park administration
- dual major or minor in public administration is available
- natural resources recreation management
- natural resources interpretation
- planning and resource development
- travel and tourism
- sports administration

For more information, contact:
North Carolina State University
Dr. Phillip S. Rea, Head, or Dr. Roger Warren, Undergraduate Coordinator
Parks, Recreation and Tourism Management
Box 8004
Raleigh, NC 27695-8004

(919) 737-3276

Employment

Although the public has often been accustomed to relying upon volunteers for recreation leadership, recreation and parks professionals now are being employed at all levels of government. Federal and state government positions are not as numerous as jobs in local governments, but they have increased significantly in recent years.

Local government positions in city, county and district recreation agencies constitute a major source of employment, ranging all the way from direct leaders to departmental administrators. Professionals are becoming employed by such commercial recreation enterprises as; private golf courses, ski resorts, tennis clubs, private camps, beach and boating resorts, sport clubs and health spas. Other agencies that employ recreation leaders with specific qualifications are; hospitals (therapeutic recreation), correctional institutes, military, industrial organizations and voluntary youth service agencies.

Federal Government Employment

A few decades ago, the National Park Service planned its services to handle 25 million visitors a year. Today, close to 200 million people annually jam our parks. The U.S. Forest Service had 60 million visitors in 1926. Today, another 200 million people use its facilities. All of this spells the need for a large number of additional professionals who are well qualified in the planning and management of outdoor resources.

In the past, most federal agencies have given primary attention to graduates whose educational emphasis was in the biological sciences; However, personnel with majors in recreation, social science, physical science, physical education, landscape architecture and engineering have also been hired. The present philosophy of government administrators seems to favor personnel with dual talents who can effectively relate people to resource settings. They want professionals who are competent in working with all kinds of natural and man-made areas.

Opportunities for employment with the Heritage Conservation and Recreation Service (formerly the Bureau of Outdoor Recreation) primarily are available to those who qualify as outdoor recreation planners. Duties include: make studies of recreation resource needs; prepare recommendations of transportation proposals; evaluate federal land acquisition programs; review and comment on federal environmental statements; evaluate state comprehensive outdoor recreation plans; consult with state officials on outdoor recreation programs, and; evaluate requests for financial assistance. The HCRS is primarily an agency for coordinating, planning, and financing public outdoor recreation.

In the recruitment of employees, the HCRS seeks candidates who have completed a four year course of study leading to an appropriate bachelor's degree in the areas of; biological Sciences, natural resource management and conservation, social science, design and planning, earth science and outdoor recreation. Eligibility for appointment to the HCRS staff is dependent upon the candidate's performance on the Professional and Administrative Career Examination (PACE), which is administered by the Civil Service. Information about taking the examination may be obtained from your local post office or any CSC office. Additional information about employment opportunities with HCRS may be obtained from the HCRS headquarters, Department of the Interior Building, Washington, D.C., or from any of the seven HCRS regional offices.

The National Park Service (NPS) has a permanent staff of approximately 6,000 year-round employees, managing about 300 national park areas throughout the nation. For those entering the NPS employment opportunities are available in the following positions; park ranger, park naturalist, historian, archaeologist and designer. The administrative positions are held by longtime service employees. The park Service hires numerous summer employees, and a person contemplating a National Park Service career ought to have at least one summer of park service employment while pursuing a college degree. Similar to the HCRS, the NPS selects its employees from the Civil Service Commission's list of candidates who have scored high on the PACE. The U.S. Forest Service, a division of the Department of Agriculture, employs a large number of resource management personnel. A small proportion of these employees are involved primarily in the planning and management of outdoor recreation. Schools of forestry now offer specialization in outdoor recreation and the graduates of these programs constitute the main source of recreation personnel hired by the U.S. Forest Service. With the national forests being used more and more for recreation, there will continue to be a steady increase in demand for competent forest recreation personnel. The Forest Service also selects its employees from candidates identified through the Civil Service Commission.

Other federal agencies that offer limited opportunities for employment in outdoor recreation are; the U.S. Fish and Wildlife Service, the Bureau of Reclamation, the U.S. Army Corps of Engineers, the Bureau of Land Management and the Tennessee Valley Authority.

State Government Positions

Every state has a department which manages the state park system and some of these departments also offer recreation consultation services. Every state has a wildlife management agency that manages other state owned natural resources. Further, every state has a tourism office and a designated office which coordinates the state's recreation functions with the Federal Heritage Conservation and Recreation Service.

Most of the personnel in these state departments and divisions are prepared professionally in recreation providing many opportunities for employment of specialists in the field.

Most of the recreation related positions are in outdoor recreation or natural resource related recreation. The positions are relatively few in each state, with the more populated states generally providing better employment opportunities. Most state positions of this kind are filled by applicants processed through the State Civil Service Office. However, it is beneficial to also contact the particular department of government where you wish to be employed to be sure that your interests and qualifications are known.

Recreation Therapy

Numerous hospitals of various kinds have recreation therapy programs. The programs are designed to encourage positive attitudes and high morale among the patients, while at the same time developing their personalities. The smaller hospitals often have only one recreation specialist on the staff, while some of the larger hospitals have several specialists with one of them serving as coordinator or supervisor of the program. In such cases as state or federal ownership, the employment conditions of recreation therapists are defined by Civil Service specifications.

Those seeking recreation therapy positions need to prepare themselves by completing a specialized program in this field at a four year college or university. A few positions are available for people who have completed an associate or two year college program.

Therapeutic recreation has been one of the fastest growing areas of professional recreation. However, there is a definite limitation on the number of professionals in this field because of the restricted hospital population. Working with hospital patients is extremely satisfying to some people, while others cannot adapt to it. In trying to determine whether this type of employment is for you, it is important to be very analytical of your own personality. Hospital field experience early in your professional training program can be valuable in helping you decide whether this is the field for you.

Industrial Recreation

Certain industrial organizations provide a recreation program for employees and dependents as part of the employee benefits. Sometimes the program is sponsored by the employees' organization, usually known as an association or club. Industrial recreation agencies often own such specialized facilities as a private park, a golf course or a hunting club. Such programs involve a variety of leagues and tournaments designed to furnish participation opportunities to employees and family members. The exact responsibilities and working conditions of industrial recreation leaders vary from each other considerably because each industrial organization is independent and different. Further, the norms of professional qualifications and working conditions are less defined in this area of recreation than most others. For more information, contact:

National Industrial Recreation Association
20 North Wacker Drive
Chicago, Illinois 60606.

Commercial Recreation

As in any business, commercial recreation is based upon a free enterprise system. The individual or company prepares and distributes services and products in an effort to make a profit. This fact of business life (operating at a profit) forces the successful operator to remain sensitive and responsive to the public being served.

Job opportunities in commercial recreation are quite varied and relatively sparse. However, it is believed that the increasing recreation needs of Americans will not be met effectively in the future by the combined efforts of local, state, and federal government agencies. This will result in increased opportunities in commercial recreation.

Jobs in this field include: manager of a boy's or girl's ranch; manager or guide for a wilderness tour or expedition organization; employee of a recreation travel agency; manager of a bowling alley or an amusement park; manager or employee of an outdoor recreation enterprise; private consultant for the planning of recreation areas, facilities and programs, and; manager or employee of a commercial waterfront, ski resort, an aquatics center or a skating rink.

Those going into commercial recreation need to be somewhat cautious and plan very carefully. Certain characteristics and abilities are vital to a successful entrepreneur. Commercial recreation firms that qualify can obtain federal financial assistance (low interest loans) and planning assistance through the Small Business Administration and the Farmer's Home Administration. Also, certain states have assistance programs available to recreation and tourism enterprises.

Tourism

The travel industry is much broader than just its recreational aspects. However, travel for pleasure is a very significant part of the industry and therefore, should be identified as a field of recreational employment opportunity. It is interesting that in 46 of the 50 states, tourism ranks as one of the top three industries. This would seem to imply a gigantic number of job opportunities, but one should not be overly optimistic about this because most tourists travel by private automobile and make their own travel arrangements. However, about 20 percent of the tourist travel occurs on airlines, buses, and trains. A large portion of these programs involves organized tours. These tours may be sponsored and organized by nonprofit groups such as schools, religious, political, cultural, civic, professional and community organizations. Those employed in the tourist industry are involved mainly in arranging transportation, food, lodging and entertainment. Anyone interested in tourism job opportunities needs to be interested in and prepared for promotional work, business management, personnel management, and public relations. Your state office of tourism would be a good place to obtain specific information about tourism statistics and trends.

Employment Conditions

In the future, leisure time career opportunities within the broad spectrum of parks, recreation and conservation will involve critical issues ranging from the inner city ghettos to the wilderness of the great outdoors.

Women and Minorities

Approximately 40% of the college students majoring in recreation and park curricula are women. Employment opportunities for women are excellent. A woman who is well qualified for this field of work will find plenty of opportunity for gainful employment, if she is willing to locate herself in the areas where the opportunities exist.

In the past, employment of minorities in the field of recreation has been concentrated in large cities, but is becoming more widespread. Federal agencies are bound by law to give equal opportunity to members of minority groups.

Generalist or Specialist

It has been illustrated that there are certain positions in this field which require a high degree of specialization, whereas other positions require more generalized preparation. Whether you should prepare to be a specialist or a generalist depends on the nature of the position to which you aspire. Obviously, if you want to be a golf or tennis pro, you must be a specialist of the highest order. Conversely, if you are preparing to be a recreation supervisor or eventually the director of a program, generalized preparation covering a broad scope of the field would give you a stronger base for achieving your aspirations. The earlier in your professional preparation you can decide what you want to accomplish in your profession, the better prepared you will be to determine the degree of specialization or generalization you should pursue. There are places in this field for both, but these two kinds of employment require quite different preparation and experience.

Salaries

Salaries for full-time recreation positions range from approximately $10,000 to more than $45,000 per year. The salary scale for positions in municipal programs (the largest employment area in recreation) parallel rather closely the salaries for public school teachers in the same geographic area. This means that beginning salaries for employees with a bachelor's degree would range from $12,000 to $18,000 for 11 months. Jobs with youth agencies and hospitals have similar ranges.

Those employed by the federal government in recreation positions would receive salaries comparable to other federal employees of the same experience and rating. These are civil service jobs and the salaries are determined by the civil service pay scale. Generally, federal employees in the field of recreation would receive between $13,000 and $27,000 per year. A few of the top positions would also receive salaries comparable to their counterparts at the state level. Typically, state government employees receive $1,000 to $2,000 less per year than their federal government counterparts.

The highest paid people in the profession are the executives of large municipal programs. The one in charge of the program in a city of one million population, for example, would receive a salary of more than $35,000. The summer salaries of student employees would be $5.00 to $8.00 per hour, and the same would be true for year-round part time employees. However, summer positions that pay considerably better than this are available to better prepared employees, such as school teachers.

The Future

Even though the future of the recreation and park profession appears generally bright, it is important to understand that this field does not present a plethora of employment opportunities. It will undoubtedly experience consistent growth and the profession will gain improved status. During the past decade the market for college trained recreation and park personnel has expanded at a steady and healthy rate, and there is no reason to expect that this trend will change. In view of the recent past the following points are important: If you want to make a career of this field you need to prepare yourself expertly so you can compete in the job market, and; The leaders of the profession need to strive for more effective development and enforcement of standards.

Recent Changes and Current Trends

Much has been said regarding the future of recreation in a country where leisure is becoming common. U.S. News and World Report claims that Americans spent $200 billion in 1980 on leisure oriented activities and that by 1995 the expenditure will exceed $300 billion. The Chicago Tribune recently printed an article based on projections by the Bureau of Labor Statistics and listed opportunities in recreation and leisure as one of the top ten career prospects in the country today.

Future Participation Trends

During recent years the overall participation in recreation activities has increased about 50 percent faster than the population. This has been due primarily to increased leisure time, increased means and a more favorable philosophy toward participation in recreational activities. With people's increased awareness about the need to maintain an acceptable level of physical fitness and health, leisure time will become increasingly occupied by activities which promote fitness. There will be more joggers, more cyclists, more golfers, more tennis players and more participants in practically every popular form of fitness activity. Hopefully, there will also be more emphasis on other aspects of the healthy life such as weight control and discretion in the use of tobacco, alcohol, drugs, and other harmful substances. Recently there has been an upsurge in private campgrounds, luxury marinas, tennis complexes, resort villages, hunting and fishing preserves, and amusement complexes. Future technology will contribute to continued change with the prospects of plastic snow for skiing and plastic ice for skating, double and triple deck golf driving ranges, artificial surfs for swimming and surfing, artificial white water courses, programmed travel packages, underwater exploration vehicles and a multitude of other leisure time innovations. We can only speculate about how rapidly these and other innovations will take hold and what changes they will cause in leisure time patterns.

Trends and Issues

Education for the worthy use of leisure will become an important responsibility of schools and other educational agencies. Creative leadership will be required in connection with programs and class content. There will be a strong trend toward increased use of schools and other public facilities for recreational activities when the facilities are not in use for their primary purposes.

The market for services, supplies and equipment used in leisure activities will boom. This will result in considerable expansion of job opportunities in leisure related manufacturing and business.

There will be an accelerated trend toward creativity in the design of playgrounds, play equipment and recreational centers. There will be a steady trend for job applicants to have better credentials. In response to this, professional preparation programs will become more stringent. In turn, this will cause college programs to become more standardized. There will be a more even spread of facility use during the week as compared to weekends. This is due to a combination of factors including: the increased percentage of the retired population; later entry by youth into the job market; the trend toward more involvement with the four day work week, the continued reduction in the average work week.

With the attitude toward more stringent controls on government spending and with projected continued financial affluence, there will be a marked increase in commercialized recreation. Those with good business minds will find many opportunities to capitalize on people's leisure time interests in terms of financial profit.

Publications

Journal of Leisure Research
(Quarterly)
National Recreation and Park Association
3101 Park Center Drive
Alexandria, Virginia 22302

Journal of Physical Education and Recreation (Monthly)
American Alliance for Health, Physical Education, Recreation and Dance
1900 Association Drive
Reston, Virginia 22091

Park and Recreation Magazine
(Monthly)
National Recreation and Park Association
3101 Park Center Drive
Alexandria, Virginia 22302

CLUB Industry
1415 Beacon Street
P.O. Box C9122
Boston, MA 02146

(617) 277-3823

Recreation Resources
50 South Ninth Street
Minneapolis, MN 55402

(612) 333-0471

Federal Agencies

Department of Agriculture
Washington, D.C. 20250

contact:
Extension Services
Forest Service
Soil Conservation Service

Department of Defense
Washington, D.C. 20301

contact:
All branches of the military
U.S. Army Corps of Engineers

Dept. of Health, Education, and Welfare
Washington, D.C. 20201

contact:
U.S. Office of Education
Office of Environmental Education

Department of Housing and Urban Development
Washington, D.C. 20410

Department of the Interior
Washington, D.C 20240

contact:
Bureau of Sports, Fisheries and Wildlife
National Park Service
Bureau of Land Management
Bureau of Reclamation

Department of Transportation
Washington, D.C. 20990

State Divisions with Parks and Recreation Responsibilities

- Department of State Parks
- Department of Wildlife
- Department of Forests
- Travel and Tourism Division
- Water Resources Division

Additional Resources

American Alliance for Health, Physical Education, Recreation and Dance
(AAHPERD)
1900 Association Drive
Reston, VA 22091

(703) 4763400

Canadian Association for Health, Physical Education and Recreation
(CAHPER)
333 River Road
Vanier (Ottawa), Ontario, KIL 8B9

National Employee Services and Recreation Association
(NESRA)
2400 S. Downing Avenue
Westchester, IL 60154

(708) 562-8130

Today's sports official needs to be a little bit athlete, negotiator, psychologist, and sometimes, an unbiased arbitrator. Photo: **Athletic Achievements.**

18

Specialty Sports Careers

The best thing is to play, the second best is to coach, and the third best is to officiate the sport you love.

Dr. Henry Nichols
NCAA & Olympic Basketball Referee

Not every sports related career can be classified under the preceding headings. However, there are other career endeavors that also will provide opportunities in sports related fields. Some may be more traditional in nature but may not have received as much notoriety while others are still relatively new and are still developing.

Sports Officiating

For many years officials were the frequent target of verbal and, on occasion, physical abuse from coaches, players and fans. More recently a growing respect, almost admiration, has transpired at all levels fro the men and women who make the game possible by enforcing the rules. With a more educated awareness on the importance of officials, not only is there a greater appreciation for their thankless work, but there also has been increasing interest in becoming a member of the unknown better coined as the zebra corps.

Most officials earn their livelihood as educators; self-employed business people; or in careers that feature flexible work hours making it possible to officiate afternoon sporting events and travel on week nights. While 95 percent of all officials serve in a part time capacity and consider the profession more of an avocation, a select few will qualify and pursue it as a full-time career.

The road to the professional officiating ranks has many of the proverbial dues to be paid. The first phase in the attainment of skills will be in acquiring experience at the lower levels of play. This could begin very well by working with youth programs as well as the high schools which could eventually lead up the collegiate ranks or even the minor leagues. Countless nights are spent on lonely distant highways obtaining the necessary nurturing that must take place before one may even be considered for the big show. This often trying lifestyle should be of a major consideration when contemplating a career in officiating. Unless you are a football referee who performs only on weekends, the remainder of the officiating corps will travel extensively for months at a time. Being away from family or close acquaintances has been more than a strain on many referees' marriages and personal well being.

Officiating, like so many other occupations, requires a certain personality type as it definitely can be said that it is not for everyone. The ideal sports official is a saint... no one but a saint could exhibit all the psychological traits necessary to be a competent referee or umpire". These personality characteristics include tolerance, humility, self confidence, objectivity, and an ability to make quick, decisive decisions under fire.

"If officiating is so demanding, why then do people do it?" Dr. Roy Askins, a professor of social psychology who officiates part time, has discovered several reasons. The most common motivation for pursuing the interest was earning extra money, remaining close to athletics, and enjoying a sports position identified with status and power.

Referee magazine, the only publication dedicated to officials, has a list of guidelines that you should consider before getting started:

- Am I competitive and hard driven enough?
- Am I in control under pressure?
- I like to be a tough guy with an I'll show you type attitude?

- Do I consider myself confident, or do I come off cocky and arrogant in my presentation to others
- Does crowd reaction affect me or do I hear everything said by having rabbit ears?
- Do I think before I act or speak?

The above questions are merely rhetoric. If you're not sure about how you may react to intense situations, there's no better way to find out than to simply go out and do it.

Getting Started

To get a taste of the officiating scene, call upon a local recreation center, an adult intramural program, or any school sponsored league in dire need of officials. You may pick up a rule book and basic equipment for a minimal cost at a sporting goods store and attend referees' clinics that are sponsored by municipal athletic departments.

There is and always will be a shortage of referees for the lower levels of play and, while the pay won't get you rich, it will provide you with valuable experience in addition to giving you a better understanding of the game in which you are participating.

Remember though, there is no substitute for knowledge of the rules at any level of competition. Also, by dressing the part and presenting a firm yet tolerable disposition, you will ward off a majority of the problems that you may have encountered earlier during the contest by gaining the respect of the players.

Once you become seriously interested in this profession, it is highly recommended to consider membership in a local officials' association and to contact your state's high school athletic league to become certified (if necessary).

Officiating also provides excellent part time employment for the sports-oriented student who has the necessary flexible schedule to officiate during the afternoon hours. As novice officials improve their level of competency, they will have the opportunity to take on higher caliber games, which may lead to a major tournament or championship event. Even though there never seems to be enough qualified officials, nevertheless the upward movement to the collegiate ranks is slow and involves a very selective process. Officials must have worked numerous major tournaments to even be considered for Division II & III assignments. It is during these events that prospective referees are critiqued and receive recommendations from coaches and conferences for possible upward mobility. The next step involves applying to major Division I conferences which have their own individual criteria and requirements for acceptance. An official should be careful not to wait too long in his career to make this move or he/she may become entrenched in one level of play and never be given further consideration.

College officials receive very good per game stipends including travel expenses for out of town contests. Most business people enjoy college officiating because the greater share of its schedule is played on evenings and weekends.

Opportunities are abundant in all areas of officiating especially within women's sports and non-revenue athletic activities that are less publicized. With the rapid growth in soccer, referees in this sport can practically pick their own schedules, while club sports that utilize judges, such as gymnastics and figure skating, also are in demand of qualified officials. Salaries vary widely among sports, but most high school varsity contests will pay $30 to 50 per event. Small college games usually will have stipends ranging from $50 to $175 per game plus traveling expenses. On the professional front, the following scales are representative of each prospective sport.

Baseball

MLB has 60 full-time umpires who will usually earn a minimum of $50,000 in their rookie season with the veteran crews taking home over $100,000. Crew chiefs are awarded an additional $4,000 per season while the play-offs will provide a large bonus pool to be divided among the chosen umpires.

Baseball umpires get assignments from the Umpire Development Program, which accepts graduates from only three schools; the Harry Wendelstedt School for Umpires in Ormond Beach, Florida, the Joe Brinkman Umpire School in Cocoa, Florida and the New York School of Umpiring in Riverdale, New York. The schools offer a five week or six week training courses. The Brinkman School is open January and February in Cocoa, Florida while the well known Wendelstedt School is open during the months of January and February in Daytona Beach, Florida. Likewise, the New York School of Umpiring is open during June, July and August at Fordham University in New York. Students go to classes to learn the rules of baseball and the right positions for umpires. There also is the opportunity to exercise and go through drills on playing fields to learn stance, voice control, ball and strike calls, the handling of players and the use of equipment. After you learn the basics, they practice by umpiring high school and college games. Umpires advance from rookie leagues through class A, class AA, and class AAA leagues while some may go on to the major leagues. Salaries in the rookie leagues begin at $1,400 a month plus minimal expense monies. Pay and expense money increase as umpires work their way up. They earn $1,500 per month in the long A league, $1,600 in the double A league, and over $2,000 in the triple A league.

At first glance, this pay seems good. Minor league umpires, however, work only during the baseball season. Some umpires give up the work and take full-time jobs elsewhere. Others continue to umpire and work at other jobs in off-seasons.

Basketball

Most NBA officials will earn a minimum of $75,000 per year. However, the competition is fierce to attain a contract as most referees will spend as many as 15 years in the amateur ranks waiting for the professional opportunity. The International Association of Approved Basketball Officials Referee School in West Hartford, Connecticut, offers four referee schools each summer in various locations. At the four day sessions, officials go to morning classes for lectures, films, workshops, and tests on the fine points of officiating basketball games. They then referee afternoon and evening games at players camps held in conjunction with the referees schools. Cost of the program is $195.

Officials (IAABO) have a membership of more than 13,500 men and women basketball officials. It promotes the welfare of basketball, its players, and its officials. To become a certified member of IAABO, an applicant must have a satisfactory record of health and character, and must pass a written and practical floor examination with a grade of 86 percent or higher.

Football

The NFL employs 112 referees each season. First year officials receive close to $1,500.00 per game. Referees possessing 20 years or more of experience earn over $2,000.00 per contest with $2,500.00 given per man for the Pro Bowl, $5,000.00 for each play-off game, and $7,500.00 for the honor of being selected to work the Super Bowl.

National Football League (NFL) applicants must have at least ten years officiating experience with at least five of these being spent with major college varsity teams. During a season, NFL scouts watch officials work games. Of the 110 to 125 they scout each year, six will be selected. These six then take an open book test of 220 questions on NFL rules in addition to study film clips from games of the past year. All veteran officials must complete the rules questions and film study prior to the clinics. New officials also attend clinics whereby they discuss rules, review field mechanics, and study films. During the regular season, officials (who work as a crew) constantly study and review rules, take written tests, and watch films of the games.

At each game, an NFL observer and the coaches of both teams grade the work of the officials. They rank every call on a point system from one through seven. At the end of the season all officials are ranked according to their total grades. Highly rated officials get post-season assignments. Those with poor ratings are not rehired.

Candidates for NFL game officials must, besides meeting other requirements, belong to an accredited association of football officials while also being able to verify their collegiate schedules for the past two seasons and for the coming season.

Hockey

After spending an average of 78 years performing in the minor leagues, a hockey official who is promoted to the NHL will have a base pay of $45,000.00 plus performance and play-off incentives. There are 12 referees and 21 linesmen under contract in the NHL. Seasoned officials of 10 years or more of experience will earn $125,000 $150,000 annually in addition to their contract incentives.

Officiating Schools

A study of readership of *Referee* magazine indicates that most officials enter the profession for the purpose of staying in his/her's spurt while receiving a side income. They become proficient by attending local clinics and as they progress, future officials will receive more sophisticated developmental instruction through formal officiating schools. This form of training will also provide additional credibility when applying to various conferences.

Listed below are camps and schools that provide specialized instruction in becoming a seasoned official:

Wendelstedt Umpire School

Harry Wendelstedt, who has worked in World Series, All Star, and Championship Play-off competition, is regarded by baseball people as one of the game's most competent officials. The school's specific purpose "...is to provide supervised training for young people to qualify for umpire positions in professional, college or amateur baseball." Class sessions run for five weeks from January to February. Even though no jobs are promised, some exceptional students do receive appointments right after completion of the program while others may be called upon at a later date. For information, contact:

    Harry Wendelstedt, Jr.
    88 South Street Andrews Drive
    Armond Beach, FL 32074

    (904) 872-4879

Joe Brinkman Umpire School

This famed American League umpire holds two five week sessions yearly one in California, and one in Florida at the previous home of the Houston **Astros**. With the use of video equipment, lead instructors John McSherry (N.L.) and Nick Brenigan (A.L.) will personally teach you every aspect of umpiring necessary to make it in the professional circuit. For information, contact:

    Joe Brinkman Umpire School
    1021 Indian River Drive
    Cocoa, FL 32922

    (305) 639-1515

Mickey Owen Umpire School

This site of American's internationally recognized baseball camp is also the home of an established umpire school. The school, which runs from May to July in 1 or 2 week segments, is operated in a cooperative effort with the National Baseball Congress' National Association of Umpires. Both novice and seasoned umpires from the ages of 15 to 50 have attended the schools headed by former pro umpire Carl Lewton. The basic format includes rules study, mechanics instruction, and considerable field experience. For a free information packet, contact:

    Mickey Owen Umpire School
    Dept. NS85
    Miller, MO 65707

    (417) 452-3111

Academy of Professional Umpiring

The Academy offers a comprehensive training program that prepares the student mentally, physically and psychologically for the demanding challenges of professional umpiring. A carefully designed curriculum that provide you a thorough understanding of baseball rules and a practical philosophy of enforcement. You will learn the latest mechanics, signaling, and procedures accepted in professional baseball.

In order to realize your full potential as an umpire, you will be taught techniques that are sure to increase your self confidence and competency. The daily regimen is demanding. In the early phases of training, you will be spending an average of 3 hours per day in a classroom environment and up to 6 hours on the field. Night sessions, batting cage work, and organized group study will also be required during the course. The goal of the Academy is twofold: To prepare professional aspirants in the most thorough and effective manner possible, and to educate amateur umpires to the real world of professional umpiring and provide them with the skills that enhance their amateur endeavors.

For information, contact:

Jim Evans
Academy of Professional Umpiring
P.O. Box 164164
Austin, TX 78716

(512) 346-9555

Basketball Officials Opportunities

The 800 officiating program, which is under the direction of Bob Murrey, represents more than just a basketball camp. This unique camp offers its participants opportunities in coinciding vacations with learning seminars, optional investment plans, leads for job placement, and the flexibility of choosing sites and dates convenient to the basketball official. 800 has been organized at the request of officials throughout the United States who have expressed a desire to improve themselves as referees, regardless of their level of experience. Every official will attend lectures, officiate a minimum of twice a day, and spend time learning from Division I instructors in one-on-one situations. To learn more about the 800 program, contact:

Basketball Officials Opportunities
617 S. Brentwood Blvd. S267
St. Louis, MO 63144

(314) 968-4232

Blue Chip Officials Camp

Each year Mr. Ed Traxler is invited to put on his three day clinic at numerous sites throughout the country in football, basketball and softball. This traveling camp has recently returned from Germany and the Far East and is expected to offer a full slate each summer.

If you would like to schedule a camp in your area or wish to attend the nearest sponsored clinic, contact:

Mr. Ed Trexler, Director
Blue Chip Officials Camp
2076 Minton Drive
Tempe, AZ 85282

(602) 965-3526

Publications

If you cannot take the time to attend a formal program or simply want to enjoy your involvement more as a hobby, one of the best ways to stay on top of officiating is to subscribe to *Referee* magazine. This monthly publication contains updates, current issues, profiles of successful officials, and tips for improvement.

For information on obtaining a subscription, write:

Referee
P.O. Box 161
Frankville, WI 53126

(414) 632-8855

Doing It

While gaining experience, attempt to master the rules of your sport by keeping abreast of recent changes, interpretations, and emphases. This technical knowledge is important, but so is the development of your personality traits as an official. Continually self critique your performances.

When you feel you are ready to make a move to the collegiate ranks or professional minor leagues, write to the administrative office of the league in which you might like to officiate and ask about the criteria they require. Each conference has an assigning secretary and you may obtain an address in the directory section of this book. A couple of special addresses are as follows:

National Football League Officials Association
609 Brainerd Place
Exton, PA 19341

(215) 3631733

Amateur Softball Association
2801 N.E. 50th
Oklahoma City, OK 73111

National Association of Basketball Referees
475 Park Avenue South
Philadelphia, PA 19103

(215) 5687368

Major League Umpires Association
1 Logan Square, #1004
New York, NY 10016

(212) 7251800

Despite the criticism officials receive, there exists a quiet admiration for the role they provide. Al McGuire, former Marquette University basketball coach, sums it up best. "Nobody, but nobody, got on officials more than I... Conversely, no one has more respect for these dedicated people and the difficult, thankless job they do so well."

Strength and Conditioning Coaches

This speciality is fast becoming a vital position in both the professional and amateur circles. Today's athletes are not only required to cooperate in off-season programs for increased performance, but it also has been proven that weight and agility training can serve as a preventive force to certain types of injuries. As a return benefit to the athlete, this increased attention to bodily functions may also prolong a playing career. Strength coaches in the past have served as both part time exercise specialists, and as team coaches. However, now they are hired in full-time capacities with no additional duties. These fitness specialists may be required to serve as psychologists of sorts since the ability to motivate athletes is vital to the success of any rehabilitative or strength program. When working with an injured athlete, strength coaches will work in conjunction with a physical therapist, a trainer, or a doctor. A strong background in anatomy and exercise physiology along with personal weight lifting expertise, are necessary requirements to enter this field. There is currently a movement to require strength coaches to become members of the National Strength Coaches Organization (NSCA) as a means to set up their own certification program.

Professional consultants are paid handsomely for their services. However, due to the budding nature of this career, many collegiate strength coaches are compensated from only $16,000 to $25,000 annually.

The Optimum Performance Professionals

The NSCA is the professional membership organization of persons involved in the conditioning of athletes to levels of optimum performance. More than 12,000 professionals in the United States and 40 other countries share the commitment to total conditioning of athletes. This group represents such various disciplines as: strength and conditioning coaches, athletic trainers, physical therapists, sports medicine physicians, sports science researchers, health club personnel and, the athletes themselves. The NSCA publishes the world's premier conditioning journal. The NSCA Journal is your link between the sports science research lab and the strength training facility. It bridges the gap between theory and practice, and gives you the opportunity to share information and education with experts around the world.

National Strength & Conditioning Association
P.O. Box 81410
Lincoln, NE 68501

(402) 472-3000

Groundskeepers

With the onset of artificial surfaces, the landscaping artists of yesteryear are fast becoming a dying breed. Yet if you talk to any of today's professional athlete who competes on natural grass, they will be quick to tell you which fields and groundskeepers have the best reputations. Many state run universities offer courses in agronomy the science of grass and soil management which can prepare students for numerous occupations requiring this knowledge. A person need not have a degree in agronomy to become a groundskeeper, but advancement is not as easily attainable without one.

It is not uncommon for a major golf course to pay its head groundskeeper $40,000 to $50,000 annually. On the other hand, a groundskeeper at a major university or with a major league stadium generally will not receive more than $30,000 yearly. The importance of these imaginative people is best illustrated by professional football franchises who may have to share a facility with several other sports tenants or compete in an unpredictable climate. Upon completion of a successful season, teams have been known to share their respect for the groundskeeper by sharing their play-off monies.

Equipment Managers

At times this can be a thankless position (as many of you ex-high school and college managers know), but this occupation does allow for the sports enthusiast to display much expertise and creativity without any long, involved training. These support staff members at the college and professional levels are required at times during peak seasons to perform around the clock. An equipment manager must know equipment, its styles and its safety measures. He/she must also keep in tune with the latest technology and latest market lines. And when a piece of equipment does not meet the needs or body configuration of an athlete due to injury or comfort, the equipment specialist will become an improviser able to modify equipment without jeopardizing safety. It is at times like these that you may have to consult a trainer or go directly to the manufacturer. In a sense, you need to be a part time counselor: understanding the players, their needs, their whims, and their frustrations. Many times the improvisation of the equipment will give athletes a sense of added confidence knowing that the adjustment may have made them a half-step faster.

There is no way to prepare for this job, no courses to study, and no degrees to obtain. It's more or less an education of on-the-job training. For the college student, it provides an excellent means of supplemental income or a way to receive a scholarship.

Equipment people must be reliable, punctual, quick thinkers considering that by missing even one play, a player's absence could cost the outcome of the game.

There are many job opportunities with a wide open market existing for women. Those at the college level can expect salaries in the $12,000 to $18,000 range, while professional equipment personnel will receive wages from $18,000 to $22,000 with many receiving bonuses beyond their basic rates. For further information, contact:

Athletic Equipment Managers
 Association
723 Keil Court
Bowling Green, OH 43402

(419) 352-1207

Cinematographers

The use of film and video recording has increased in all sports over the last decade. No longer are football coaches the only ones who may benefit from this training aid. No other skill oriented activities coaches have come to realize, its advantages for performance analysis, teaching, scouting, and even injury prevention.

Almost every professional organization hires cinematographers to cover their games and, on occasion, their practices. The typical cinematographer will double as both a lab technician and a film librarian. Becoming an assistant to an established cinematographer is one means of getting started. Experience is a vital factor here and may be the only aspect evaluated when you solicit contracts. This technologically skilled area presents benefits to a team that can't be accomplished within their organization.

With the emergence of videos and the popularity of the NFL films series and team highlights, opportunities will arise for the individual with innovative talent.

Resources

Society of Motion Picture & Television Engineers
9147611100
Society for Technical Communications

(202) 737-0035

Trainers as a Para-Professional

The most noted forms of trainers are those that work with horses in the racing scene and those who perform a multitude of duties with boxers.

Horse Trainers

The majority of horse trainers have a veterinarian background, and much like the human exercise physiologist, trainers will be well versed on nutrition, biomechanics and anatomical functions. Horse trainers are well compensated, but their hours are long and consuming. To enter this field, one must have a sincere interest in the well being of the animal population and be willing to be committed to continually keeping abreast of veterinary advancements. Opportunities will be more abundant in states where pari-mutuel betting is legal. However, be ready to start on the ground floor, which may result in some very undesirable duties.

Boxing Trainers

The recent rebirth of boxing's popularity has allowed for the opening of gyms across the country. The boxing trainer acts as a manager coach for the boxer, preparing his or her protege in the technique of the sport and scheduling fight cards.

The more proficient trainer will have a knowledge of exercise principles, athletic training, film analysis, and expertise in dealing with the media. But before you get any grandiose ideas of being in the next Rocky movie, visit a local gym to see if you could be of any assistance. A boxing background would be most helpful for, if nothing else, credibility's sake. Keep in mind that few trainers make a living in this career; in fact, most will do this as a hobby rather than as a steady job.

St. Thomas University of Miami, Florida is one of the most recognized educational programs in the sports sciences. Photo: courtesy of **St. Thomas University.**

19
Specialized Training & Education in Sports Administration

When applying for a position in sports administration or any other sports related field, it is not essential that one's training or educational background come from a specialized sports curriculum. More times than not, sports related positions are created to meet organizational needs thus requiring the individual to possess diverse qualifications and experiences that could invariably be acquired from a variety of academic institutions or business field. As was mentioned earlier, the field of sports administration is nothing more than being employed as a business administrator in a sports atmosphere. A good example of the expectations for an aspiring sports enthusiast is this statement from the former chairperson of both the Madison Square Garden as well as the New York Yankees, Michael Burke: "We do not expect young people coming to the **Yankees** right out of college to have any technical knowledge that can be immediately applied. Rather, we are eager to acquire young people who are bright, willing and able to apply their general talents to any number of assignments as they learn the baseball trade."

For those who have not yet started a career and for those who have time to attend classes in sports administration, there are universities and colleges offering courses that make the difference in securing a position. While no school can guarantee placement in a job upon graduation, many of these institutions have outstanding success records, especially in attaining internships with major university and professional programs. The professional and collegiate ranks rely on specialized institutions for their employment needs since in reality, the schools perform the all important screening process of their prospective employees.

The Curriculum in Sport Management

Undergraduate Programs

Colleges and universities offer a number of different degrees in different majors. Some institutions with sport management programs offer a sport management degree. Other institutions offer a specialization, concentration or emphasis in sport management with the degree itself granted in another area. Since many sport management programs are housed in physical education or in education departments, students may sometimes be required to take course toward teacher certification which may or may not be useful. Sport management is a broad field serving many different types of work settings. Each type of setting requires a somewhat different preparation. The curriculum should provide flexibility for various options. Colleges and universities have many course requirements for graduation in addition to the courses in sports management. The percentage of the total number of credits needed that are specifically assigned to sport management courses is important. Typically, at least 25% of the total credits should be in sport management courses.

The curriculum in sport management should contain three major components. The foundational areas of study include courses typically taught in business departments or schools. Included are courses in management, marketing, finance, advertising, public relations, etc. The second component is the applied area of study which includes courses in management, marketing, finance, etc. These are typically taught by the sport management faculty. The third component is the field experience which includes the internship. The internship is the culminating experience and is the transition into employment in the field.

Questions to Ask:

- What degree do graduates of the sport management program receive?
- Is teacher certification a required a part of the course of study in sport management?
- Does the curriculum provide for different career options in sport management?
- What percentage of the total credits for the degree program will be in sport management courses?
- What courses offered specifically apply to sport management?
- How many courses are included in a core that everyone in the department takes?
- Is there a supervised sport management internship that is part of the program?
- How are the sport management internships arranged?
- What type of internship sites are available?

Graduate Programs

It is highly desirable that a student entering a graduate program in sport management have academic background in several areas of business and other allied fields. Many programs may require undergraduate coursework in economics, finance, management, marketing, advertising, and public relations. If this coursework is absent, the institution may require that this background be acquired concurrently with the graduate program.

All graduate programs should require a research methods course which can provide the tools needed to critically read the literature, as well as to write research and scholarly publications. In addition, the graduate program should provide courses to cover the breadth of the field while providing in-depth exposure in several areas.

The field experience in sport management, i.e., the practical and/or internship, should be a mandatory experience for graduate students who have had no previous internship in the field. It is desirable for all graduate students because of the placement potential this experience has for entry into the field.

Additional Questions
- What undergraduate prerequisites are required for admission to the program?
- Is a research methods course required?
- Is a project of thesis required as part of the graduate degree program?
- Is a comprehensive examination, exit orals, seminar, or some other culminating experience required in the program?
- Is a graduate internship available? Is it required?

Questions to Ask Prior to Enrolling in a Sport Management Program

Undergraduate and graduate students investigating careers in sport management need to determine whether prospective sport management programs provide the necessary curricula and curricular resources to adequately prepare them for work as a professional. The following insights and questions are suggested for students to use during interviews or correspondence with faculty and administrators at prospective colleges and universities with sport management programs. The questions will determine: The admission, retention, and placement practices. The access the student will have to physical and human resources. The scope of the curriculum in sport management, and the reciprocity the program enjoys with academic areas outside the department.

Questions to Ask:
- What are the criteria used for admission to the sport management program?
- How many students are accepted into the sport management program each year?
- What screening process (if any) is used to select the students to be admitted to the program?
- What are the criteria used to be retained in the program?
- What are the requirements for graduating from the program?
- How many persons have graduated from the sport management program over the last five years?
- How does the institution assist in placement of the sport management graduates?
- Where are some of the graduates of your sport management program employed?

Durham College

The Sports Administration Program at Durham College remains unique in its content and approach as it is the only two year diploma course of its kind in Canada. This approach is not designed to develop coaches, trainers, or athletes. Instead, the program focuses its attention on the skills of the administrator who must relate to all aspects of the Canadian sports scene. Graduates may aim at many responsible positions with professional sports teams, amateur sports organizations, recreational agencies, and private facilities within the sporting goods industry.

With the very rapid development of sport, form the international to the local level, both amateur and professional, and the emergence of government support to traditionally volunteer agencies, new possibilities for full-time employment are expanding. No single educational institution other than Durham College offers a practical, skills oriented program to satisfy this need. Training in this program focuses upon the development of knowledge, understanding, skills and values in both functional and general administrative areas, and in specific sport related areas. The course is conducted in an atmosphere of lecture, workshop, practical assignment and discussion situations combined with extensive second year field work experience.

For further information regarding Durham College, contact:

Paul de Souza, Dept. Head
Administrative, Communication & Applied Arts Division
Durham College of Applied Arts & Technology
P.O. Box 385
Oshana, Ontario, Canada

(416) 576-0210, Ext. 377

Robert Morris College

Robert Morris College offers undergraduate (B.S., B.A.) and graduate (M.B.A., M.S.) degrees in business with a concentration in sports management. The concentration is aimed at preparing the sport manager in the business, social, and legal aspects necessary to operate in the modern sports industry.

The department, started in 1977, has steadily developed in courses, students, and faculty. The curriculum offers a core of required courses as well as elective courses in which students can explore individual interests. There is also an emphasis on practical, "hands-on" experience through opportunities available on campus and with sport organizations in the Pittsburgh area. Three full-time faculty are drawn from sports organizations. Robert Morris' campus location just 17 miles outside Pittsburgh, a major sports market, allows for extensive use of guest speakers and student visits to sports settings.

A strength of the department is an extensive internship program, which has seen students placed from Florida to New Hampshire and North Carolina to Colorado. Sample intern placements including professional sports (Boston Celtics, Minnesota North Stars, Pittsburgh Pirates), colleges (Tulane University, George Mason University), associations (ECAC, MLB Players Alumni Marketing Association, U.S. Olympic Committee), resorts (Innisbrook, Kiawah Island), Faculties (RFK Stadium), and sporting goods (Converse). RMC sport management alumni work in all of these fields.

Students also have the opportunity to spend a semester abroad through a sports management exchange program with Deakin University in Melbourne, Australia.

For additional information, write or call:
Dr. Susan Hofacre
Department of Sport Administration
Robert Morris College
Narrows Run Road
Coraopolis, PA 15108

(412) 262-8416
(800) 762-0097   (Admissions Office)

St. Thomas University

The rapidly changing world of sports now seeks highly trained managers and administrators who are prepared to meet the challenges of tomorrow. The Bachelor of Arts and the Master of Science degree programs in Sports Administration at St. Thomas University in Miami, Florida prepare students with the management skills necessary to meet those challenges.

In 1973, an experienced group of nationally known, well-respected sports executives helped St. Thomas University pioneer a degree program in the business of sports. The first four-year school in the United States to offer a bachelor's degree in Sports Administration, St. Thomas University combines liberal arts, management and sports business courses along with seminars, internships and opportunities for practical experience. The 36 hour master's degree program is designed to allow students to accumulate 30 credit hours of course work within a calendar year. The final six credit hours may be earned by satisfactorily completing the requirements for an internship or by completing two additional courses. In addition to the full-time faculty, a highly qualified adjunct faculty includes professionals from college athletic departments, professional sports organizations and/or community recreation programs.

Nestled in an area rich with sports events, St. Thomas offers students numerous opportunities to engage in volunteer and part-time work experiences. St. Thomas' Main Campus proudly bears the title of "Home of the Miami **Dolphins**" and the surrounding South Florida area hosts events such as the Doral Ryder Golf Tournament (PGA), Lipton International Players Championships (tennis), the PharMor at Inverrary (LPGA), Miami Grand Prix, and other opportunities within the athletic departments at the University of Miami, Florida, Atlantic University and St. Thomas University which allow students to enhance their skills and direct them toward additional career opportunities.

The internship is an integral part of full educational preparation and is the vehicle by which classroom theory is applied and practiced. Recent sponsors include professional baseball, basketball, football, hockey and soccer teams, arenas, college athletic departments, and Conference league offices. The number of local and out-of-town internships has expanded as sports organizations continue to recognize the value of our well-prepared interns.

For further information on this exciting challenging career please contact:

Dr. Janice A. Bell, Coordinator of Sports Administration
St. Thomas University
16400 NW 32 Avenue
Miami, Florida 33054
Phone: (305) 628-6634

Admissions Office Toll free in Florida: 1-800-367-9006
Toll free outside of Florida: 1-800-367-9010

Western Illinois University

Western Illinois University was the second university to establish a graduate Program in Sport Management. Since 1972, this interdisciplinary degree program with the College of Business, has included course work not only in Sport Management and Business, but also in closely aligned fields of Psychology, Communications, Computer Science, Recreation, and Sociology. Students in the program complete both course work and an internship selected from a variety of locations including collegiate athletic programs, professional sports, business, and industry. Graduates of the program have been employes in all areas of sport management including the following: Chicago White Sox, Chicago Cubs, Green Bay Packers, Detroit Pistons, University of Iowa, Arizona State, Nebraska, and Texas A & M. For more information regarding this program, contact:

>Dr. Beatrice Yeager, Graduate Coordinator
>College of HPER
>Brophy Hall 214
>**Western Illinois University**
>Macomb, Illinois 61455-1396
>
>(309) 298-1332 or (309) 298-1981
>Fax: (309) 298-2981

Bowling Green State University

Bowling Green State University's sport management program is one of the largest and most diversified undergraduate sport management programs in the nation. It prepares students for a variety of sport and fitness related careers. The major has three options from which to choose: exercise and sport science with an emphasis in sport, physical fitness or athletic training; sport information management with an emphasis in sport information or sport marketing; and sport organization management with an emphasis in sport enterprise. An aquatics minor and an athletic training certification program are also offered through the sport management program. For additional information about the program in sport management, contact:

>**Bowling Green State University**
>School of Health, Physical Education and Recreation
>201 Memorial Hall
>Bowling Green, Ohio 43403
>(419) 372-2876

Other Leading Sports Administration Programs

The listing below is comprehensive but by no means complete. New programs are continually being developed while others are being expanded and revised. Athletic Achievements will continue to research this field in the quest to provide future sports practitioners with a maximum amount of useful information regarding sports management programs.

University of Massachusetts

One of the oldest and most respected Sport Management programs in the country, the University of Massachusetts at Amherst offers a Master's and Doctorate degree as well as a Bachelor's degree in Sports Studies. In addition to courses in the sociology and history of sport, the UMass Sport Management Program offers coursework in Sport Marketing, Computer Science, Sport Law, Sport Business and Finance, Media Relations, Event Management and Spectator Facility Management.

In addition, UMass Sport Management majors will learn managerial accounting, policy and the sport enterprise. All courses are offers within the department which boasts nine full-time faculty members. All faculty members have experience in the sports industries and utilize a network of Alumni to aid current students.

The extensive internship program for both graduate students and undergraduate students is one of the major, unique and positive aspects of the UMass Sport Management program. The internship is on-the-job training and allows the student to gain valuable experience and contacts within their discipline. Interns are available in professional and college sports, sport marketing and promotion companies, public relations, faculty management, sporting goods, international sports, and health fitness and private clubs.

Additional information may be obtained by writing:

Professor Glenn M. Wong
Department of Sports Studies
Curry Hicks Building
University of Massachusetts
Amherst, MA 01003

(413) 545-0441

Ohio University

Ohio University has grown into a leader in higher education in a number of cutting edge areas. The most spectacular example of Ohio University's leadership in program development is the graduate program in Sports Administration and Facility Management. Mr. Walter O'Mally of the Los Angeles **Dodgers** perceived a growing demand for very specific training in facility and sports management. Thus, in 1966 the first graduate program of its kind in the world was born at Ohio University recognizing "...that professionally prepared individuals were needed to give direction to sports organizations." Much of the program's success arises from the extraordinary depth and diversity of its students and alumni. Graduates of the program are experiencing rapid advancement and are well positioned for future success. For more information, contact:

Ohio University
Sports Administration and Facility Management Program
Dr. Charles R. Higgins, Coordinator
Athens, OH 45701

(614) 593-4666

St. John's University

St. Vincent's College of St. John's University in New York was the first university level school to offer a four year bachelor's degree in athletic administration. According to St. John's, the administration of athletics requires well-educated, dynamic, intelligent individuals. Its program offers special training in the areas of supervision and executive management. Courses concentrate in public and media relations, player contacts, personnel management, advertising, and purchasing. An internship in some area of athletic administration is a key addition to the program. For further information regarding this program, contact:

Dean Beglane
Athletic Administration Program
St. Vincent's College
St. John's University
Grand Central and Utopia Parkways
Jamaica, NY 11439

(212) 990-6161

Wayne State University

The Masters of Arts degree in Sports Administration at Wayne State University is designed to prepare the student for a career within the broad spectrum of professional, commercial and academic sports organizations. Students may select from four basic areas of specialization: Interscholastic, Intercollegiate, Professional or Commercial sports. Flexibility is the key to setting up individual programs with only three required classes. Depending on personal goals and previous experience the student, with the help of an advisor, can select the remaining courses for their program from within Health, Physical Education and recreation, or from other departments such as Marketing, Journalism, Business, Education, Labor Relations and a variety of other related fields.

The internship is one of the most valuable learning experiences available in the field of Sports Administration. One of the strengths of the program at Wayne State University is its location in the Detroit area. All four major professional sports leagues are represented: the Detroit Tigers, Pistons, Lions, and Red Wings. Other local professional organizations include the Detroit Rockers of the Major Indoor Soccer League, the indoor lacrosseTurbos, the Jr. Red Wings, and the Drive of the Arena Football League. Many opportunities for internships in intercollegiate athletics exist within thirty minutes of campus including the University of Detroit, Eastern Michigan University, and the University of Michigan. The metro Detroit area also has an extensive number of amateur and commercial sports organizations for students interested in those areas.

For further information, contact:

Dr. Todd Seidler or Mr. Tim Domke
Sports Administration
260 Matthaei Bldg.
Wayne State University
Detroit, MI 48202

(313) 577-4265

Wayne State College

Wayne State College offers a four year bachelor's degree and a masters degree in Sport Management. The Curriculum was designed to follow the most recent <u>Guidelines for Sport Management Programs</u> approved by NASPE.

The 58 hours undergraduate major includes 28 hours of physical education (Sport Law, Sport Administration, Sport Information Systems, Sport Management Practium, etc.), 15 hours of Journalism and Communication, 12 hours of Business and 3 hours of Economics.

Our Staff is extremely satisfied with our internship program which is essential to an excellent program. For more infromation contact:

Dr. Ralph Barclay or Mr. Lenny Klaver
Wayne State College
Wayne, NE 68787

(402) 375-7301

University of South Carolina

The department of Sport Administration is uniquely located in the College of applied Professional Sciences with its mission to prepare students for careers in sports business. An equally distinguishing characteristic os the USCS program is its full-time faculty of practitioners who are responsible for the design and implementation of the program.

Another component that separates USC from traditional programs is its commitment to providing ongoing research and information dissemination services for the sports industry with its International Conference on Sports Business. For more information contact:

Dr. Guy Lewis, Chairman
University of South Carolina
Dept. of Sport Administration
College of Applied Professional Sciences
Columbia, SC 29208

(803) 777-4690

United States Sports Academy

Since its inception, the United States Sports Academy has experienced tremendous growth in becoming the largest producer of sport-related master's degree recipients in the nation. "America's Graduate School of Sport" offers program concentrations in Sport Management, Sport Coaching, Sport Fitness Management, Sports Medicine, and Sport Research. Within the Sport Management department, additional emphasis in Facilities, Journalism, and Travel & Tourism are available. A Doctor of Education in Sport Management is also offered.

The innovative program allows students to earn their master's degree in one year with opportunities for practical "hands-on" experiences from respected sport leaders. In addition, the various delivery options are designed to meet every student's needs. Resident study, Mentor study, Cluster study, and the new Distance Learning program are among these options. A full range of financial aid services are made available to students. For further information contact:

United States Sports Academy
Office of Student Services
One Academy Dr.
Daphne, AL 36526
(205) 626-3303

University of St. Thomas

To meet the need for a comprehensive business management education, the University of St. Thomas has devised a MBA concentration in Sports Management which specifically addresses significant issues facing the industry. These issues range from sports marketing in an extremely competitive entertainment industry, to long-range and strategic planning encompassing risk management and cost-containment. The sports management track will focus on such topics as sports law, labor relations, ethical issues, the social dimensions of American sports, organizational design and human resource management.

Sports Management Curriculum:

The Sports Management concentration utilizes St. Thomas' Graduate School of Business faculty along with leaders in the sports field. This unique curriculum builds on the overall MBA degree foundation and enables students, in conjunction with the concentration director and an academic advisor, to design a degree plan that meets individual career goals and educational needs.

Concentration Objectives:

The sports marketplace concentration strives to create a learning environment that:

- Provides graduate education in business management through quality courses integrating theory and application.

- Broadens an understanding of the unique issues facing the sports industry by involving students in participatory discussions.

- Enhances each student's ability to function in a leadership role within a sports-related business.

For More Information:

To learn more about the Sports Management concentration, contact:

John T. Wendt
Director, Sports Management
Graduate School of Business
University of St. Thomas
1000 LaSalle Ave.
Minneapolis, MN 55403-2005

(612) 962-4250

Additional program listings for you to contact directly

Adelphi University
Dr. Ronald S. Feingold, Chair
Woodruff Hall
Garden City, NY 11530

Akron, University of
Wyatt M. Webb, Dept Head.
Dept. of PEHE, College of Ed.
Ackron, OH 44325-5103

Alabama-Birmingham, Univ. of
Dr. Peggy Harrison, Dir. HEPE
Dept of HEPE, University Station
Birmingham, AL 35294

Alabama, University of
Dr. Joe F. Smith
P.O. Box 1967
University, AL 35486

Alcorn State University
Dr. Rose Chew, Act. Chair
P.O. Box 513
Lorman, MS 39096

Appalachian State University
Jamie Moul, Dir.
Varsity Gym
Boone, NC 28608

Arkansas, University of
Mel R. Fratzke, Area Coordinator
Fayetteville, AR 72701

Averett College
Dr. Robert B. Turner, Assistant Professor
Danville, VA 24541

Baldwin-Wallace College
June Baughman, Coord
Spt/Dance/Arts Mgmt Prog.
Berea, OH 44017

Ball State University
John E. Reno, Dir.
Helath & Phys Act. Bld
Muncie, IN 47306

Baylor University
Dr. Nancy Goodloe, Dir.
Box 7313
Waco, TX 76798-7313

Bemidji State University
A.P. Loeffler, Chair
Dept HEPE
Bemidji, MN 56601

Bowling Green State University
Dr. Janet B. Parks, Chair
School of HPER
Bowling Green, OH 43403-0248

Brooklyn College
Kenneth Cohen, Ph.D., Director
City University of New York
Brooklyn, NY 11210

Bucknell University
Lewisburg, PA 17837

California at Berkeley, Univ. of
Dr. Linda S. Koehler, Coordinator
200 Hearst Gymnasium
Berkeley, CA 94720

California State University at Fullerton
Dr. Anne Marie Bird, Chrprsn
Dept of HPER
Fullerton, CA 92634

California State University at Long Beach
Douglas Young, Grad Coord
1250 Bellflower Blvd.
Long Beach, CA 90840

Campbell University
Dr Wm. Freeman, Chair
Box 414
Buies Creek, NC 27506

Canisius College
Dr. Gregory Reeds, Grad Coord.
2001 Main St.
Buffalo, NY 14226

Capital University
Dr. Steve Strome, Chrprsn
2199 E. Main St.
Dept. of Health and Sports
Columbus, OH 43209

Central Michigan University
Walt Schneider, Dir.
Rose Center
Mount Pleasant, MI 48859

Central Missouri State University
Dr. Roger Denker, Coord.
Morrow 101
Warrensburg, MO 64093

Central Washington University
Dr. John Gregor, Chmn.
Dept of PEHLS
Ellensburg, WA 98926

Chadron State College
Ann Smith, Dept. Chair
10th & Main
Chadron, NE 69337

Cleveland State University
Dr. Annie Clement, Coordinator
Euclid Avenue at E. 24th St.
Cleveland, OH 44115

Colby-Sawyer College
Dr. Judith P. Newcombe, Chair
New London, NH 03257

Columbus College
Dr. Michael Mangum, Asst Prof.
Dept. of Phys Ed./Leis Mgt.
Columbus, GA 31993-2399

Concordia University
George D. Short, Director
7141 Sherbrooke St. W.
Montreal, Quebec H4B 1R6

Connecticut, University of
William M. Servedio, Dept Head
2095 Hillside Road, U-110
Storrs, CT 06269-1110

Davis & Elkins College
Dr. Jean Minnick, Chmn
Sycamore St.
Elkins, WV 26241

Dayton, University of
John Schleppi, Dir
300 College Park
Dayton, OH 45469-1210

Delta State University
Dr. Milton Wilder, Dir.
Box B-2
Cleveland, MS 38733

Eastern Illinois University
Dr. Kevin Lasley, Assoc. Prof
Charleston, IL 61920

Eastern Kentucky University
Bobby Barton, Chmn
202 Weaver Building
Richmond, KY 40475

East Stroudsburg University
Dr. F. Michael Pullo, Chmn PRPE
Koehler Fieldhouse
East Stroudsburg, PA 18301

Elon College
Dr. James P. Drummond, Dir.
Campus Box 2500
Elon College, NC 27244-2010

Evansville University
Sue Lantz, Admn
1800 Lincoln Ave.
Evansville, IN 47702

Florida International University
Ted Wasko, Coord
Tamiami Trail
Miami, FL 33199

Florida State University
Dr. Charles Imwold, Dir.
Dept. of Phys Ed.
Tallahassee, FL 32306

Florida, University of
Dr. Sue Whiddon, Coordinator
305 Florida Gym
Gainseville, FL 32611

Georgia Southern University
Dr. Patrick Cobb, Coordinator
Landrum Box 8076
Statesboro, GA 30460

Georgia State University
Dr. Jeff Rupp, Chmn
University Plaza
Atlanta, GA 30303

Georgia, University of
Dr. Stan Brassie
Dept of Phys Ed.
Athens, GA 30602

Gettysburg College
Gareth Biser, Chmn
Hauser Athl Complex
W. Lincoln Ave.
Gettysburg, PA 17325-1486

Grambling State University
Dr. Willie Daniel, Director
Campus Box 4244
Grambling, LA 71245

Greenville College
Phyllis Holmes, Dir.
315 S. College Ave.
Greenville, IL 62246

Guildford College
Joyce Clark, Assoc. Prof. Spts St.
5800 W. Friendly Avenue
Greensboro, NC 27410

Harding University
Dr. Karyl Bailey, Program
Coordinator
900 E. Center
Searcy, AR 72143

Houston, University of
Dr. Shayne P. Quick, Coord.
123 Melcher Gymnasium
Houston, TX 77204-5331

Idaho, College of
Jim Fennell, Chmn Phys Ed.
2112 Cleveland Blvd.
Caldwell, ID 83605

Idaho, University of
Dr. Cal Lathen, Dir.
Memorial Gym #109
Moscow, ID 83843

Illinois State University
Dr. Sandra Little, Coord
Dept. of HPERD
Normal, IL 61761

Illinois, University of
Dr. Rollin G. Wright, Prof.
126 Freer Hall
906 S. Goodwin Ave.
Urbana, IL 61801

Illinois at Chicago, University of
Dr. Michael McGovern, Dir.
Box 4348
Chicago, IL 60680

Indiana State University
Dr. Thomas H. Sawyer, Dir.
Phys. Ed. Dept.
Terre Haute, IN 47809

Indiana University
Dianna Gray, Coord.
HPER Building Ste 112
Bloomington, IN 47405

Iowa State University
Gary R. Gray, Ed.D.
Phys. Ed. Dept.
Ames, IA 50011

Ithaca College
Wayne Blann, Coord. Spt Mgt.
School of HSHP
Ithaca, NY 14850

James Madison University
Joel Vedelli, Ed.D., Program Coord.
Godwin Hall
Harrisonburg, VA 22807

Jersey City State College
Eugene E. Bacha, Chmn
2039 Kennedy Blvd.
Jersey City, NJ 07305

Kansas, University of
Dr. James La Point
104 Robinson Center
Lawrence, KS 66045

Keene State College
Dr. Rebecca Brown, Ed. D., Dir.
229 Main St.
Keene, NH 03431

Kennesaw State College
Dr. Fred Whitt, Chmn HPER
P.O. Box 4444
Marietta, GA 30061

Kent State University
Dr. Carl Schraibman, Coordinator
264 Memorial Annex
Kent, OH 44242

Laurentian University
Prof. G. Zorbas, Dir.
School of Sports Admn.
Ramsey Lake Rd.
Sudbury, Ont, CN P3E 2C6

LeTourneau University
Dr. Richard Beach, Dir. Phys Ed.
P.O. Box 7001
Longview, TX 75607-7001

Liberty University
Dr. Dale Gibson, Dir. Spt. Mgmt.
Box 20000
Lynchburg, VA 24506

Loras College
Robert Tucker, Chair
1450 Alta Vista Dr.
Dubuque, IA 52004

Louisville, University of
Brenda Pitts, Dir. of Spt. Mgmt.
Belknap Gym
Louisville, KY 40292

Luther College
Dr. Kent Finanger, Dept. Head
Fieldhouse
Decorah, IA 52101

Mankato State University
Dennis Erie, Grad. Coord.
MSU P.O. Box 28
Mankato, MN 56002-8400

Marshall University
Dr. Don Williams
College of Education
Huntington, WV 25701

Maryland, University of
Dr. Jerry Wrenn, Dir. Spts Mgmt.
Kinesiology Dept.
College Park, MD 20742

Massachusetts at Boston, University of
Gail Arnold, Director of P.E.
Harbor Campus
Boston, MA 02125

Michigan State University
Dr. John Haubenstricker, Dir.
134 1M Sports Circle
E. Lansing, MI 48824

Michigan, University of
Joyce Lindeman, Chrpsn.
Central Campus Recreation Bld.
Ann Arbor, MI 48109-2214

Mississippi, University of
Dr. Don Creek, Chmn.
Turner Complex
University, MS 38677

Missouri Western State College
Bonnie Greene, Asst. Professor
4525 Downs Drive
Saint Joseph, MO 64507

Montana State University
Gary F. Evans, Professor
Romney Gym, Rm. 225
Bozeman, MT 59717

Mount Union College
James E. Thoma Ph. D., Dir.
Sports Mgmt. Program
Alliance, OH 44601

New Brunswick, University of
Garth A. Paton, Ph.D.
Fredericton, New Brunswick
Canada E3B 5A3

New Hampshire, University of
Dr. Michael Gass, Chmn.
New Hampshire Hall
Durham, NH 03824

New Haven, University of
Frank Flaumenhaft, Coord.
300 Orange Ave.
W. Haven, CT 06516

New Mexico, University of
Dr. Bill DeGroot, Director
Dept of HPPELS
Albuquerque, NM 87131

New York University
Dr. James Santomeier, Dir.
239 Greene St., Ste 635
Washington Square
New York, NY 10003

New York University
Janatha Pollock, Dir.
48 Cooper Square, Rm 108
New York, NY 10003

Newberry College
Dr. Dennis Obermeyer, Chr.
2100 College St.
Newberry, SC 29108

North Carolina State University
Dr. Phillip Rea, Dept. Head
Box 8004
Raleigh, NC 27695-8004

North Carolina at Chapel Hill, University of
Dr. John Billing, Chmn
CB#8700, 209 Fetzer Gymnasium
Chapel Hill, NC 27599-8700

Northeastern University
Dr. Carl Christiansen, Chmn
360 Huntington Ave.
3 Dockser Hall
Boston, MA 02115

Northern Colorado
Dr. David K. Stollar, Dir. Spt.
School of Kinesiology
Greely, CO 80639

Northwestern College
Dr. Kevin Lasley, Chair
3003 N. Snelling Avenue
St. Paul, MN 55113

Ohio Northern University
Dr. Ron Beaschler, Coord.
King-Horn Center
Ada, OH 45810

Ohio State University
Dr. Dennis Howard, Prog. Mgr.
453 Larkins Hall
Columbus, OH 43210

Okalahoma State University
Dr. George Oberle, Dir.
103 Colvin Center
Stillwater, OK 74078-0616

Old Dominion University
Dr. Paul Heine, Prog. Dir.
Dept of HPER
Norfolk, VA 23529-0196

Oral Roberts University
Scarlet Johnson, Coordinator
7777 South Lewis
Tulsa, OK 74171

Ottawa, University of
Graduate Coordinator
Ottawa, Ontario K1N 6N5

Pacific Christian
Lee Erickson, Psy Ed.
2500 E. Nutwood Ave.
Fullerton, CA 29631

Pacific, University of
Dr. Linda Koehler, Coord.
Spt. Mgmt. Program
Stockton, CA 95211

Pennsylvania State University
Dr. Lawrence Revo, Spts. Mgmt
109 White Building
University Park, PA 16802

Pfeiffer College
Jack Ingram, Dir.
Sports Management Prog.
Misenheimer, NC 28109

Quincy College
John Ortwerth, Dir.
1800 College Ave.
Quincy, IL 62301-2699

Rice University
Jessie Wilde, Dir.
P.O. Box 1892
Houston, TX 77251

Richmond, University of
Donald W. Pate, Ph.D., Coordinator
Robins Center
Richmond, VA 23173

Rockford College
Richard Bromley, Chair
5050 East State Street
Rockford, IL 61108

Rutgers University
Dr. Edward J. Zambriski, Chmn
PO Box 270
New Brunswick, NH 08903-0270

Saginaw Valley State University
Dr. Douglas Hansen
Dept. of PHE
University Center, MI 48710

San Francisco, University of
Dr. Gary Moran, Prog Dir.
2130 Fulton St.
San Francisco, CA 94117

Seattle Pacific University
Dr. Dan Tripps, Prog Dir.
3414 3rd. W.
Seattle, WA 98119

Slippery Rock University
Gary S. Pechar, Chair
Slippery Rock, PA 16057

South Carolina, University of
Guy M. Lewis, Chmn
Carolina Coloseum, Rm. 2012
Columbia, SC 29208

Southeastern Louisiana University
Dr. Betty Baker, Dept. Head
P.O. Box 845
Hammond, LA 70402

South Illinois U. at Carbondale
Dr. John A.W. Baker, Assoc. Prof.
Dept. Of Phys Ed.
Carbondale, IL 62901

South Mississippi, University of
Dr. C. Newton Wilkes
Box 5142, Southern Station
Hattiesburg, MS 39406

Spring Arbor College
Ted Comden, Chrm
Dept of Exer & Sports Sciences
Spring Arbor, MI 49283

Springfield College
Dr. Betty L. Mann, Dir Grad.
Dr. Nicholas Moutis, Dir. Under
263 Alden St.
Springfield, MA 01109

St. Johns University
Bernard P. Beglane, Dir.
Grand Central & Utopia Pkwys.
Jamaca, NY 11439

St. Leo College
Marilyn Schaeffer, Dean
P.O. Box 2038
Saint Leo, FL 33574

S.U.N.Y. Brockport
Dr. William Stier, Dir.
B-304 Tuttle N.
Brockport, NY 14420

S.U.N.Y. Cortland
Suzanne Wingate
PO Box 2000
Cortland, NY 13045

Tampa, University of
Dr. Robert Birrenkott
401 Kennedy Blvd.
Tampa, FL 33606

Temple University
Bonnie Parkhouse, Coord.
Seltzer Hall 316M
Philadelphia, PA 19122

Tennessee State University
Bernard Crowell, Chmn.
3500 John Merritt Blvd.
Nashville, TN 37209-1561

Tennessee, University of
Dr. Dennie Kelley
Dr. Ken Krick, Co-Directors
1914 Andy Holt Avenue
Knoxville, TN 37996-2700

Texas, Austin, University of
Dr. Dorothy Lovett, Chair
Bellmont 222
Austin, TX 78712

Texas Wesleyan College
Dr. Ed. Olson, Athl Dir.
1201 Wesleyan St.
Fort Worth, TX 76105

Tiffin University
Bonnie Hamryka, Adm.
155 Miami St.
Tiffin, OH 44883

Toledo, University of
Coordinator of Exer. Sci. & P.E.
2801 W. Bancroft St.
Toledo, OH 43606

Towson State University
Dr. Raymond Stinar, Chmn
Towson Center, Rm 200
Towson, MD 21204

Tulane University
Dr. Peter FArmer, Dept. Chair
Reiley Rec. Center 105
New Orleans, LA 70118

Utah, University of
Dr. James R. Ewers, Dir.
HPR N-245
Salt Lake City, UT 84112

Valparaiso University
Dr. Jerome Stieger, Chmn
254 Ath-Rec Center
Valparaiso, IN 46383

Virginia Tech College of Education
Dr. Margaret L. Driscoll
War Memorial Gym
Blacksburg, VA 24061-0326

Virginia University
Dr. William L. Alsop
263 Coliseum
Morgantown, WV 26506

Virginia, University of
Cyndy Kelly, Dir.
405 Emmett St., Ruffner Hall
Charlottesville, VA 22903

Washburn, U. of Topeka
James H. McCormick, Chmn
Dept. of HPED
Topeka, KS 66621

Washington State University
Joanne Washburn, Coordinator
Dept. of P.E., Sport & Leisure
Pullman, WA 99164-1410

West Chester University
Charles Pagono, Chmn
Dept. of Phys Ed.
W. Chester, PA 19383

West Virginia University
Dr. Dallas Branch, Jr. Prog Coord.
PO Box 6116, Rm 265 Coliseum
Morgantown, WV 26506-6116

Western Carolina University
Dr. Susan C. Brown, Dir.
Reid Gym, Spt. Mgmt
Cullowhee, NC 28723

Wheaton College
Dr. Tony Ladd, Chmn
Athletic Dept.
Wheaton, IL 60187-5593

Winston Salem State University
Tim Grant, Coordinator
Station A
Winston-Salem, NC 27110

Wisconsin, La Crosse, Univ. of
Dr. Mary McLellan
Dr. John Porcari, Grad. Dir.
129 Mitchell Hall
La Crosse, WI 54601

Whittenberg University
Dr. Tom Martin, Chmn
Box 720
Springfield, OH 45501

Wyoming, University of
Ward Gates, Dean of Phsy Ed.
Box 3196, University Station
Laramie, WY 82071-3196

Youngstown State University
Richard Walker
Youngstown, OH 44555

Not only has the race track industry become high-tech in the advanced training of its business professional, but likewise in its sophisticated approach in the recruitment of its personnel. Photo: courtesy of **Canterbury Downs.**

20
Specialized Job Search Services

Career Development Firms

The sports industry is extremely competitive if you don't have the right contacts, resources, and an understanding of **where to go, whom to see, and how to access decision makers and unpublished jobs** it's virtually impossible to build a career path.

SPORTS CAREERS

SPORTS CAREERS is a fast-paced educational program developed for the millions of eager and qualified professionals who would do just about anything for a career in sports, if only the knowledge and opportunities were available.

SPORTS CAREERS mission statement is simple: To help interested and qualified professionals build and enhance a career path in the sports industry. SPORTS CAREERS has aroused the interest of thousands of career-oriented Americans. The fields of interest within the sports marketplace are changing rapidly and many professionals currently working in sports-related areas are looking for new trends, niches and opportunities to explore.

National Job Search Conference

The Sports Career Conference is a demanding three day program of intensive how-to information designed to eliminate the confusion surrounding the many opportunities available in the sports industry.

The Conference has quickly become known as the sports industry's *job fair* where job seeker and employer come face-to-face. Attendees that actually acquire jobs as a result of the Conference and its newsletter.

I have attended many conferences, but SPORTS CAREERS tops them all - first class in every respect.

–Sam Ketchman, President, Athletic Enterprises

Congratulations on putting together one of the finest rosters of speakers that I have ever seen come together in one place.

–Maria Dennison, Executive Director/VP
Sporting Goods Manufacturers Association (SGMA)

The biggest names in the sports industry cover the most progressive topics. Speakers have included David Falle, Vice Chairman - Pro Serv and Jeremy Handelman, VP - CBS Sports. These leaders will share their techniques and years of experience, while being completely available after lectures, at roundtable discussions during one-on-one coaching sessions.

Special Interest Career clusters to be addressed

- Sports Journalism/Media
- Sports Administration
- Sports Marketing and Sales
- Athlete Representation
- Sports Entrepreneurship / Business Ventures
- Sports Education
- Opportunities for Women / Minorities
- Job Search Consulting
- Sports Health and Recreation

Your panelists qualify to be some of the most distinguished managers in the world.

–John Junker, Executive Director, John Hancock Bowl

Conference Format

- General keynote sessions, panel discussions, specialized break-out sessions, and small group encounter session
- One-on-three sessions with authorities in various sports-related fields
- Unlimited networking possibilities with professionals across the U.S.
- Sessions for job interviews for some of the most exciting opportunities in the country.

Who Should Attend

This job fair concept is loaded with proven strategies, techniques and tips that will enable those who register, no matter what their experience level to build or enhance a career path in the sports industry. The contacts, resources, and jobs opportunities available will be especially beneficial for:

- Veteran sports professionals looking for more industry contacts, networking opportunities or contemplating a change in direction.
- Educators looking to expand their departments or to develop entirely new programs for learning institutions at any level.
- Counselors and human resource professionals searching for new candidates and resources in order to maximize their own opportunities.
- Students and recent graduates wishing to build an entire career in sports.
- Professional and student athletes searching for ways to stay in a sports career.
- Employers looking for a captive audience of qualified candidates in a forum set up for the entire hiring process.
- Sports journalists: television, radio, sportswriting, publishing, video, production and technical personnel.
- Athletic administrators: coaching, teaching, sports administration, facility management, sports information, publicity, officiating, development/marketing, sports physiology, athletic trainers,
- Sports marketers: special event, management, corporate, sports departments
- Advertising: promotion, public relations, professional sports organizations, sporting goods, sales representatives.

- Athlete representatives: agents, contract negotiations, legal, financial planning, career counseling, endorsements.
- Sports entrepreneurs: sports team ownership, business ventures, sporting goods, manufacturing and retail, promoting sporting events.

Right after the Conference, I received the offer I was looking for. This opportunity would not have been possible without SPORTS CAREERS.

–Gilbert Garcia, Sporting Goods Agent

The SPORTS CAREERS Newsletter

I love it. It's exactly what I've needed for my career in sports. I anxiously await each new issue.

–Margaret Carpenter, Greensboro, NC

The unique, monthly publication is dedicated to enhancing employment opportunities within the sports industry.

Each special interest group is covered in every issue and sub-divided to put more focus on each of its eight areas of discipline. For example, sports journalism is broken down into television, radio, print and technical.

The editorial format revolves around a scouting report, opportunities, star qualities and a game plan necessary for success in each of these areas. In addition, eight of the 12 pages list jobs currently available. This format allows readers to focus their total attention on what should be the #1 priority — to find a better job in the sporting industry.

The information provided will be available to anyone interested in the unlimited number of opportunities in the Sports World.

–Robert Helmick, Former President, U.S. Olympic Committee

The SPORTS CAREERS Newsletter is the only publication of its kind that:
- Focuses on sports issues and trends for the sake of creating jobs and opportunities.
- Lists real jobs and opportunities.
- Shows you how to acquire the jobs and opportunities.

For more information on **Sports Careers** or the *SPORTS CAREERS Newsletter*, contact:

Stratford American Sports Corp.
P.O. Box 10129
Phoenix, AZ 85064

(800) 776-7877
(602) 954-8106 (Phoenix)

SportSearch... Retained Career Development Consulting

SportSearch is an executive recruiting and consulting firm specializing in placement services for companies and candidates seeking senior level sales, marketing and administrative positions in sporting goods, media, sports organizations and professional sports teams.

SportSearch believes the executive search field in sports must change to meet the need of new relationships and human resource programs. SportSearch offers a process of consulting and networking with clients and candidates, which ultimately creates and preserves mutual interests.

The SportSearch Team

Mark Tudi is recognized as one of the leading authorities on career development in the sports industry. With over 15 years of diversified sports marketing experience, he has contacts and resources in virtually every niche of the sports industry.

Mark is the founder of the Sports Careers concept, an educational program dedicated to help qualified and interested individuals build a career path in the sports industry.

For more information, contact:

SportSearch
Mark Tudi
702 E. Osborn S - 180
Phoenix, AZ 85014

(602) 241-9890

Job Search Agencies

Sports Jobs

This resume registry service matches job applicants with positions within the sporting goods industry. The goal is to assist job seekers in their job search within the sporting goods community whether they are actively seeking a new position or would like to be considered should a more interesting job become available. The registry of job candidates covers all levels of applicants from entry level to senior management.

There is no placement fee if a position is secured and there is no charge to companies who use our service. The only charge is a $39 listing fee to the job applicants for each six month period. In today's market this is quite a valuable service when you consider the cost of mailing out a stack of resumes to individual companies.

Vaughn and Peggy Baker are the people behind Sport Jobs. They have been involved with many facets the sporting goods industry for over 25 years. Their sales and marketing firm dealt directly with most of the departments found in a large sporting goods company and they learned first hand the staff requirements needed to keep that company headed in the right direction.

For further information, contact:
Sport Jobs
Peggy Baker
P.O. Box 841
Medina, OH 44258-0841

(216) 722-9096

ATHLETICS EMPLOYMENT WEEKLY

This weekly publication, staredt in 1986, provides a valuable service to colleges, coaches, students and alumni interested in athletic careers. The newsletter lists all levels of athletic vacancies nationwide on the junior and four year college level.

For further information, contact:
RDST Enterprises
Ms. Ruth Fugate
Rt. 2, Box 140
Carthage, IL 62321

(217) 357-3615

NCAA Weekly Hotline

In addition to having one of the finest editorial publications on the market, this weekly newspaper offers both a job listing in its marketplace section as well as providing a more in-depth wire service.

For information, call: NCAA Weekly (913) 339-1906

Additional Placement Resources

Executive Career Options
1125 Golfview Road
Glenview, IL 600253166

(708) 657-1073

SherCo (Retail Sporting Goods)
114M Reynolds Village
Winston Salem, NC 27106

(919) 722-9183

Teamwork Consulting
3306 Maynard Road
Shaker Heights, OH 44122

(216) 751-3306

Dunhill Sports Group
4700 Six Forks Road, Suite 320
Raleigh, NC 27609

(919) 881-8400

Search Solutions
4540 Woodland Avenue
Western Springs, IL 60558

(708) 246-7949

Additional Job Listing Agencies

Sports Jobline

Featuring hundreds of exciting opportunities in marketing, sales, radio, television, journalism, public relations, health, fitness, sporting goods, administration and coaching. To sample current job openings, call

1-800-SPORT41

or write:

117 West Harrison Street
Suite 605
Chicago, IL 60605

Athletic Administration

Northeast Athletics Job Link
7512 Co. Road 19
Wauseon, OH 43567

(419) 446-2131

5 State Athletic Employment Bulletin
P.O. Box 411
Archbold, OH 43502

(804) 330-3168

Mid-Land Job Bulletin
301 7th St. N.W.
Sioux Center, IA 51250

(712) 722-4545

Southland Job Hotline
P.O. Box 2397
Temple, TX 76503

To Order: (409)756-5393

**Broadcasting & Mass Media
American Radio Job Market**
1553 N. Eastern
Las Vegas, NV 89101

The Hot Sheet
P.O. Box 1476
Palm Harbor, FL 34682

(813) 786-3603

Television Careers
P.O. Box 6637
New Orleans, LA 70174

(504) 467-0652

Media Line
P.O. Box 51909
Pacific Grove, CA 93950

(800) 237-8073

Telephone Job Placement Agencies

The Pipeline	(900) 456-2626
Broadcast Job Line	(900) 990-6865
National Media Services	(303) 839-1770
JOBPHONE	(900) 234-INFO
NIKE Hotline	(503) 644-4224
Advertising Jobs	(900) 990-6865
Sales Agents	(919) 722-9183

International Conference on Sports Business

Through seminars, panels and roundtable talks, participants will examine a range of sports topics related to the importance of sport in business. Topics include:
- Government and Politics of Business and Economic Development
- Sports Event and Franchise Acquisitions
- Entrepreneurial Ventures in League and Event Creation
- Facility Development and Operation
- Legal Issues
- Advertising
- Event Performance Accountability
- Travel and Tourism
- Marketing
- Forecasting
- Corporate Sponsorship
- Management
- Media
- Promotions
- Feasibility Studies
- Public Relations
- Organizational Behavior
- Finance

The sharing and networking that takes place among participants make this dynamic conference a unique opportunity for individuals from all segments of the sports industry to exchange ideas on contemporary sports business matters. For information, contact:

Dr. Guy Lewis
USC Department of Sport Administration
Carolina Coliseum Room 2012
Columbia, SC 29208
(803) 777-4690

Newsletters

Sports Industry News

Each week, *Sports Industry News* provides 10 pages of in-depth reporting on the business of sports including:

- new ventures
- expansion plans in all sports
- divestitures, endangered franchises and mergers
- college sports as viewed from the business of sport
- broadcast and cable sports
- player management relations
- sports related marketing, sponsorship and advertising
- court cases
- drug testing and sports medicine
- hard-to-find statistical data on vital areas such as salaries, ticket pricing, gate receipts, attendance and other areas that are the lifeblood of sports industry.

Readers learn how others are using lucrative —but little publicized — sports and events to cut through the commercial clutter on network TV. Follow the growing trend toward the globalization of sports as U.S. leagues seek new markets overseas.

Sports Industry News will help career-minded sports enthusiasts determine how those negotiations will affect player salaries, ticket prices and advertising rates. *Sports Industry News* stories and statistical data have been frequently picked up by newspapers and wire services coast-to-coast. *The New York Times, Chicago Tribune, USA Today, Sports Features Syndicate* and *Los Angeles Times* often run information that appeared in *Sports Industry News*. To subscribe, contact:

Ray Swan
Game Point Publishing
P.O. Box 946
Camden, Maine 048430946

(207) 236-8346

Sports Marketing Letter

A concise monthly report for the progressive thinking sports marketing individual. The *Sports Marketing Letter* covers every aspect of the ways companies use sports to highlight their goods and services such as: marketing, merchandising, promotion, licensing, public relations, advertising, distribution— all the marketing disciplines as they apply to sports. For subscription information, contact:

Brian Murphy
1771 Post Road East, Suite 180
Westport, CT 06880

(203) 255-1787

Skybox magazine represents the new wave of sports publication targeted to address the business of sports. Photo: courtesy of **Skybox** magazine.

21
Sports Magazines, Newspapers & Periodicals

The following is a list of nationally sold publications which will provide in-depth knowledge of current trends, issues, and happenings within the magazine's topic area. Each particular magazine contains potential contacts and information about industry trends as well as leads to future employment opportunities. If a publication is not easily found on newsstands, most publishers will usually send you one complimentary inspection copy if you write the editor directly. I am often asked to recommend publications and trade journals that will enhance an individual's knowledge of a career area. In addition to specific resources suggested throughout this book particular sports careers, there are several periodicals that I highly recommend for the serious sports practitioner. Some of these magazines and journals, though out of print, will serve as invaluable resources for gaining in-depth understanding the sports marketplace. It may be difficult track back-dated issues, but the effort will be well worth it. Don't forget to check you local libraries. They may own some of out-of-print periodicals.

Physical Education Digest

For the "serious" student of the physical sciences, this periodical is considered to be one of the foremost resources for both instructors and practitioners. Its up to date and well researched manuscripts has made it "must reading" for the progressive minded career enthusiast.

> Physical Education Digest
> Dick Moss, Publisher
> 111 Kingsmount Blvd.
> Sudbury, Ontario Canad,a P3E 1K8
> (705) 675-7055

NCAA News

A weekly that is a must for any individual who is serious about becoming a student of the collegiate market. The newspaper features stories, statistics, and most importantly, a section dedicated to job opportunities.

> *NCAA News*
> 6201 College Blvd.
> Overland Park, KS 66211-2422
> (913) 339-1906

Skybox: Inside the Sports Business

Skybox is an exclusive product that is not sold on the newsstand. It's editorial focus is on the structure of the game both its economic underpinnings as well as a detailed look at the how and why of the sports business world. Therefore, the audience of the bi-monthly magazine will be targeted to address the needs of a select people who are looking for practical solutions to the business of sport the tenants of executive suites in stadiums, arenas, and skyboxes. For the inside information on the business of sport and an opportunity to be a part of an exclusive group of sports practitioners, contact:

> *Skybox Magazine*
> 1328 Elam Avenue
> Cincinnati, OH 45225-9945
> (513) 541-0269

The Sporting News

Considered by many to be the sports bible of current happenings in the sport scene, this weekly newspaper is considered as priority reading by the industry's most successful and visionary individuals. For more information, contact:

> *The Sporting News*
> 1212 N. Lindbergh
> St. Louis, MO 63132
> (314) 997-7111

Sports, Inc.
The Sports Business Weekly *out of print*

This weekly magazine provided some of the most in-depth features on the business of sport ever written. For two years business professionals were treated with up-to-date research and facts compiled by the leaders of the sports marketplace. ABP A Times Mirror Business Publication

Sports Travel
out of print

This monthly publication represented the industry's only magazine that provided coverage of facilities, transportation, and demographics of sports sites from around the world.

Murdock Magazine
500 Plaza Drive
Sicaucus, NJ 07096

(201) 902-2000

Nationally Sold Publications (listed alphabetically)

Athletic Journal
1719 Howard Street
Evanston, IL 60202

(312) 328-8545

Auto Racing Digest
990 Grove Street
Evanston, IL 602014370

(312) 491-6440

Baseball Digest
990 Grove Street, 3rd Floor
Evanston, IL 60201

(312) 491-6440

This compact directory has everything from sports enthusiast could ask for in a reading format.

The Basketball Clinic
Princeton Educational Publisher
117 Cuttermill Road
Great Neck, NY 11021

(516) 466-9300

Basketball Times
P.O. Box 960
Rochester, MI 48063

(313) 879-1676

Baseball Weekly
17820 E. Warren Avenue
Detroit, MI 48224

(313) 881-9554

Bicycling
33 E. Minor Street
Emmaus, PA 18098

Black Sports
31 East 28th Street
New York, NY 10016

Boating and Sailing
224 W. 57th St.
New York, NY 10019

(212) 262-8244

Bowling Digest
990 Grove Street, 3rd Floor
Evanston, IL 60201

(312) 491-6440

Boxing Scene
Box 42
Palisades, NY 10964
(212) 840-0660

Coach and Athlete
220 S. Hull Street
Montgomery, AL 36104

Cyclist
20916 Higgins Court
Torrance, CA 90501

(213) 328-5700

Fit News (Running)
9310 Old Georgetown Road
Bethesda, MD 20814

Football News
17820 E. Warren Avenue
Detroit, MI 48063

(313) 879-1676

Golf Digest
5520 Park Avenue
Trumball, CT 06111

(203) 373-7000

Golf Illustrated
3 Park Avenue
P.O. Box 6057
New York, NY 10016

(212) 340-9673

Golf
Times Mirror Magazine, Inc.
380 Madison Avenue
New York, NY 10017

(212) 687-3000

Hot Rod Magazine
Peterson Publishing Co.
8490 Sunset Blvd.
Los Angeles, CA 90069

(213) 657-5100

High School Sports
1230 Avenue of the Americas
Suite 2000
New York, NY 10020

(212) 765-3300

Inside Sports
990 Grove St., 3rd Floor
Evanston, IL 60201

(312) 4916440

International Gymnast
P.O. Box G
Oceanside, CA 92054

(612) 722-0030

Karate Illustrated
1847 W. Empire Avenue
Burbank, CA 91504

Motor Trend Magazine
Peterson Publishing Co.
8300 Santa Monica Blvd.
Los Angeles, CA 90089

(213) 854-2222

Muscle & Fitness
P.O. Box 4009
Woodland Hills, CA 91367

(213) 8846800

National Coach
P.O. Box 1808
Oscala, FL 32678

(904) 6223660

National Masters News (Running)
P.O. Box 2372
Van Runs, CA 91404

Runner
P.O. Box 2730
Boulder, CO 80321

Runner's World
33 E. Minor St.
Emmaus, PA 18049

(215) 967-5171

Running Commentary
441 Brookside Drive
Eugene, OR 97405

Running Research News
P.O. Box 27401
Lansing, MI 48909

Running Times
2022 Opitz Blvd., Suite 1
Woodbridge, VA 22191

(703) 491-2044

Scholastic Coach
Scholastic Coach, Inc.
730 Broadway
New York, NY 10003

SKI
P.O. Box 52013
Boulder, CO 803212013

303) 442-3410

Skin Diver
Peterson Publishing Co.
8490 Sunset Blvd.
Los Angeles, CA 90069

Soccer Digest
990 Grove St., 3rd Floor
Evanston, IL 60201

Sport
McFadden Bartell Corporation
119 W. 40th St.
New York, NY 10018

(212) 869-4700

Swim Magazine
523 S. 26th Rd
Arlington, VA 22202

(703) 549-6388

Swimming World
Swimming World, Inc. Box 45497
Los Angeles, CA 90045

Tennis
5520 Park Avenue
Trumbull, CT 06611

(203) 373-7000

The Ring Magazine
130 W. 37th St.
New York, NY 10018

(212) 736-7464

Track and Field News
P.O. Box 296
Los Altos, CA 94023-0296

(415) 948-8188

Triathlete
Triathlete Publishers, Inc.
8461 Warren Drive
Culver City, CA 90230

(213) 558-3321

Triatholon
8461 Warner Dr
Culver City, CA 90230

(213) 558-3321

Ultra Sport
Raben Ultrasport Partners
711 Boylston St.
Boston, MA 02116

(617) 236-1885

USA Gymnastics
1099 N. Meridian St.
Indianapolis, IN 46204

USA Today
Call: (800) USA-0001

Volleyball Monthly
Straight Down, Inc.
P.O. Box 3137
San Luis Obispo, CA 93403

(805) 541-2294

Winning: Bicycle Racing Illustrated
1127 Hamilton Street
Allentown, PA 18102

World Tennis
P.O. Box 359009
Palm Coast, FL 32035-9978

22

Resources Directory

The following directory of major professional franchises and league offices provides you with addresses and where available the name of the person to contact when inquiring about possible employment or internship opportunities. With the continuing development of new leagues and teams, some of the resources listed here may have moved to new headquarters or even ceased to operate by the time you read this book. If the postal service returns one of your letters, write to the Commissioner's Office and request the team's new address.

New teams, franchise, arenas, sports facilities and services are constantly being developed. The staffs of these organizations book events all over the country. Don't neglect your local chamber of commerce for contacts and information on any new sports-related events occurring in your area.

Minor league baseball is the real training ground for the majors and has produced many of the top executives in the sport. Never overlook this route—even though the pay may be minimal, the experience isn't. This abbreviated directory contains much valuable information but is not comprehensive. Use your initiative to make contacts. Any one of them could be your starting point. It is up to you. Remember send out as many personalized letters as possible and talk to as many people as you can. The road to success may be rough, but the rewards can be very satisfying. If you have time, please write us regarding your attempt to enter the sports world. Tell us about how using this book has affected career search.

General Resources

Directory of College & High School Contacts
The National Association of Collegiate Athletic Directors (NACDA) and the National High School Federation publish yearly directories of all their members and leagues. Guides may be purchased for $14.95 from:

Ray Franks Publishing
P.O. Box 7068
Amarillo, TX 79114

(806) 355-6417

The *Sports Bible* of Athletic Addresses
The comprehensive directory of sports addresses is published annually by Global Sports Productions. From contacts in the amateur and professional sports world home and abroad, the latest developing sports leagues, publications, commissions, and associations, there is no better source of potential job contacts. A required tool for anyone who serious about becoming part of the sports marketplace. To obtain a copy, send $15.95, plus $3.50 for postage and handling, to:

Athletic Publishers
3036 Ontario Road
Little Canada, MN 55117

(612) 484-8299

Head Offices - Amateur Organizations

Amateur Athletic Union
Attn: Jay Kleindorfer
3400 W. 86th St.
Indianapolis, IN 46268

(317) 872-2900

The Athletic Congress (TAC)
P.O. Box 120
Indianapolis, IN 46206

(317) 638-9155

International Olympic Committee
Chateau De Vidy
CH1007
Lausanne, Switzerland

41-212-532-7132-72

U.S. Olympic Committee
Baaron Pittenger, Executive Director
Olympic House
1750 E. Boulder Street
Colorado Springs, CO 80909

(719) 632-5551

Arenas

International Association of Auditorium Managers
Attn: William Federa
One Illinois Center
111 E. Wacker Drive
Chicago, IL 60601

Major League Baseball

Office of the Commissioner
350 Park Avenue
New York, NY 10022

(212) 371-7800

American League
Robert W. Brown, President
350 Park Avenue
New York, NY 10022

(212) 371-7600

Baltimore Orioles
Edward Bennett Williams, President
Memorial Stadium
Baltimore, MD 21218

(301) 243-9800

Boston Red Sox
John L. Harrington, President
Fenway Park 4 Yankee Way
Boston, MA 02215

(617) 267-9440

California Angels
Gene Autry Chairman
State College Blvd.
Anaheim, CA 92806

(213) 625-1123

Chicago White Sox
Eddie Einhorn, President
32 W. 35th Street
Chicago, IL 60616

(312) 924-1000

Cleveland Indians
President
Cleveland Stadium
Cleveland, OH 44114

(216) 861-1200

Detroit Tigers
Jim Campbell, President
Michigan & Turnbull Avenues
Detroit, MI 48216

(313) 962-4000

Kansas City Royals
Joe Burke President
P.O. Box 1969
Kansas City, MO 64141

Milwaukee Brewers
Bud Selig, President
Milwaukee County Stadium
Milwaukee, WI 53214

(414) 933-4114

Minnesota Twins
Jerry Bell, President
501 Chicago Avenue South
Minneapolis, MN 55415

(612) 375-1366

New York Yankees
Michael Lyczkovich, Executive
Vice President
Yankee Stadium
Bronx, NY 10451

(212) 293-4300

Oakland Athletics
Oakland Alameda County Coliseum
Oakland, CA 94621

(415) 635-4900

Seattle Mariners
Woody Woodward, President
P.O. Box 4100
Seattle, WA 98104

(206) 628-3555

Texas Rangers
Michael H. Stone
P.O. Box 1111
Arlington, TX 76010

(817) 273-5222

Toronto Blue Jays
Pat Gillick
P.O. Box 7777
Adelaide St.
Toronto, Ontario M5C 2K7

(416) 595-0077

National League
Bill White
350 Park Avenue
New York, NY 10022

(212) 371-7300

Atlanta Braves
Stan Kaston, President
P.O. Box 4064
Atlanta, GA 30302

(404) 522-7630

Chicago Cubs
Donald Grenesko, President
1060 West Addison Street
Chicago, IL 60613

(312) 281-5050

Cincinnati Reds
Marge Scott, President
100 Riverfront Stadium
Cincinnati, OH 45202

(513) 421-4510

Houston Astros
William Wood, General Manager
P.O. Box 288
Houston, TX 77001

(713) 799-9500

Los Angeles Dodgers
Peter O'Malley, President
1000 Elysian Park Avenue
Los Angeles, CA 90012

(213) 224-1500

Montreal Expos
Claude Brochu, President
P.O. Box 500, Station M
Montreal, Quebec H1V 3P2

(514) 253-3434

New York Mets
Fred Wilpon, President
Shea Stadium
Flushing, NY 11368

(212) 507-6387

Philadelphia Phillies
Bill Giles, President
P.O. Box 7575
Philadelphia, PA 19101

(215) 463-6000

Pittsburgh Pirates
Carl Burger, President
Three Rivers Stadium
Pittsburgh, PA 15212

(412) 323-5000

St. Louis Cardinals
August Busch, Jr., President
250 Stadium Plaza
St. Louis, MO 63102

(314) 421-3060

San Diego Pirates
Dick Freeman, President
P.O. Box 2000
San Diego, CA 92102

San Francisco Giants
Al Roger, President
Candlestick Park
San Francisco, CA 94624

(415) 468-3700

Minor League Baseball

National Association of Professional Baseball Leagues
P.O. Box A
St. Petersburg, FL 33731

Class AAA

American Association
Ken Grandquist, President
2nd & Riverside Drive
Des Moines, IA 50309

(614) 871-1300

International League
Harold Cooper
P.O. Box 608
Grove City, OH 43123

(614) 871-1300

Mexican League
Pedro Treto Cisneros
Angel Pola No. 16
Col. Periodista C.P. 11220
Mexico, D.F.

(905) 557-1007

Pacific Coast League
Bill Cutler, President/Secretary/
Treasurer
2101 E. Broadway Road
Tempe, AZ 85282

Class AA

Eastern League
Charles Eshbach
P.O. Box 716
Plainville, CT 06062

(203) 747-9332

Southern League
Jimmy Bragan
235 Main St., Suite 103
Trussville, AL 35173

(205) 655-7062

Texas League
Carl Sawatski
10201 W. Markham St.
Little Rock, Arkansas 72205

(501) 227-7703

Class A

California League
Joe Gagliardi
P.O. Box 26400
San Jose, CA 95159

(408) 977-1977

Carolina League
John Hopkins
4241 United Street
Greensboro, NC 27407

(919) 273-7908

Florida State League
George MacDonald, Jr.
P.O. Box 414
Lakeland, FL 33802

(813) 644-2909

Midwest League
George Spelius
P.O. Box 936
Beloit, WI 53511

(608) 364 1188

New York-Pennsylvania League
Leo A. Pinckney
168 E. Genesee St.
Auburn, NY 13021

(315) 253-2957

Northwest League
Jack Cain
P.O. Box 30025
Portland, OR 97230

(503) 256-0085

South Atlantic League
John H. Moss
P.O. Box 49
Kings Mountain, NC 28086

(704) 739-3466

Rookie Classification

Appalachian League
Bill Halstead
157 Carson Lane
Bristol, VA 24201

(703) 645-2300

Arizona League
Bob Richmond
8340 E. San Benito
Scottsdale, AZ 85258

(602) 483-8224

Gulf Coast League
Thomas J. Saffell
11 Sunset Drive, Suite 501
Sarasota, FL 33577

(813) 966-6407

Pioneer League
Ralph C. Nelles, President,
 Secretary/Treasurer
P.O. Box 1144
Billings, MT 59103

(406) 248-3401

Basketball

Continental Basketball Association
Jay Ramsdell, Commissioner
425 S. Cherry St., Suite 230
Denver, CO 80222

(303) 331-0404

National Basketball Association
David Stern, Commissioner
645 5th Avenue
New York, NY 10022

(212) 836-7000

Atlanta Hawks
100 Techwood Drive, NW
Atlanta, GA 30303

(404) 681-3600

Boston Celtics
Boston Garden at No. Station
Boston, MA 02114

(617) 623-6050

Charlotte Hornets
2 First Union Plaza, Suite 2600
Charlotte, NC 28282

(704) 376-6430

Chicago Bulls
333 North Michigan Avenue
Chicago, IL 60601

(312) 346-1122

Cleveland Cavaliers
P.O. Box 355
Richfield, OH 4286

(216) 659-9100

Dallas Mavericks
Reunion Arena
777 Sports Street
Dallas, TX 75027

(214) 748-1808

Denver Nuggets
P.O. Box 4286
Denver, CO 80204

(303) 893-6700

Detroit Pistons
Pontiac Silverdome
1200 Featherstone Road
Pontiac, MI 48507

(313) 338-4667

Golden State Warriors
The Oakland Coliseum Arena
Nimitz Freeway and Hegenberger Road
Oakland, CA 94621

(415) 638-6300

Houston Rockets
The Summit
Houston, TX 77046

(713) 627-0600

Indiana Pacers
920 Circle Tower
5 East Market Street
Indianapolis, IN 46204

(317) 632-DUNK

Los Angeles Clippers
LA Memorial Sports Arena
3939 S. Figuerou St.
Los Angeles, CA 90037

(213) 748-0500

Los Angeles Lakers
The Forum
P.O. Box 10
Inglewood, CA 90306

(213) 419-3100

Miami Heat
Mr. Lewis Schaffel
The Miami Arena
Miami, FL 331364102

(305) 577-4328

Milwaukee Bucks
901 North Fourth Street
Milwaukee, WI 53203

(414) 272-6030

Minnesota Timberwolves
500 City Place
730 Hennepin Avenue
Minneapolis, MN 55403

(612) 332-DUNK

New Jersey Nets
Brendan Byrne Arena
East Rutherford, NJ 07073

(201) 935-8888

New York Knickerbockers
Four Pennsylvania Plaza
New York, NY 10001

(212) 563-8000

Orlando Magic
Mr. Pat Williams
P.O. Box 76
20 North Orange Avenue
Orlando, FL 328020076

(407) 649-3200

Philadelphia 76ers
Veterans Stadium
P.O. Box 25040
Philadelphia, PA 19147

(215) 339-7600

Phoenix Suns
2910 N. Central Avenue
Phoenix, AZ 85012

(602) 266-5753

Portland Trail Blazers
700 NE Multnomah Street
Suite 950, Lloyd Building
Portland, OR 97232

(503) 234-9291

San Antonio Spurs
Hamis Fair Arena
P.O. Box 530
San Antonio, TX 78292

(512) 2240-4611

San Diego Clippers
San Diego Sports Arena
3500 Sports Arena Blvd.
San Diego, CA 92110

(916) 261-275

Seattle Supersonics
C Box 12102
Seattle, WA 98114

(202) 628-8400

Utah Jazz
Salt Palace
100 S.W. Temple
Salt Lake City, UT 84010

(801) 355-5151

Washington Bullets
One Harry S. Truman Drive
Landover, MO 20785

(301) 350-3400

World Basketball League
Steven E. Ehrhart, Commissioner
3767 New Getwell Road
Memphis, TN 38118

(901) 795-9334

College Basketball

National Association of Collegiate Directors of Athletics
Michael J. Cleary, Executive Director
P.O. Box 16428
Cleveland, OH 44116

(216) 892-4000

National Collegiate Athletic Association (NCAA)
U.S. Highway 50 & Nall Ave.
Box 1906
Shawnee Mission, KS 66201

(913) 384-3220

National Association of Intercollegiate Athletics (NAIA)
Jefferson Farris, Executive Director
1221 Baltimore Avenue
Kansas City, MO 64105

(816) 842-5050

National Junior College Athletic Association (NJCAA)
George Killian, Executive Director
1825 Astin Bluff Pkwy
Colorado Springs, CO 80918

(719) 590-978

National Little College Athletic Association
Gary Dallman, Commissioner
1884 College Hts
New Ulm, MN 56073

(507) 354-8221

Major College Conferences

Atlantic Coast Conference
Eugene Corrigan
6011 Landmark Ctr. Blvd
P.O. Drawer ACC
Greensboro, NC 274196999

(919) 854-8787

Atlantic 10 Conference
Mr. Ron Bertovich
10 Woodbridge Center Dr.
Woodbridge, NJ 07095

(201) 634-6900

The Big East
David R. Gavitt
321 S. Main St., Heritage Building
Providence, RI 02903

(401) 272-9108

The Big Eight
Carl C. James
104 W. 9th St., Suite 408
Kansas City, MO 64105

(816) 471-5088

Big Ten Conference
James E. Delany
1111 Plaza Dr., Suite 600
Schaumburg, IL 601734990

(312) 605-8933

Big Sky Conference
Ron Stephenson
1816 Shoshone Avenue
Boise, ID 83704

(208) 342-3429

Headquarters:
Ron Stephenson
P.O. Box 1736
106 N. 6th, Suite 202
Boise, ID 83701

(208) 345-5393

Big West Conference
All California Schools
James A. Henry
1700 E. Dyer Rd.
Suite 140
Santa Ana, CA 92705

(714) 261-2525

Central Collegiate Conference
George G. Dales
1705 Evanston St.
Kalamazoo, MI 49008

East Coast Conference
Ernest C. Casale
Drexel University
Dept. of Athletics, Building 14
Philadelphia, PA 19104

(215) 222-2700

Eastern College Athletic Conference
Clayton W. Chapman, Commissioner
1311 Craigville Beach Road
Centerville, MA 02636

(508) 771-5060

Ivy League
Jeffery Orleans, Commissioner
70 Washington Road, Room 22
Princeton, NJ 08540

(609) 452-6426

Metro Atlantic Athletic Conference
Don D. Julia
One Lafayette Circle
Bridgeport, CT 06604

(203) 368-6969

Metropolitan Collegiate Athletic Conference
Ralph McFillen
1 Ravinia Dr., Suite 1120
Atlanta, GA 30346

(404) 395-6444

Mid-American Conference
James W. Lessig
Four Sea Gate, Suite 102
Toledo, OH 43604

(419) 249-7177

Mid-Eastern Athletic Conference
Kenneth A. Free
P.O. Box 21205
Greensboro, NC 27420-1205

(914) 275-9961

Mid-Western Collegiate Conference
James Schaffer
201 S. Capital Avenue, Suite 500
Indianapolis, IN 46665

(317) 237-5622

Missouri Valley Conference
J. Douglas Elgin
200 N. Broadway, Suite 1905
St. Louis, MO 63102

(314) 421-0339

Mountain West Athletic Conference
Sharon M. Holmberg
Eastern Washington University
Anderson Hall
Cheney, WA 99004

(509) 359-6437

Ohio Valley Conference
R. Daniel Beebe
50 Music Square West, Suite 307
Nashville, TN 37203

(615) 327-2557

Pacific 10 Conference
Thomas C. Hansen
800 South Broadway, Suite 400
Walnut Creek, CA 94596

(415) 932-4411

Southeastern Conference
Harvey W. Schiller
3000 Galleria Tower, Suite 990
Birmingham, AL 35244

(205) 985-3686

Southern Conference
Dave Hart
Ten Woodfin St.
Suite 206
Asheville, NC 28801

(704) 255-7872

Southwest Athletic Conference
Fred Jacoby
1300 W. Mockingbird, Suite 444
Dallas, TX 75247

(214) 634-7353

Mailing Address:
P.O. Box 56940
Dallas, TX 75356-9420

Sun Belt Conference
Victor A. Bubas
1408 N. Westshore Blvd.
Suite 1010
Tampa, FL 33607

(813) 872-1511

Trans American Athletic Conference
Lou McCullough
Butler Building, Suite 215
Athens, GA 30605

(404) 548-3369

West Coast Athletic Conference
Michael Gilleran
400 Oyster Point Blvd., Suite 221
South San Francisco, CA 94080

(415) 873-8622

Western Athletic Conference
Dr. Joe Kearney
14 West Dry Creek Circle
Littleton, CO 80120

(303) 795-1962

Football

Arena Football
James E. Foster, President
2250 E. Devon Avenue, Suite 337
Des Plaines, IL 60018

(312) 390-8660

The National Football League
Commissioner
410 Park Avenue
New York, NY 10022

(212) 758-1500

American Football Conference

Buffalo Bills
One Bills Drive
Orchard Park, NY 14127

(716) 648-1800

Cincinnati Bengals
200 Riverfront Stadium
Cincinnati, OH 45202

(513) 621-3550

Cleveland Browns
Cleveland Stadium
Cleveland, OH 44114

(216) 696-5555

Denver Broncos
5700 Logan Street
Denver, CO 80216

(303) 296-1982

Houston Oilers
P.O. Box 1516
Houston, TX 77251

(713) 797-9111

Indianapolis Colts
Box 535000
Indianapolis, IN 46253

(317) 297-2058

Kansas City Chiefs
One Arrowhead Drive
Kansas City, MO 64129

(816) 924-9300

Los Angeles Raiders
332 Center Street
El Segundo, CA 90245

(213) 322-3451

Miami Dolphins
4770 Biscayne Blvd.
Suite 1440
Miami, FL 33137

(305) 576-1000

New England Patriots
Sullivan Stadium, Rte. 1
Foxboro, MA 02035

(616) 543-7911

New York Jets
598 Madison Avenue
New York, NY 10022

(212) 421-6600
practice: (516) 538-6600

Pittsburgh Steelers
Three Rivers Stadium
300 Stadium Circle
Pittsburgh, PA

(412) 323-1200

San Diego Chargers
San Diego Stadium
P.O. Box 20666
San Diego, CA 92120

(619) 280-2111

Seattle Seahawks
11220 NE 53rd Street
Kirland, WA 98033

(206) 827-9777

National Football Conference

Atlanta Falcons
Suwanee Road at 185
Suwanee, GA 30174

(404) 945-1111

Chicago Bears
250 N. Washington Road
Lake Forest, IL 60045

(312) 295-6600

Dallas Cowboys
1 Cowboy Parkway
Irving, TX 75063

(214) 556-9900

Detroit Lions
1200 Featherstone
P.O. Box 4200
Pontiac, MI 48057

(313) 335-4131

Green Bay Packers
1265 Lombardi Avenue
Green Bay, WI 54303

(414) 494-2351

Los Angeles Rams
2327 Lincoln Drive
Anaheim, CA 92801

(714) 535-7267

Minnesota Vikings
9520 Viking Drive
Eden Prairie, MN 55344

(612) 828-6500

New Orleans Saints
1500 Podyras Street
New Orleans, LA

(504) 587-3034

New York Giants
Giants Stadium
East Rutherford, NY 07073

(201) 463-2600

Philadelphia Eagles
Broad St. & Patterson Avenues
Philadelphia, PA 19148

(215) 463-2500

Phoenix Cardinals
51 W 3rd
Tempe, AZ 85281

(602) 967-1010

San Francisco 49ers
4949 Centennial
Santa Clara, CA 95054

(415) 365-3420

Tampa Bay Bucaneers
One Buccaneer Place
Tampa Bay, FL 33607

(813) 870-2700

Washington Redskins
P.O. Box 17247
Dulles International Airport
Washington, D.C. 2004

(703) 471-9100

Canadian Football League

Canadian Football League
Roy McCurtry, Chairman/CEO
110 Eglinton Ave., 5th Floor
Toronto, Ontario,
Canada M4R 1A3

(416) 928-1200

B.C. Lions Football Club
Joe Galat, General Manager
765 Pacific Blvd. S.
Vancouver, B.C. V6B 4Y9

(604) 681-5466

Calgary Stampeder Football Club
Norman Kwong, General Manager
McMahon Stadium
Calgary, Alberta T2M 4M5

(403) 289-0205

Edmonton Eskimo Football Club
Hugh Campbell, General Manager
9023 11th Avenue
Edmonton, Alberta T5B 0X3

(403) 429-2821

Hamilton TigerCat Football Club
Joe Zuger, President
75 Balsum Avenue North
Box 172
Hamilton, Ontario L8N 3A2

(416) 547-2418

Ottawa Rough Rider Football Club
Paul Robson, General Manager
Lansdowne Park
Ottawa, Ontario K1S 3W7

(613) 563-4551

Saskatchewan Roughrider Football Club
Bill Baker, General Manager
2940 10th Avenue
Regina, Saskatchewan S4P 3B8

(306) 569-2323

Toronto Argonaut Football Club
Bob O'Biilovich, General Manager
Exhibition Stadium
Toronto, Ontario M6R 3C3

(416) 595-9600

Winnipeg Blue Bomber Football Club
Cal Murphy, General Manager
1465 Maroons Road
Winnipeg, Manitoba R3G 0L6

(204) 786-2583

Hockey

The National Hockey League
John Ziegler, Commissioner
650 5th Avenue
New York, NY 10019

(212) 398-1100

Boston Bruins
Boston Garden
150 Causeway Street
Boston, MA 02114

(617) 227-3206

Buffalo Sabres
Memorial Auditorium
140 Main Street
Buffalo, NY 14202

(716) 856-7300

Calgary Flames
P.O. Box 1540
Station M
Calgary, Alberta T2P 3B9

(483) 261-0475

Chicago Black Hawks
Chicago Stadium
1800 West Madison Street
Chicago, IL 60612

(312) 733-5300

Detroit Red Wings
Joe Louis Sports Arena
600 Civic Center Drive
Detroit, MI 48226

(313) 567-7333

Edmonton Oilers
Northlands Coliseum
7424 118 Avenue
Edmonton, Alberta T5B 4M9

(403) 474-8561

Hartford Whalers
One Civic Center Plaza
Hartford, CT 06103

(203) 728-3366

Los Angeles Kings
The Forum
Box 17013
Inglewood, CA 90306

(213) 419-3160

Minnesota North Stars
Met Center
7901 Cedar Avenue South
Bloomington, MN 55420

(612) 853-9333

Montreal Canadiens
The Forum
2313 St. Catherine St., West
Montreal, Quebec H3H 1N2

(514) 932-2582

New Jersey Devils
Byrne Meadowlands Arena
P.O. Box 504
East Rutherford, NJ 07033

(201) 935-6050

New York Islanders
Nassau Veterans Memorial Coliseum
Uniondale, NY 11553

(516) 794-4100

New York Rangers
Madison Square Garden
4 Pennsylvania Plaza
New York, NY 10001

(212) 563-8036

Philadelphia Flyers
The Spectrum
Pathson Place
Philadelphia, PA 19148

(213) 465-4500

Pittsburgh Penguins
Civic Arena
Pittsburgh, PA 15219

(412) 642-1800

Quebec Nordiques
Colisee de Quebec
2205 Avenue du Colisee
Quebec, Que G1L 4W7

(418) 529-8441

St. Louis Blues
The Arena
5700 Oakland Avenue
St. Louis, MO 63110

Toronto Maple Leafs
Maple Leaf Gardens
60 Carlton Street
Toronto, Ontario M5B 1L1

(416) 977-1641

Vancouver Canucks
Pacific Coliseum
100 North Renfrew St.
Vancouver, B.C. V5K 3N7

(604) 254-5141

Washington Capitals
Capital Center
Landover, MD 20785

(301) 386-7000

Winnipeg Jets
Winnipeg Arena
151430 Maroons Road
Winnipeg, Manitoba R3G 0L5

(204) 772-9491

American Hockey League
218 Memorial Avenue
West Springfield, MA 01089

(413) 781-2030

International Hockey League
8650 Commerce Park Place
Suite D
Indianapolis, IN 46268

(317) 872-1523

Soccer

Major Indoor Soccer League
Bill Kentling, Commissioner
7101 College Blvd., Suite 320
Overland, KS 66210

(913) 339-6475

Sports and Athletic Organizations

The following organizations can offer information concerning the sport or activities with which they are associated. Many will be able to provide dates of contests, requirements for certain jobs, and additional sources of information.

National Archery Association of the U.S.
1750 E. Boulder St.
Colorado Springs, CO 80909

(303) 578-4576

American Amateur Baseball Congress
215 E. Green
Marshall, MI 49058

(616) 781-6002

American Baseball Coaches Association
P.O. Box 3545
Omaha, NE 68103-0545

(402) 7330374

Association of Professional Ball Players of America
12062 Valley View St.
Suite 211
Garden Grove, CA 92645

Association of Baseball Players
Donald Fehr, Executive Director
805 3rd Avenue
New York, NY 10022

(212) 826-0808

American Baseball Coaches
c/o Jerry Miles, Executive Director
P.O. Box 3545
Omaha, NE 68103-0545

(402) 733-0374

Major League Baseball Players Alumni Association
Jim Kaat, President
500 S. Florida Avenue, Suite 600
Lakeland, FL 33801

(813) 858-3886

International Baseball Association
Dr. Robert E. Smith, President
Pan American Plaza, Suite 490
201 S. Capitol Avenue
Indianapolis, IN 46225

Little League Baseball, Inc.
Dr. Luke L. LaPorta
P.O. Box 3485
Williamsport, PA 17701

(717) 326-1921

National Baseball Congress
Bob Rich, President
338 S. Sycamore
Wichita, KS 67213

(316) 267-7333

U.S. Baseball Federation
2160 Grenwood Avenue
Trenton, NJ 08609

(609) 586-2381

Baseball Statistics
Elias Sports Bureau, Inc.
500 5th Avenue, Suite 2114
New York, NY 10036

(212) 869-1530

Society for American Baseball Research
Gene Sunnen, President
P.O. Box 10033
Kansas City, MO 64111

(816) 523-1961

Major League Scouting Bureau
Donald F. Pries, Director
23712 Birtcher Drive, Suite A
El Toro, CA 92630

(714) 458-7600

National Basketball Players Association
Alex English, President
15 Columbus Circle, 6th Floor
New York, NY 10023

National Association of Basketball Coaches
Clarence Gaines
P.O. Box 307
Branford, CT 06045

(203) 488-1232

International Basketball Association
Ben Hatskin, COB
1037 E. Dorothy Lane
Fullerton, CA 92631

(714) 525-5070

U.S. Basketball League
Daniel T. Meisenheimer, President
P.O. Box 211
117 North Broad St.
Milford, CT 06460

(203) 877-9508

Women's Basketball Association
Jason Frankfort, President
2 Penn Plaza, Suite 1500
New York, NY 10001

(212) 643-6677

Women's Basketball Coaches
Gooch Foster, President
1687 Tullie Circle, Suite 127
Atlanta, GA 30329

(404) 321-2922

NBA Properties, Inc.
Rick Wells, President
Olympic Tower
645 5th Avenue
New York, NY 10022

(212) 826-7000

NBA Entertainment, Inc.
Ed Desser, V.P. & GM
38 E. 32nd Street
4th Floor
New York, NY 10016

(212) 532-NBAE

Billiards Organizations

Billiard Congress of America
Charles Robertson, President
1901 Broadway St.
Suite 110
Iowa City, IA 52240

(319) 351-2112

U.S. Billiard Association
Carl Strassburger, Executive Director
757 Highland Grove Dr.
Buffalo Grove, IL 60089

(312) 459-7042

American Motorcyclist Association
Ed Youngblood, President
33 Collegeview Avenue
Westerville, OH 43081

(614) 891-2425

Bicycle Federation of America
William C. Wilkerson, Executive Director
1818 R. Street, NW
Washington, D.C. 20009

(202) 332-6986

International BMX Federation
Ross Fisher, President
9th Floor
343 Little Collins Street
Melbourne, Vic. Australia 3000

U.S. Cycling Federation
Richard DeGamro, President
1750 E. Boulder Street
Colorado Springs, CO 80909

(719) 578-4581

U.S. Professional Cycling Federation
Fred Mengori, President
Route 1, Box 1650
New Tripoli, PA 18066

(215) 298-3262

Sport Fishing Institute
1010 Massachusetts Ave. N.W.
Washington, DC 2001

(202) 878-0770

National Football League Alumni
2866 E. Oakland Park Blvd.
Ft. Lauderdale, FL 33306

(305) 564-6118

National Football League Players Association
2021 L Street N.W.
Washington, D.C. 22036

(202) 463-2200

American Football Coaches Association
7758 Wallace Road, Suite 1
Orlando, FL 32819

(305) 351-6113

Pop Warner Junior League Football
1315 Walnut Street
Building, Suite 1632
Philadelphia, PA 19107

Golf Coaches Association of America
583 D' Onofrio Drive, Suite 1
Madison, WI 537192004

(608) 833-6824

Golf Writers Association of America
P.O. Box 37324
Cincinnati, OH 45222

(513) 631-4400

National Association of Collegiate Gymnastics Coaches

Men's Gymnastic Coaches
c/o Mark Pflughoeft, President
1440 Monroe St.
Madison, WI 57311

(608) 262-6370

Women's Gymnastic Coaches
c/o Leah Little
Alumni Gym
University of Kentucky
Lexington, KY 40506

(606) 257-6483

U.S. Gymnastics Federation
Pan American Plaza
Suite 300
201 S. Capitol Avenue
Indianapolis, IN 46625

(317) 237-5050

American Athletic Association for the Deaf
1134 Davenport Dr.
Burton, MI 48529

(313) 239-3962

National Handicapped Sports and Recreation Association
1145 19th St. NW
Suite 717
Washington, D.C. 20036

(202) 652-7505

National Wheelchair Basketball Association
110 Seaton Bldg.
University of Kentucky
Lexington, KY 40506

(606) 257-1623

Special Olympics
1350 New York Avenue, N.W.
Suite 500
Washington, D.C. 20005

(202) 628-3630

Amateur Hockey Association of the United States
997 Broadmoor Valley Road
Colorado Springs, CO 80906

(303) 576-4990

American Trainer's Association & Certification Board
660 West Duarte Road
Arcadia, CA 91006

(818) 445-1978

Thoroughbred Owners and Breeders Association
P.O. Box 4367
Lexington, KY 40544

(606) 276-2291

United States Harness Writers' Association
horse racing
P.O. Box 10
Batavia, NY 14020

United States Thoroughbred Trainers of America
19363 James Couzens Highway
Detroit, MI 48235

United States Amateur Jai Alai Players Association
100 SE Second Avenue
Miami, FL 33131

United States Committee Sports for Israel
275 S. 19th St.
Philadelphia, PA 19103

(215) 546-4700

The LaCrosse Foundation
Newton H. White, Jr.
Athletic Center
Baltimore, MD 21218

(301) 235-6882

National Paddleball Association
P.O. Box 712
Flint, MI 48501

United States Modern Pentathlon Association
P.O. Box 8178
San Antonio, TX 78208

(512) 228-0055

People-to-People Sports Committee
610 Cutter Mill Road
Great Neck, NY 11021
(516) 482-5158

North American Society for the Psychology of Sport and Activity
c/o Dr. Maureen Weiss
131 Esslinger Hall
University of Oregon
Department of Physical Education
Eugene, OR 97403

(503) 686-4106

American Ski Teachers Association
14 Yorkstown Road
Pottsville, PA 17901

(717) 223-0730

Professional Ski Instructors of America
133 S. Van Gordon
North 240
Lakewood, CA 80228

(303) 987-9390

International Softball Congress, Inc.
6007 E. Hillcrest Circle
Anaheim Hills, CA 92807

(714) 998-5694

U.S. Slo-Pitch Softball Association
Box 2047
Petersburg, VA 23804

(804) 520-3042

National Intercollegiate Soccer Officials Association
c/o Raymond Bernabel
541 Woodview Dr.
Longwood, FL 32779-2614

National Soccer Coaches Association of America
P.O. Box 5074
Stroudsbury, PA 18360

(717) 421-8720

National Academy of Sports
220 E. 63rd Street
New York, NY 10021

American Swimming Coaches Association
1 Hall of Fame Drive
Ft. Lauderdale, FL 33316

(305) 462-6267

Intercollegiate Tennis Coaches Association
David A. Benjamin
Lenz Tennis Center
P.O. Box 71
Princeton, NJ 08544

(609) 452-6332

Lawn Tennis Writers' Association of America
Washington Post
Sports Department
1150 15th Street NW
Washington, D.C. 20005

United States Track Coaches Association
745 State Circle
Ann Arbor, MI 48104

United States Track and Field Association
30 N. Norton Avenue
Tucscon, AZ 85719

Professional Association of Divers Instructors
1251 E. Dyer Road, Suite 100
Santa Ana, CA 92705

(714) 540-7234

United States Volleyball Association
557 4th Street
San Francisco, CA 94107

National Wrestling Coaches Association
P.O. Box 8002
Foothill Station
Salt Lake City, UT 84108

(801) 581-3836

Attention Sports Enthusiasts, Educators, Librarians, Career Counselors, and Sports Professionals.

You can order additional copies of this book for your reference library, as a gift, or for course work. Quantity discounts area available.

Use the form below to send for your copy, or call **Athletic Achievements** for information about this and other sport careers reference books, job fairs, and special events.

Please send my copy(s) today!

DEVELOPING A ....CAREER IN SPORTS _____ COPIES @$19.95 ea. = _____

_____ MN Res. add 6% tax = _____

Shipping And Handling _____ ITEMS @$3.75 ea. = _____

TOTAL ENCLOSED _____

Ship To:

Name _____

Address _____

City _____ State _____ Zip _____

Daytime Phone (_____) _____

Attach Check or Money Order, made out to Athletic Achievements and mail to:

Athletic Achievements, Inc.
3036 Ontario Rd., Little Canada, MN 55117
612-484-8311